The Official Guide to
Ultima Online

Credits

Authors	Tuesday Frase, Melissa Tyler
Additional Writing	Marko Agterberg (Player Guilds), David Biggs (Relvinian news), Andrew P. Morris (Pentameron), Ken Scott (Developing Your Character), David Ladyman, Chris McCubbin, Jennifer Spohrer
Editor	David Ladyman (aka. Stat-Monkey)
Additional Editing	Chris McCubbin, Ken Scott
Interior Design	Wendi Dunn
Cover Design, Interior Layout	Jennifer Spohrer
Many thanks to	Richard Garriott, Starr Long, Joye McBurnett, Keith McCurdy, Michelle Bratton, Brian Martin, Raph Koster, Marshall Andrews, Mark Franz, Kristen Koster, Todd McKimmey, Designer, Kevin Schlipper, David Biggs, Dan Rubenfield, Chuck Zoch, Bob White, Andrew Morris, Richard Zinser, Mike McShaffry, Scott Phillips, Rick Delashmit, Jason Spangler, Jeff Posey, Herman Miller, Gary Scott Smith, Ragnar Scheuermann, Jeff Wofford, Jennifer Davis, Bruce Lemons, Clay Hoffman, Cari Oberstar, Scott Jones, Chuck Crist, Micael Priest, Brendon Wilson, Jonathan Price, Bob Frye, Michael Morlan, Matt Sheffield, Terry Manderfeld, Mark Rizzo, Brandon Williams, John Moreland, Todd Wachhaus, Brett Bonner, Timothy Bell, Rick C. Holtrop, Artie Rogers, Paul D. Sage, Russ Wilkins, Robert Windisman, Hal Milton, Monte Mathis, Paul Vaden, Evan Brandt, Rich Vogel, Tyler Cannon

ORIGIN Systems, Inc.
5918 West Courtyard Dr.
Austin, TX 78759

	® is a registered trademark of Prima Publishing, a division of Prima Communications, Inc.		® and Prima Publishing® are registered trademarks of Prima Communications, Inc.		is a trademark of Incan Monkey God Studios.

97 98 99 00 BB 10 9 8 7 6 5 4 3

ISBN: 7615-0926-7

Library of Congress Catalogue Card Number:

Printed in the United States of America

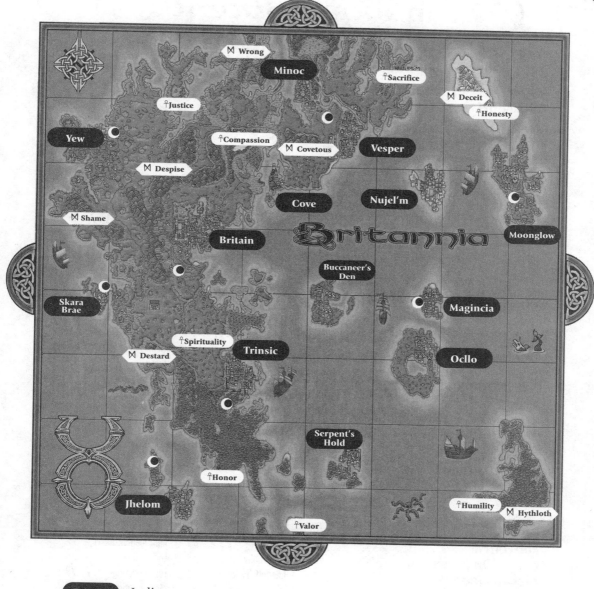

Trinsic   Indicates a town.

⬦ Shame   Indicates a dungeon.

⬧ Valor   Indicates a shrine.

◑   Indicates a moongate.

Table of Contents

Hear ye, Hear ye ...

Due to the ever-changing nature of *Ultima Online*, all details given in this book — statistics, specific locations and names and everything else — are subject to change at any time. For updates check www.primagames.com

Town Cryer

LORD BRITISH INCREASES SHRINE FUNDING

Lord British yesterday announced plans to upgrade the shrines that were recently constructed across Britannia. "The economy is doing well, and the time seems ripe to increase awareness of the eight Virtues among the people of Britannia," British said at a meeting with Your Correspondent. "I believe strongly that by teaching the Virtues to our children, Britannia will become a better, more educated and peaceful place for all of us in the years to come."

Lord Blackthorn, Lord British's most vocal opponent, believes that Britannia's ruler isn't being honest with his subjects. "British wants is everyone to accept what he thinks is good and forget about individual thought. But it's not all black and white. Something that is wicked to some is helpful and good to others. I know he has the best intentions, but the more he tries to mold everyone into his vision, the more discontentment there will be."

"I'm wondering where he's gonna get the money," one citizen said, after the announcement had been made. "If he ups the taxes to put more into his pet project, I, for one, will throw every bit of support I can behind Lord Blackthorn. I don't care a fig about either side of their argument, I ain't for or against the Virtues, I mean, but I don't need my taxes raised again. I have enough trouble tryin' to make a profit as it is!"

That sentiment was echoed around Britain, as word about the announcement spread. "I had to hire personal guards last week because of all the stealing here in Britain," one merchant complained. "Why doesn't he take all that money, wherever he gets it from, and do something useful with it? Like hire more guards to protect us and ours. And yeah, now that I got people on the payroll, I certainly can't afford higher taxes!"

"The shrines are fine the way they are," opined Gladiolas, an adventurer recently arrived from Magincia. "They do what they're supposed to do. I'm mighty glad they're there, but I don't see any need to add on to them. Everyone in Britannia knows about them by now. More advertising won't accomplish a thing."

Brother Paul from Empath Abbey was among those that support Lord British's policies. "It's because of Lord British's wise rule that we're a civilized, relatively peaceful community of humans today. Not long ago we'd have just as soon strangled one another as we would the orcs in the forest.

(Continued on next page)

NEW GRANDMASTER MAGE ANNOUNCED

The Guild of Arcane Arts today announced that another mage had achieved Grandmaster status in the city of Britain. Known only as Relvinian, the new initiate into the highest level of the arts has been called an "incredible natural" and "extremely talented." Still, there are some that accuse him of being "just weird."

"He's ... disturbing," according to Kandace the Lovely, another grandmaster mage. "He's really into all of the summoning spells. He dabbles too much with the darker magics. I don't know. He's earned his position, certainly, I just don't want to be in the same room with him."

Relvinian's tutor, Grandmaster Luthior, agreed with Kandace. "Yes, Relvinian does tend to deal more with lesser used or altogether forgotten spells, but he means well. He's trying to find ways to help Britannia as a whole, not just on a one-to-one basis. I think he'll be a very positive addition to our community, and I believe Britannia will be hearing more from him."

A small reception will be held in Relvinian's honor at the mage's guildhall in northern Britain. ▨

ASK DEATHDEALER

Destructor wrote to me from Britain, where he's just getting started in his career. He asks: "What can I do to become the best $%#@ fighter in Britannia?"

Well, Destructor, first you need to take your knife, find a training dummy, and practice. Then, practice some more. When you're through with that, you should probably practice some. You may get lucky and some experienced warrior will give you a decent weapon. If that happens, take that weapon and — you guessed it — practice.

At some point you'll be ready to collect your first kill, so go into the woods (but not out of town, mind you, you'll get jumped by people who are better than you) and kill a rabbit. That's right, a bunny. A cute little, cotton-tailed varmint. If you can't find one, take some other woodlands creature out. This'll get you some real-world experience with using your weapon, which is somewhat different than the stuffed dummies.

What I would then do (and this is where most warriors tend to start differing in their advice), is sell what I could from my kills, buy some armor and maybe a better weapon, and go find some brigands or thieves. Some warriors are working toward Paladin-hood, which is all well and good and I respect their wish not to just go out and randomly kill humans, but I gotta tell ya, brigands tend to have stuff on 'em, and no one's gonna miss 'em when they're gone.

By that time you can pretty much figure it out for yourself. There are a dozen dungeons to explore, tons of wilderness and islands, and lots of money to be had. If you can save enough, find a warrior or weapons trainer who is better than you are and ask for him or her to teach you. That can sometimes help a bunch.

Good luck on your journeys, hope I helped some, and if you can't hack it, remember — you can always be a mage. 🔳

All opinions expressed in this column are my own, nobody else's, and take it or leave it, I don't care, just don't call me a liar. Ever.

CLASSIFIEDS

12 ACRES, two planted fields, nice two-room house, close to major transport routes. Located southwest of Britain. Leave a note for Glen at the Salty Dog.

SWF seeks strong, willing warrior to show me his inner dungeons. Let's explore together and find treasures galore! Contact Malinda at the Unicorn's Horn in Britain.

DUNEDAIN GUILDMEMBERS WANTED. Brave Rangers, Mages, and Warriors needed to join the ranks of the Dunedain. Come to Cove and help us protect this coastal town from utter annihilation! The Dunedain is a new guild with opportunities for advancement and high standards for all members. If you posses honor, courage and strength, then travel to Cove to help save the innocent!

(SHRINE FUNDING, CONT.)

But the foundation on which the Virtues rest helped set us on this path to enlightenment. Whatever Lord British has planned is just the next step on our road of bettering ourselves."

The work should begin near the end of the month, according to an official spokesperson for the shrine project. The upgrade is scheduled to last a month per shrine, and will not interrupt the shrines' regular traffic. 🔳

BABY DRAGON ESCAPES

Keep an eye out for the young, fire-breathing and curious.

During a routine training session, Master Animal Tamer Duroc of Britain was distracted from his baby dragon, Caustic, by the call of a passing stranger. Without warning, the animal leapt to its feet and hurried toward the city.

According to Duroc, he began to chase the beast, to no avail. "These animals are very fast, especially at a tender, young age" reports Duroc. "Luckily, my colleague happened to accompany me, and I commandeered his steed and was able to follow Caustic into town."

Duroc informed onlookers that the animal was curious and harmless, but townsfolk were quite rattled by the event. Guards were finally able to lure Caustic into a cage with a slab of raw ribs. No townsfolk were injured, and some broken stands were all that resulted from this young, adventurous dragon's "raid." 🔳

Hints

GENERAL TIPS

Ultima Online is a big game, and the folks testing it (both testers here at ORIGIN and Beta testers throughout the world) have come up with a lot of useful information for you. Some of these tips are available in the online docs, but they bear repeating to make sure you're aware of them. **Of course, as with all material in this book, any particular tip might be out of date by the time you try it.** However, most tips are based on broader principles, so even if a specific tip no longer applies, consider the more general principle behind it.

Character Creation

⚨ It helps to plan ahead when assigning skills to a new character. One sample strategy (out of many) is to start a character with *Animal Taming* (to attract pets), *Peacemaking* (to resolve trouble) and *Archery* (to attack from a distance). When trouble strikes, try to calm the belligerents. If that doesn't work (for instance, if players are involved), send in your pets to attack and launch a ranged weapon attack from a safe distance. If the battle becomes too heated, you have a better chance of escaping with your life.

For more tips on character creation, see **Developing Your Characters** (later in this chapter, on p. 20) and **Skills** (beginning on p. 40).

Character Advancement

⚨ You can learn skills by watching others who are proficient in that skill. If you want to learn to bake, spend time with a baker. If you want to develop your combat skills, watch the guards, or other fighters, in action.

⚨ To find someone to teach you skills, stick close to the towns. Save money and work on the simpler skills that you can learn without a teacher. After you've earned some cash, work on your basic combat skills. Training dummies are free (check out the Warriors' Guild building in each town), and you can always watch the town guards to learn quite a bit about *Tactics*.

Buying

⚨ If at all possible, try to purchase items from other players rather than from shops. Players nearly always have lower prices than a shop, and they are often willing to compromise or trade for something you don't need.

⚨ In particular, forges are a great place to trade and buy things. There are always pleny of folks gathered around, using the forge. They will often sell armour and weapons at a cut rate.

Combat

⚘ An obvious but useful tactic is to hide behind a large object, such as a tree or corner of a building, then use a bow or crossbow. The person you're attacking has trouble getting at you to return the attack, especially without a ranged weapon and the skill to use it.

⚘ It is sometimes necessary to slay someone intent on killing you. While player-killing is not advocated, there are steps you can take to cover your tracks:

Change your clothing after slaying someone

Don't give your character an easy-to-remember name.

⚘ Conversely, pass on the names of troublesome players to other players.

⚘ You regain one lost hit point every 5 to 15 seconds. The better fed you are, the faster your hit points are restored.

Adventuring

⚘ Never travel between cities alone. If you form traveling parties, make sure all members have offensive and defensive skills and armaments that complement each other. You should also include at least one member who is armed with a bow or crossbow.

⚘ When you're in the wilderness, stay near the trail. It makes it easier to run from large monsters if you have to.

⚘ It's a simple truth, but one easily forgotten in the rush to adventure: There is strength in numbers. If you don't have friends, consider hiring guards or buying large, fierce animals to protect your back. Just make sure you have plenty of gold and/or food, to keep them happy.

Ships

⚘ Although a boat costs a fair amount of gold (2800+ gold pieces), it is well worth the investment. If you're interested, but short of money, try assembling a small band of people, around 3 to 6, to pool money for the ship deed.

⚘ Once you've bought the boat, go to the nearest dock, double-left-click on the ship deed in your backpack, and place the boat on the water. Make sure that the outline of the boat doesn't touch the land, and that the side of the boat can be reached from the dock — otherwise you won't be able to board.

⚘ And before you start *building* a boat — make sure that you'll be able to navigate the finished boat out of its construction location! If you build between two bridges or other structures, you might be unable to sail out of port.

Magic

⚕ Targetable spells (spells that require you to specify a target) display cross hairs when you cast them. Place the cross hairs over a target, then left-click.

⚕ When casting area effect spells (spells that affect everyone/everything within a certain radius), it's better to target the *ground* near the middle of your objectives rather than the objectives themselves. This "grounds" the spell and distributes its effects more evenly.

⚕ Some monsters are almost completely immune to certain spells. A Fire Elemental is virtually immune to all fire spells, for example. Be ready to change offensive spells to compensate.

⚕ Always keep a large supply of reagents on hand. The last thing you want to do is face a life-or-death situation with a shortage of bloodmoss or ginseng.

⚕ Never waste your mana and reagents on a high-level spell when something cheaper will do the job just as well. Mana regenerates slowly in the game, and as a mage, you'll be more vulnerable when your mana level is low.

⚕ It's handy to keep your spellbook open all of the time. Minimize it, leaving the closed book visible. This will save time when you're scrambling to cast a spell.

⚕ Work with another mage whenever possible. The best magical combination is to have one mage working on offensive spellcasting, while the other concentrates on healing and protecting the first mage or accompanying warriors.

⚕ Keep a backup magic item handy (an item with magical charges) whenver possible, in case your mana or reagents run low.

⚕ Mana regenerates at a flat rate of one point every five seconds.

⚕ Casting offensive spells in town, including the *Summon* and *Field* spells and those listed below, is forbidden and subject to punishment:

Clumsy	*Feeblemind*	*Mass Curse*	*Poison*
Curse	*Mana Drain*	*Paralyze*	*Weaken*
Earthquake	*Mana Vampire*		

First Circle

⚕ If you're a mage fighting another mage, you can temporarily lower his Intelligence by casting a *Feeblemind* spell. This lessens your opponent's chances of hitting you with a spell, since casting abilities are affected by Intelligence. (Similarly, striking a warrior with a *Clumsy* or *Weaken* spell will lower her ability to hit you.)

⚕ While a target is suffering from a spell that lowers attributes — e.g., *Weaken* or *Feeblemind* — no other such spells can be cast on the target.

Second Circle

⚜ If you're fleeing from someone, run through a door and then cast *Magic Trap* the door you've run through. If you are pursued through the door, the pursuer takes damage.

Third Circle

⚜ *Magic Lock* only works on chests, boxes and other containers. It will not work on doors.

⚜ Use *Wall of Stone* to temporarily block a door. For a truly underhanded method of doing someone in, lure your victim into a room that contains a monster or other nasty character, then run out and block off the door with a *Wall of Stone*.

⚜ *Field* and *Wall* spells are very sensitive to the direction in which they are cast. They'll appear perpendicular to the direction you are facing when you cast them. Be sure that you're pointing the right way before you cast.

Fourth Circle

⚜ A *Curse* will lower intelligence, dexterity and strength simultaneously.

⚜ When you find yourself involved in a magical battle, try casting *Mana Drain* or *Mana Vampire* on your enemy. They're very effective and temporarily eliminate an opposing mage's ability to cast high-level spells.

⚜ With a marked object, you can use *Recall* or *Gate Travel* to teleport to the place where you originally cast *Mark* was cast on that object. Simply click on the marked item.

⚜ Mass-effect spells — *Mass Curse, Archcure, Chain Lightning* and so forth — work well over a densely populated area. A maximum of nine characters can be affected at once if they're packed into a tight group, standing shoulder-to-shoulder. Target the ground at the center of the group instead of the group itself for the maximum effect.

Fifth Circle

- When a summoning spell is cast, creatures always appear about three feet to the north (directly up and to the left of where the caster is standing). If something is standing at the place where the creature should appear, you won't be able to summon it until you move to a clearer location.

- If you've become infamous, some NPCs may refrain from talking to you or selling you goods. If you run into this problem, use *Incognito*. The effects are only temporary, but should last enough for you to learn or buy what you want.

- When fighting a magical battle, set up a *Magic Reflection* of yourself. Your reflection only rebounds a single spell, so you may need to recast the spell several times during battle. if your enemy casts a *Mana Vampire* at your reflection, you'll end up with all of *her* mana instead of her gaining *yours*. This makes her completely vulnerable and gives you the upper hand in battle.

- Be judicious when you're using the *Mind Blast* spell. The damage it inflicts is based on the difference between your intelligence and your victim's intelligence. If your target happens to have a higher intelligence than you, then you'll take damage, not him. (Of course, this can work to your advantage if someone of a lower intelligence casts this spell at you.)

- *Dispel* and *Mass Dispel* are useful tools to rid an area of undead. Occasionally, you can successfully cast this spell against elementals and daemons.

- *Blade Spirits* are geared to track and attack warrior types — namely, characters with high *Tactics* and *Parrying* skills. Similarly, *Energy Vortex* tracks and kills mages and other characters with high intelligence.

  Both spells are particular about their targets. While your opponents can ward off or destroy *Blade Spirits*, *Energy Vortex* spells can not be physically countered. Your best defense against either spell is to run and lure it past nearby characters in hopes that the spell finds someone else a more suitable target than you.

- *Blade Spirits* and *Energy Vortex* can have a devastating effect in a crowded room. Stand near the door, casting one of destructive spells, then trap your opponents in the room with *Magic Lock* or *Wall of Stone*.

- The field spells (*Energy Field*, *Fire Field*, *Poison Field*, *Dispel Field* and *Paralyze Field*) double as both offensive and defensive weapons. Most monsters tend to shy away from fields.

Sixth Circle

⚧ If you can cast *Mark*, it can provide a quick teleport getaway in an emergency. From your home (or wherever you want the spell to take you to), cast the spell on an object small enough to carry in your backpack. It will record your exact location.

⚧ You may want to cast *Mark* on several items, just so that you have several safe points to which to escape (your home, your guild hall, a healing shrine, etc.).

⚧ When you make yourself invisible, you see yourself as a gray apparition on the screen. However, other players can not see you for the duration of the spell (excepting, of course, mages who cast *Reveal*).

⚧ Use *Reveal* if you suspect that an invisible character is lurking nearby. It works over a large radius and exposes invisible characters.

⚧ Invisible targets can be hit by mass-effect spells.

Seventh Circle

⚧ *Gate Travel* opens a ten-second gate between your current location a specified marked object. This spell is useful for moving an entire party of people between points, but be careful — some monsters can (and will) follow you through the gate.

⚧ *Gate Travel* only works in one direction — once you elect to return to a *Marked* location, you can't gate back to your previous location.

⚧ An *Energy Field* is impassable, but the other field spells can be passed through with some detrimental effects. *Energy Field* is the most dangerous, as merely touching it incurs great damage. Because of this, it's the best one for blocking off an exit from a dangerous room.

Eighth Circle

⚧ During battle, *Summon* a creature, then access its status window by double-clicking on the creature. The name box will say something like "Daemon" or "Fire Elemental." Erase that identifying name by clicking in the name field and typing in a new name. Now, you can treat the creature like a pet — order it to attack, follow, retrieve, etc. Its loyalty will be at maximum, although the creature will disappear after a short time.

⚧ *Earthquake* is a destructive spell, but it can also help you make a grand escape. A wide-radius spell, it causes all characters within the area (except the caster) to flop around on the ground and injure themselves. *Earthquake* lasts long enough to allow you to flee the area.

Non-Player Characters

- Non-player characters (NPCs) have 225 different ways of saying "I don't understand."

- When you're talking to NPCs, speak to them in complete sentences. Their vocabularies are based on keywords and context. The more words you use, the better the chance they will have of correctly understanding you.

- Conversely, there are a few keywords that must be spoken in isolation — the **bold-face** words in the keywords lists (starting on p. 125) can not have any other words spoken with them.

- You can ask NPCs for directions to a specific place of business. They will recognize "blacksmith," "tavern," "stable" and words for other common trade shops and locations. (See **Keywords**, p. 125.)

- NPCs speak differently according to how intelligent they are. Educated NPCs will tend to have larger vocabularies and more refined grammar, while some peasants will have a strong dialect and a narrow vocabulary.

- Innkeepers, bards and tavernkeepers usually have the latest rumors on where magic items are located in that region.

- You can ask any NPC what time it is in game hours. Just make sure to include the word "time" in your question.

- You can talk to scholars, tavern keepers, bards and mages about "Relvinian" to find out the history behind the hedgemaze and the wizard who created it. The news articles in this book give part of the story as well.

- The NPC names include the first name of every employee at ORIGIN.

- NPCs answer to normal greetings like "Hi" and "Hello." They'll also answer to "Yo," "Hiya" and "Howdy!" (We are from Texas, after all ....)

Miscellaneous

- If you slay a creature, make sure you dress your kill. You can make money by selling the hides of certain animals, and nearly all creatures have ribs you can sell to a butcher. If you don't know where the nearest butcher is, simply ask any town-dwelling NPC, "Where is the butcher?"

- Player-killers (those who make a career out of attacking players, especially new players) often stake out the starting points where new players enter the game. Once you're in the game, move away from the starting area.

- Name your pet something you can type quickly and easily. Many of the pet commands involve using the pet's name, and it's a lot easier to type "Igg" or "Flu" rather than "Ignatius" or "Fluellicello."

- If you have *Peacemaking* and *Musicianship* skills (and an instrument to play on), the wilderness isn't as dangerous as it might be to other players. Creatures are particularly affected by your music and will usually remain peaceful. After you spend some time in the woods playing your instrument to calm rabbits and other small creatures, you'll improve your *Peacemaking* skill enough to return to the city and use it as a defense.

- Wisps can only be harmed by magical attacks, but they are susceptible to the calming powers of music. A tacky bard trick involves luring other players into the expanses between Britain and Yew, where many wisps live. As a skilled bard, you can peacefully walk among the wisps, playing your instrument. When you quit playing, the other players are attacked by the wisps, and you inherit whatever they are carrying.

- (Conversely, beware of bards bearing lutes between Britain and Yew!)

- Knowing how much meat and hide (resource units) different creatures provide can be especially important if you intend to hunt them and sell the animals' by-products — a cow yields 10 resource units of leather, for example. See **Creature Descriptions**, starting on p. 137.

- If you need a large place in which to meet, try Trinsic. There's a hall there, suitable for guild meetings and other large congregations of people. You don't have to reserve it — all you need to do is occupy it. Look for the large building with the second story balcony and large garden. (See **Trinsic**, p. 272.)

- The barrier island off the coast of Trinsic is based in part on the American island of Chincoteague. If you want to tame a wild horse, it's a good place to visit.

- A shrine will fully resurrect you, but no more than once a day (that's once every two hours, with the current game/real time ratio). Contrary to common rumors, a shrine will not heal a wounded character — you must be dead for it to do you any good.

Counselors

Some experienced players have volunteered to answer questions and help new players get started in *Ultima Online*. These *counselors* are recognizable by the blue robes they wear. A counselor can usually answer your game-related questions immediately, or can find someone who knows the answer.

Counselor characters do not actively participate in the game, so don't expect to find them adventuring. (On the other hand, a counselor might locate herself near a shrine or dungeon, to help players in those areas.) Players who run counselor characters should create another character to actively participate in the game.

Counselors' Guildhalls

Each major town has a Counselors' Guildhall (Britain and Trinsic each have two). These are marked on the town maps (starting on p. 246), in the Guild category. Visit the guildhall for help if you don't see any blue-robed characters nearby. (Unlike the game guilds (p. 51), you won't find a guildmaster there, and you can't use the the guildhall to join the "Couselors' Guild.")

Becoming a Counselor

If you're interested in becoming a counselor, check the website for more information.

Easter Eggs

A favorite pastime of game designers is to throw hidden surprises into the game. They can be small or large, but they're always interesting. In some cases, the surprises (a.k.a. "Easter Eggs") reflect actual events or inside jokes among the development team members.

☥ If you speak to non-human species (such as orcs), you'll often get responses like "Glugbugzugboog!" Occasionally, however, they'll respond with "Me jabber incomprehensibly!" or the like. They know words like "Ultima" and "game," and will be offended if you say certain things to them.

☥ If you charter a ship, have a conversation with the tillerman. He has some great stories, including one about a lass who braided fox tails into her hair (and who was actually a character played by one of the game's designers). Another story talks about a fellow who is sucked into a whirlpool, and whose hair turns white — an allusion to Edgar Allen Poe's *Descent Into the Maelstrom*.

- Most daemon names come from an old book on black magic. Other daemon names in the game are derived from many sources, from the traditional "Be'elzebub" to his whimsical country cousin "Be'elzebubba." You'll also find "El Chupacabra," which you might remember from an episode of a popular, supernatural-phenomenon series, several names from the works of H. P. Lovecraft, and "Starr," the name of the game's associate producer.

- Some of the Orc names include "Digdug" (a classic videogame), "Frug" (a dance), "Gomoku" (a board game) and "Ignatz."

- Magincia Council Members often carry magic items.

- Pizza is a food item in the game.

- You'll find a book describing some of the late night meals eaten in ORIGIN meeting rooms — such as the Star Chamber, Mosh Pit and Glass House.

- Some books link together to form an ongoing story about a former paladin guildmaster and a girl he loved when he was young.

- The book about a dragon exploding describes something that actually happened to a programmer as a result of a bug (i.e., a problem with the game reported during testing).

- Very rarely, you'll meet an NPC who describes his job as "mystic llama-herder."

- Try speaking the mantra of Spirituality three times on the top stair near the Shrine of Spirituality. (The shrine itself is halfway down the road between Britain and Trinsic, on the west side) When uttering the mantra, type OM Enter OM Enter OM Enter, **not** OM OM OM Enter.

- You might check out a mountain range southwest of Trinsic where two rivers meet. The southern branch has a waterfall running out the side of the mountain. Follow the rivers to find something interesting.

- What's the purpose of the Hedge Maze, located southwest of Britain? We bet there's a good answer.

- Some NPCs and creatures will almost always have gold and a magic item in their inventory, including Orc Captains, Earth Elementals, Ettins, Ogres, Trolls, Gargoyles and Liches. More powerful creatures — Daemons, Dragons, Drakes, Gazers, Elementals (all but Earth Elementals) have even more.

DEVELOPING YOUR CHARACTER

by Ken Scott (Astra Irae)

When starting a new character, there are two things that you should decide before ever hitting CREATE CHARACTER: "What does this character wish to be?" and "How am I going to get there?" The fact that these questions require thought at all is one of the great innovations of *Ultima Online*. Because the system is skill-based, characters are not locked into any one career, but may follow any path, or series of paths, that they choose. A little thought before characters are introduced to the rigors and joys of Britannia can produce much more well-rounded and self-sufficient careers in the long run.

"What does this character wish to be?"

That's the easy question to answer. Most players have an idea of what their character will be. Whether it be a Doughty Fighter, a Powerful Mage, a Cunning Thief, a Skillful Ranger or something less mainstream, the game has templates set up with useful skills for all these professions. However, the skills presented in the templates are sometimes more reflective of the skills that a fully formed character of the profession should have. The player who dives right in — presses CREATE CHARACTER, selects a template and runs with it — may be in for a bit of a rude awakening. Character templates often lack skills that the new character will need to make a start in the game.

Templates — Pros and Cons

For example, a Mage starts out with *Magery, Inscription* and *Resisting Spells*. All well and good for a spellcaster at the height of her career, when people ask her to join them on grand quests for a share of the loot. Unfortunately for the lowly Apprentice Mage, there is very little potential for self-sufficiency in those skills. The same goes for the Thief template: *Snooping, Stealing* and *Lockpicking* are all the necessary skills for a good thief. But in the beginning, while the thief is at best mediocre with one of these skills, and near-pitiful with the others, he is going to spend many hours of game time seeking the services of healers for resurrection.

Similarly, unless our apprentice Mage is fortunate enough to have a band of friends who are willing and able to support her in the early stages of her career (find her spells to add to her book, give her reagents, protect her from harm when outside the city), so they might reap the benefits of having a high-circle Mage in their company later on, she's going to need a plan that gives the character time to grow, from "infancy" through adolescence to maturity. The template reflects the necessary skills of a mature Mage, but consider changing it to address the needs of an infant character.

Modifying Templates

What an infant character needs most is the ability to make money needed to purchase equipment and training. Our apprentice mage could replace *Resist Spells* with *Tailoring* (or, if she wouldn't stoop to something outside the magical arts, *Alchemy*). Tailors can buy cloth and dyes, make clothes and sell them to shopkeepers and others without ever leaving the safety of the town. (*Alchemy* can also make the mage money, but the market for potions is smaller. On the other hand, *Alchemy* will probably be more useful to the mage later in her career.)

Similarly, someone who wants to be a Ranger might start with a Bowyer template (*Parrying, Archery, Bowyer/Fletcher*), since a self-sufficient ranger will want to craft her own arrows anyway, and bows and arrows can be sold or traded. However, bows are crafted from wood. If you don't have the means to collect wood, you have to trade for it or by it, and the increased overhead lowers your profit margin and results in a longer 'infancy' for your character. One solution: replace *Parrying* in the Bowyer/Fletctemplate with *Lumberjacking*. Now you've got the skill and tools to produce marketable goods with only time and effort invested.

Saving for a Rainy Day

Once you start acquiring gold and training in the skills of your profession, build a nest-egg. Never spend everything an infant character makes — always put half of it in the bank. In the unfortunate event of an unplanned death, a penniless infant character has a harder time recovering than one with a few hundred in the bank.

Growth and Maturity

The character can now begin to venture out more often, take more risks, delve into the unknown, and train the skills that the mature character will require. Fighting monsters will raise skills far faster and farther than hitting the practice dummy or shooting at the archery butt. But don't be taken in by the headstrong enthusiasm of adolescence. Pace yourself. Don't dive headlong into the depths of Covetous the first trip into the wilderness. The adolescent character is still training, learning skills by experience, and making money along the way.

Eventually characters will approach the original conception, and become mature characters. Full-fledged characters are well-rounded, possessing the skills to ply their crafts, support themselves in time of need, and contribute to the plans and aspirations of their cohorts.

Sometimes, over the course of their growth, characters become something entirely different from what was originally sought. That's the beauty of this game, that growth and change is possible. So, when you hit that CREATE CHARACTER button, give some thought before you hit DONE. What do you want the character to be, and how are you going to get there?

OTHER PLAYERS

The thing about *Ultima Online* that sets it apart from any other roleplaying adventure in history, is the fact that you are interacting with thousands of other real people simultaneously. This is the game's main attraction, but also one of its main sources of frustration, particularly for new players.

People, you see, cannot be controlled. ORIGIN cannot write code into the game to prevent jerks from being jerks. They can take measures to limit anti-social activity and to keep malicious players from ruining the fun of the unwary, but that's about as far as they can go.

There are lots of good people in *UO* — good roleplayers, and also folks who are more interested in helping new players than in tormenting them. Meeting such people is one of the great joys of this game. But even in a perfect world, there would be some players more interested in roleplaying evil characters than virtuous ones, and so precautions would have to be taken to protect oneself. Since the world is not perfect, there will always be some players in *UO* who are simply malicious (or more often, immature), and they are far more annoying than players who are seriously trying to portray evil characters.

Below are some pointers for new players to help them protect themselves from evil characters, and avoid immature or hostile players.

Pkilling

Player killing (AKA "pkilling" or "PK") is the killing of one player-character in a multi-player game by another. There are a number of different degrees of player killing. If Harry the Dashing accosts travellers on the open road with, "Your pardon, Sirrah, but I will have either your money or your life," that is far less objectionable than Basha, who likes to train bears and sic them on unsuspecting travellers while she hides in the forest. Both are preferable to Lord of D'eth, who thinks that it is just hilarious to try out his new *Firewall* scroll in the smithy in Britain — D'eth is basically inexcusable. All three actions, however, are completely legal in the game (though D'eth will definitely face Britain's guards).

While pkillers who roleplay are far preferable to pkillers who just like slaughter for its own sake, no habitual pkiller is ever going to be popular. They are regarded by most players as an annoyance and an obstruction, and are usually invoke extreme prejudice, regardless of how well they roleplay. Unless you thrive on the hostility of others, you might want to avoid character concepts that involve pkilling.

And whatever your character concept might be, you'll definitely want to avoid pkillers. Guards provide solid protection in the towns, but if you're worried about being ambushed in town, set up a Macro so you can call the guards with a single keystroke instead of having to type in the word "Guards!"

In the wilderness, the things that will protect you against pkillers are the same things that will protect you against monsters. Travel in groups, and if travelling alone keep to the main roads. Pkillers and monsters occupy different regions, however — the worst monsters tend to congregate in the deepest wilderness, while pkillers haunt approaches to congested areas, like towns and dungeons. While shrines and moongates are guarded areas, PKs will haunt the approaches.

Stealing

Thievery is an ancient and (in its particular context) honorable fantasy profession, but that doesn't mean you have to be an easy target for it. Figure you're doing the thieves a favor by presenting them with a challenge to be overcome — or just figure you don't owe thieves any favors at all. Either way, figure on taking steps to avoid being picked blind.

First, stay out of crowds. If a stranger comes and stands close to you and appears to be doing nothing at all, chances are he's trying to *Snoop* in your inventory — move away. In town, you're not allowed to attack a thief that you catch in the act, but you can call a guard, who will do the deed for you (and you'll be first in line for the culprit's stuff — there's absolutely nothing shameful about looting the corpse of a failed thief, when you were the intended victim).

Keep your really valuable possessions in bags — or even keep the bags in bags, layered three or four deep. This not only conceals your valuables, but each container requires a separate *Snooping* check, increasing the chance a thief will be caught. A similar strategy is putting valuables under a stack of hides or something equally bulky and innocuous in your pack. This slows a thief down, and she might miss the best stuff entirely.

Looting

Gleaning useful items from the corpses of the fallen is an integral part of the game. There is no law, either social or official, guaranteeing that your possessions will still be with your body if you wander off in search of resurrection.

At the same time, a certain amount of courtesy toward the fallen is appreciated by all. If the corpse is being guarded by a hireling or pet, it is not simply prudent, but also good manners, to take that as a sign that the former owner plans to return and that you should leave the possessions alone. And, if somebody dies in town and resurrects immediately, it is extremely shoddy behavior to swarm the body and try to grab something good before the rightful owner can recover it. (The case of a failed thief, detailed above, is an arguable exception.)

If something useful is lying on the ground, it is probably open for taking, but if others are standing nearby it is polite to ask who it belongs to (of course, while you politely await an answer, someone with fewer scruples might grab the object).

ROLEPLAYING

The one thing that divides the good *UO* player from the clueless is not whether their character is good or evil, but whether the character is a *character*. In other words, roleplaying. Unlike single-player fantasy games (and "deathmatch" or "dungeon crawl" multi-player games) there's far more to *UO* than simply grabbing as much cool stuff as you can by any means available. If this is the level on which you play *Ultima Online*, you will find that its appeal fades rapidly. On the other hand, if you try to roleplay — try to create a character who is a real person, different from yourself, and react within the game as that person would act — then *UO* can continue to be fascinating experience literally forever. Roleplaying doesn't necessarily mean putting on a pose or talking with a bunch of "thees" and "thous," and it certainly doesn't mean acting like a stereotype out of an action movie, it just means acting in a consistent and believable fashion. Those who go to the effort to roleplay their character will, in time, inevitably become the most significant characters in the game, while those who don't are doomed to be regarded as simple annoyances or, at best, nonentities.

It's not your Dad's Dungeon Crawl

There is a conceptual leap that needs to be made in going from traditional computer games to Ultima Online. In an ordinary, single-player game you expect to be, and rapidly become, the center of the whole game-universe. Not only do you either start as, or rapidly become, the most dangerous entity in the game, but everything that happens happens to you or because of you. This is particularly true in the other games of the Ultima series, where you are the Avatar, the predestined champion of all the Virtues.

In *UO*, you still have formidable natural advantages, particularly when compared to NPCs, but there are also thousands of other players in the game, each with the same natural advantages, and each with the same power to alter events in the game. Also, there's no big payoff — no "level boss" to defeat and prove that you're the baddest of the bad. Most importantly, there's no save game or reset button to allow you to go back and correct your mistakes. Mistakes in *UO* are not necessarily fatal, but they are definitely indelible — once they happen, they can not be erased, only corrected.

What you gain in return for giving up these (admittedly entertaining) features of a solo game is growth, change, freedom of choice and the opportunity to participate in a real community. Understanding what *UO* does and does not offer is the key to roleplaying.

If you play *UO* with the traditional computer game goals of "get all the cool stuff, find all the secret places, beat the big bad guy and win" in mind (either consciously or unconsciously) you won't find the game entertaining for long, because you won't be roleplaying.

Roleplaying Requires a Role

On the other hand, if you go into the game planning to explore the full potential of your character, make a name for yourself among the other players, and make a lasting mark on the way the online world of *UO* expands and deepens, then you will find the game endlessly fascinating, and you will be roleplaying. It doesn't really matter if you have a flashy "high-concept" character with a deep and complicated background story (although such characters can be fun, and many of the best roleplayers prefer them). What really makes you a roleplayer is your willingness to become a member of the community.

This doesn't mean you have to be pushy or a "joiner." Your function in the community can be the solitary hunter who only comes into town to sell his hides, or the crotchety old hermit who prefers not to associate with anybody except those in great need of her skills. The point is that even such solitary characters have found a niche in the community and occupy it to their fullest potential. In order to roleplay, you must first find a role. Killing monsters for their stuff is not a role, nor is killing other players for theirs, but being Jael the Hunter, or Debrah the Bandit Princess is. Making lots of armor because that's a quick way to make cash isn't roleplaying, but being a hero so exacting in her standards that she will trust her safety only to things made with her own hands, that's a role.

Roleplaying is what you make of it

The last thing to note about *UO* is that it does not put an adventure in your face every time the plot slows down. If you're getting bored with the routine, change it — it's your routine. The adventures are out there, but it's up to you to find them and it's up to you to conquer them. Nor are they carefully pre-programmed so that the next thing you meet is guaranteed to be something you can handle. That ettin will be just as happy sucking the marrow of a newbie it flattened with one swat as it will be with a hero who almost slew it. In the traditional computer game, you wait for the adventure to come to you, and then you keep banging at it until you beat it. In *UO* you go out and find the adventure, you decide whether you're prepared to tackle it when you do find it, and you get only one shot to get it done. It's a much more fascinating experience than the average fantasy game bash, but also a much more subtle and difficult one. You can't experience *Ultima Online* passively — you have to take the initiative and find your own excitement, and this process of taking control of your own situation is also part of roleplaying. To have a goal is to have a role, and vice versa. You have to grab the adventure by the throat in *UO*, but before you can grab it, you have to know what you're reaching for. None of the maps or hints in this book can tell you where to go or what to do to have the perfect *Ultima Online* adventure, but roleplaying a real character will open up a sure path to years of ongoing fun and excitement.

LIVING IT UP IN LIMBO

When your character's hit points are reduced below zero, you die. Dying isn't necessarily a terrible thing in *Ultima Online* — you can still wander the world and spook any mortals you find. However, if you decide to stay undead, you must be willing to sacrifice your skills and attributes and give up your mortal belongings.

Newly Dead?

A great Britannian who claimed to converse with spirits once called death the "passage into life, into death, and into life again." In most respects, he was right. You are still an aware character — you just don't have as much interaction with the world as a living player character.

Should you die, here are some general facts that might make your passage a bit easier.

- No one will be able to see your (unmanifested) dead character on their screen unless, of course, they possess the *Resurrect* spell. Other ghosts will appear on your screen in full color. (Ghosts, of course, aren't colorblind to objects and people in the afterworld.)

- If you have a loyal pet or faithful hireling with you when you die, they will remain by your corpse's side, guarding it and the contents of your backpack.

- Contrary to popular belief, your ghostly character cannot pass through walls or float across water. You have to use a doorway, bridge or teleporter, just like everyone else. However, you *can* pass through closed doors.

- NPCs, monsters and animals are oblivious to your presence. Unfortunately, your loyal mountain cat Finny won't come when you call him — but then again, you don't have to worry about being attacked by dragons.

Ghostly Pranks

- Going into War mode while in a ghostly state causes you to "manifest" as a gray figure in the mortal world. Trying to manifest oneself is quite a tiring task for a ghost, so it is no surprise that fatigue sets in very shortly. Once fatigue points are exhausted, your manifestation automatically ends.

- Manifestation has been known to strike fear in the hearts of NPCs.

- No one besides other ghosts and someone using the *Spirit Speak* skill can hear your speech (see it onscreen, actually) while you're dead. While manifesting, however, anything you say to human characters or NPCs is automatically translated into ghostspeak as "Oooooh."

- Ghosts are immune to traps! For a little fun, try luring a gullible human player into a trap.

Death & Resurrection

When you die, you are immediately presented with a choice. You can wander as a spirit in search of resurrection, or you can resurrect yourself instantly. The second option seems more attractive on the face of it, but it comes at a cost — you can lose up to 25% of your skill and attribute values. A single quickie resurrection can literally undo months of hard roleplaying.

Newbies, however, have an advantage in that instant resurrection cannot lower attributes or skills beyond the point the character started with, so if you just started playing and you have the misfortune to get offed (especially if killed by an animal or dumb monster who doesn't bother to loot your corpse), go ahead and resurrect instantly. The loss of whatever trivial experience you have earned is not nearly as crippling as the loss of your starting equipment would be. Just be sure that whatever killed you has moved on before you raise yourself and start to recollect your belongings.

Sometimes, particularly in heavily overgrown terrain, a monster or creature will linger over your corpse for minutes that can seem like hours, bouncing off the surrounding scenery. In this case a rather extreme tactic that sometimes works is to resurrect yourself and *immediately* make a dash for an open area. You might get away, or the creature might catch you and kill you again, but either way in the more open area it's more likely to wander off promptly, after which you can raise yourself again and return to your first corpse for your belongings. Just remember that you have a finite maximum number of instant resurrections per day.

For more experienced characters, however, instant resurrection is a crippling experience. It should be avoided except when you have an item you absolutely cannot lose, or a schedule you absolutely must keep. This assumes, however, that appropriate precautions are taken.

When you create a character whose main worth is in her possessions, and she's killed and stripped, you've essentially lost the character. Oh sure, you could go back to town and start all over, but if you have to try to beg, borrow or steal enough money to buy some reagents, or an axe, and try to build yourself up from scratch, you're likely to be frustrated enough to say "enough already, I'll try a warrior next time around." The answer to True Death Syndrome is money in a bank.

You don't have to save enough for retirement, just enough to get you back on your feet. Decide how many reagents, or weapons, or whatever you'd want to have at a minimum, and work at making enough to tuck away for emergencies. Do it. Then, in the case of an emergency such as having your head whacked off, you'll be able to go back to town, suit yourself up, and put a bounty on your killer's head. Now *that* would feel good, wouldn't it?

SKILLS

Skills are the heart of *Ultima Online*. Nearly everything you do (other than walking and talking) is based on a skill. (In fact, even talking can be affected by skills — for example, *Begging* and *Spirit Speak*.)

Beginning Skills

Every beginning character starts by specifying three skills and assigning values to each of them. The total value of the three skills is 65 (currently), but you can spread this over the three skills you've chosen in any way you wish — 25 for one, and 20 each for the other two, or 35/20/10, or 50/10/5, or whatever works best for you.

Skill vs. Ability

However, you begin with at least minimal ability in every other skill in the game. Why? Because your actual ability with any skill is not based solely on your current skill level. It's also based on your attributes (Strength, Intelligence and Dexterity). Unless you're totally braindead, powerless and unable to walk (none of which is possible in *Ultima Online*), those attributes contribute at least a point or two toward every skill in the game. In some cases, they contribute a great deal. For example, even if you don't pick *Evaluating Intellect* as one of your first three skills, your initial *Evaluating Intellect* ability will be half of your initial Intelligence, because your ability in the skill is 50% based on your Intelligence.

Let's distinguish two terms at this point. The value for each specific **skill** is how many points you've put into that skill, either as one of the three skills you selected when creating your character, or through time spent practicing and training. Your **ability** with that skill is your base skill (what we've just described), plus any modifications based on your Strength, Dexterity and Intelligence.

The numbers that the game shows you are your *ability* levels for each skill, not the base skill level, and it's your ability level that is used when the game calculates whether you've succeeded or failed in a specific task.

Combat skills have one additional twist. Each time you strike, your chance of a successful hit is 50% based on the specific weapon ability and 50% based on your *Tactics* ability.

Ability formulas for each skill are listed in the table on p. 30, and are also listed under each individual skill description (starting on p. 54).

Practice Equipment

When you finish creating your character and begin playing, you always get the clothes on your back, a practice dagger and a backpack. You also get starting equipment based on the three skills you chose. For example, if you selected *Archery*, you begin with a practice bow and 25 arrows. If you chose *Cartography*, you begin with 4 blank maps and a sextant. Starting equipment for each skill is listed in the table on p. 31, and is also listed under each individual skill description (starting on p. 54).

Developing Your Skills

Every time you successfully use a skill, you fractionally improve your skill level. (It takes a *lot* of successes before that improvement is visible as an additional skill point.) Some skills advance more rapidly than other skills — figure that any skill you can attempt often and repeatedly (swinging an axe, *Anatomy*, or just about any combat skill) will produce significantly less improvement per success than skills that are harder to repeat (for instance, *Carpentry* or *Healing*. And no, you don't get credit for healing people who are already well.)

Your ability in a skill also improves when an underlying attribute improves, in proportion to that attribute's contribution to your ability — if your Intelligence rises two points, your *Evaluating Intellect* ability will rise a point, since *Evaluating Intellect* ability is based 50% on your Intelligence.

To encourage you to attempt new challenges and try the uncommon, and to promote diversity, your improvement will tend to be more dramatic in skills that other players aren't using very often.

Advancement at lower skill levels is much faster than at higher skill levels. In other words, it takes much longer to improve from a skill level of 90 to 91 than it does to improve from 10 to 11.

Your ability in a skill declines when you don't practice it (but never below 1).

Developing Your Attributes

Every time you successfully use a skill that is based on one of your attributes — Strength, Intelligence or Dexterity — that attribute is also fractionally improved. However, the attribute improvement is even slower than the skill improvement mentioned above. In like manner, attributes also atrophy like skills, but again, the rate of decline is much slower than the rate of decline for skills. And advancement at high levels is slower than advancement at lower levels.

Note that the total value of all three attributes can never rise above 200. Once you hit that ceiling, if one attribute increases, one of the other attributes immediately drops to keep the total at 200.

Ability Formulas

Ability	Skill%	S%	I%	D%
Alchemy	90	-	8	2
Anatomy	50	-	50	-
Animal Lore	50	-	50	-
Animal Taming	80	6	12	2
Archery *	90	-	1	9
Arms Lore	75	8	9	8
Begging	90	-	5	5
Blacksmithy	90	7	-	3
Bowcraft/Fletching	80	3	3	14
Camping	50	16	18	16
Carpentry	75	12.5	5	7.5
Cartography	85	-	12	3
Cooking	50	-	30	20
Detecting Hidden	75	-	20	5
Enticement	95	-	2.5	2.5
Evaluating Intellect	50	-	50	-
Fencing *	90	2	-	8
Fishing	75	2.5	-	22.5
Forensic Evaluation	75	-	25	-
Healing	80	-	14	6
Herding	75	6	7.5	11.5
Hiding	75	-	5	20
Inscription	90	-	10	-
Item Identification	75	-	25	-
Lockpicking	75	-	5	20
Lumberjacking	80	18	-	2
Mace Fighting *	90	8	-	2
Magery	85	-	15	-
Mining	80	14	-	6
Musicianship	90	-	2	8
Parrying	90	3	3	4
Peacemaking	95	-	2.5	2.5
Poisoning	80	-	16	4
Provocation	95	-	1	4
Resisting Spells	50	-	50	-
Snooping	75	-	-	25
Spirit Speak	50	-	50	-
Stealing	90	-	-	10
Swordsmanship *	90	5	-	5
Tactics	90	2	6	2
Tailoring	75	1	5	19
Taste Identification	50	10	40	-
Tinkering	90	2	6	2
Tracking	75	-	12.5	12.5
Veterinary	80	4	12	4
Wrestling *	90	5	-	5

* Combat ability in these skills is the average of your ability in the skill and your *Tactics* ability.

Starting Equipment List

Alchemy	mortar & pestle; 4 empty vials; 4 random reagents; red robe
Anatomy	3 bandages; robe
Animal Lore	practice shepherd's crook; green robe
Animal Taming	practice shepherd's crook
Archery	practice bow; 25 arrows
Arms Lore	random practice weapon
Begging	practice gnarled staff
Blacksmithy	random tool; brown apron
Bowcraft/Fletching	materials for 2 bows; shafts and feathers
Camping	5 kindlings; bedroll
Carpentry	carpentry tool; 10 boards; brown apron
Cartography	4 blank maps; sextant
Cooking	3 raw food items; water pitcher; flour sack; 2 kindlings
Detecting Hidden	black cloak
Enticement	random musical instrument
Evaluating Intellect	none
Fencing	practice spear
Fishing	fishing pole; brown floppy hat
Forensic Evaluation	none
Healing	5 bandages; pair of scissors
Herding	practice shepherd's crook
Hiding	black cloak
Inscription	2 blank scrolls; small blank book (to take notes)
Item Identification	practice gnarled staff
Lockpicking	5 lockpicks
Lumberjacking	practice hatchet
Mace Fighting	practice mace
Magery	spellbook; 5 random reagents; 3 random First Circle scrolls
Mining	practice pickaxe; shovel
Musicianship	random musical instrument
Parrying	wooden shield
Peacemaking	random musical instrument
Poisoning	2 poison potions
Provocation	random musical instrument
Resisting Spells	spellbook
Snooping	4 lockpicks
Spirit Speak	black cloak
Stealing	4 lockpicks
Swordsmanship	practice long sword
Tactics	none
Tailoring	sewing kit; 4 folded cloths
Taste Identification	3 random potions
Tinkering	set of tinker parts; set of tinker tools; brown apron
Tracking	practice skinning knife; brown boots
Veterinary	5 bandages; pair of scissors
Wrestling	pair of leather gloves

MOONGATE TRAVEL

Moongate travel, as the term suggests, depends on the phases of Britannia's two moons, Trammel and Felucca. There are eight known moongates in Britannia, each near a town. It is possible to travel from any moongate to any other moongate — where you go depends on the phases of the moons at the moment you step through the gate.

There are two ways to determine the current destination of a moongate you want to use. One is identify the phases of the moons directly (using a sextant), and calculate when you should use the gate by the two rings on the facing page. The other is to know the precise time, and to refer to our timetable. (Clocks can always tell you the time, or you can ask an NPC using the word "time".)

Rings

If you know the exact phase of both moons, you can use the rings for moongate travel. First, look at the **Town Ring**, below. Counting clockwise, begin with your current location and count how many steps it takes to reach your destination town. For example, counting from Jhelom to Moonglow is two steps. Counting from Moonglow to Jhelom is six steps (Be sure to count clockwise, not counterclockwise.)

Now, look at the **Phase Ring** on the facing page. Find Felucca's current phase, then count the steps (still clockwise) to Trammel's current phase. For example, if Felucca is a half moon waxing and Trammel is a full moon, Trammel is two steps ahead of Felucca. While that is the case (for ten or twenty minutes), you can travel from Jhelom to Moonglow (also two steps).

While the moons are at their current phases, all moongates will send you that many steps along the Town Ring. Keep watching the moons until Trammel is as many steps ahead of Felucca as your desired destination is ahead of your current location.

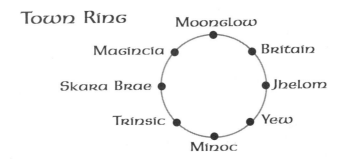

Town Ring
Moonglow
Magincia   Britain
Skara Brae   Jhelom
Trinsic   Yew
Minoc

Phase Ring

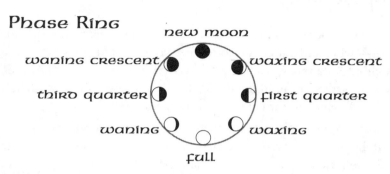

new moon

waning crescent   waxing crescent

third quarter   first quarter

waning   waxing

full

Timetable

If you know the exact time, you can use this timetable for moongate travel. First, look at the Town Ring and count the clockwise steps from your current location to your destination. Now, look up the number of steps you counted in the table below to find out when you can next use the moongate to reach your destination. (Times apply to either daytime or nighttime travel.)

Steps to destination	Times you can travel					
Nowhere	12:00-12:10	2:00-2:10	4:00-4:10	6:00-6:10	8:00-8:10	10:00-10:10
One step	12:10-12:30	2:10-2:30	4:10-4:30	6:10-6:30	8:10-8:30	10:10-10:30
Two steps	12:30-12:40	2:30-2:40	4:30-4:40	6:30-6:40	8:30-8:40	10:30-10:40
Three steps	12:40-1:00	2:40-3:00	4:40-1:00	6:40-7:00	8:40-9:00	10:40-11:00
Four steps	1:00-1:10	3:00-3:10	5:00-5:10	7:00-7:10	9:00-9:10	11:00-11:10
Five steps	1:10-1:30	3:10-3:30	5:10-5:30	7:10-7:30	9:10-9:30	11:10-11:30
Six steps	1:30-1:40	3:30-3:40	5:30-5:40	7:30-7:40	9:30-9:40	11:30-11:40
Seven steps	1:40-2:00	3:40-4:00	5:40-6:00	7:40-8:00	9:40-10:00	11:40-12:00

Shortcuts

You can always get where you want to go, but how long must you wait before doing so? At the most, the wait will never be more than two hours, and less if you use the following shortcut: you can make multiple jumps that combine to send you where you want to go. For example, if it's 4:15 when you want to get from Trinsic to Yew (two steps), you can immediately jump from Trinsic to Minoc (one step), then from Minoc to Yew (one step). If it's 11:30 when you want to get from Trinsic to Yew (still two steps), you can go from Trinsic to Magincia (six steps), from Magincia to Britain (six steps) and finally from Britain to Yew (six steps). You'll have to hurry, though, because at 11:40 the moongates shift their pattern and start giving seven-step jumps.

It's not always the case that immediate jumps can get you where you want to go, but you can usually cut your waiting period.

NOTORIETY

When you play a character in *Ultima Online*, you can choose to live life however you please — whether your goal is to rob everyone around you blind, or to wander throughout Britannia spreading kind deeds. Whatever you do, however, affects your *notoriety*, or reputation in the world. This is a measure of how others see you (mainly NPCs), which in turn affects how they respond to you.

Notoriety for NPCs is based on alignment — *Good, Evil, Chaotic* or *Neutral* (see **Alignment**, below). For players, notoriety is a numerical value from -127 to 127. This value is reflected in the game as a character's title, visible when you double-left-click on the character:

Notoriety		Male Title	Female Title
Good	121-127	Great Lord	Great Lady
	100-120	Noble Lord	Noble Lady
	80-99	Lord	Lady
	60-79	Noble	Noble
	40-59	Honorable	Honorable
Neutral	-39 to 39	No title	No title
	-40 to -59	Dishonorable	Dishonorable
	-60 to -79	Infamous	Infamous
	-80 to -99	Dark Lord	Dark Lady
	-100 to -120	Evil Lord	Evil Lady
Evil	-121 to -127	Dread Lord	Dread Lady

Alignment

Closely tied to notoriety is *alignment*, or what type of battle alliance a non-player character is most likely to make during a fight. As a player character, you start with an assigned alignment of Neutral, although your actions will change your notoriety and perceived alignment.

Non-player character alignment falls into one of four classifications:

Good	Protects Good and Neutral characters; defends self if attacked.
Neutral	Fights only if attacked, and targets attacker.
Evil	Attacks Good and Neutral characters, not Evil ones.
Chaotic	(NPCs only) Targets all characters.

In the world of NPCs, all characters have a default alignment. Nearly all NPC alignments are Neutral; in fact, alignment isn't listed in this book unless it is something other than Neutral. Those with similar alignments tend to protect their own and defend themselves against any attack. (See **Non-Player Character Descriptions**, p.162, for details.) Creatures also have alignments — most animals are Neutral, while some monsters are either Evil or Chaotic. See **Creature Descriptions**, p. 137.

Changes in Notoriety

Your notoriety rating and corresponding alignment change as you play the game, and tends to move toward zero (Neutral) over time, unless you are constantly acting to take it to one of the extremes (Good or Evil). Changes in notoriety occur as you play and interact with the game world and other characters. These shifts are weighted based on how far away you are on the scale from the opposite extreme (in other words, the "more Good" a person is, the bigger the hit to her reputation when she performs an evil deed).

The greatest shifts in notoriety occur when a knightly player performs a really evil deed. It's much harder to improve an evil reputation — this makes it harder to lightly shrug off the consequences of a dark and callous past.

Performing a good deed when you're already a Noble Lady or Lord only slightly improves your notoriety. Likewise, an already evil player that performs yet another dastardly deed won't experience much lowered notoriety.

Evil		Good
-127	0	+127

Events that edge notoriety to zero:

✞ Passage of time (without frequent Good or Evil actions)

Actions that add positive notoriety

✞ Killing Evil NPCs

✞ Giving items away to NPCs who own less than your character does

✞ Healing a Good or non-Evil NPC, or well-reputed player

✞ Completing a quest given to you by a Neutral NPC

Actions that add negative notoriety

✞ Attacking Good NPCs and Neutral players

✞ Stealing (from anyone)

✞ Healing an Evil or Chaotic NPC, or ill-reputed character

Notoriety and Interaction

Most NPCs in the game have Neutral notoriety, and will adopt an attitude toward you based on your current notoriety. They will still give you approximately the same information and ask the same questions, but you'll find that the tone of conversation reflects their opinion of you.

For example, if ask an armourer about the best way to improve your armouring skills, you'll get one of the following responses:

(To Evil players) "Oh, don't tell me thou dost want to learn armor-making. I'd be hard-pressed to train someone like thee."

(To Neutral players) "I've been known to teach some how to improve their skills, for a few coins."

(To Good players) "I'd be honored to teach thee some of what I know. 'Twould be up to thyself, though, to practice it."

Additionally, the responses change as you become famous. If you talk to an innkeeper, for example, he or she will recognize your fame:

(To famous, Evil players) "I suppose I shall have to place a sign 'pon my inn, declaring that the Great and Vile, Killer of Infants and Slayer of Guards, the Monstrous Zenkoh slept here once."

"If thou makest a solemn promise not to harm anyone while thou stayest with us, then I can offer thee a room."

(To non-famous, Neutral players) " 'Tis a pleasure to offer thee a bed and a room."

(To famous Good players) "Ah, if 'twere possible for thee to stay the night in one of mine humble rooms, perhaps my lot would improve."

Remember, notoriety is purely a measure of how you're perceived by NPCs and other players. It is a measure of fame, not a moral judgment on your character's behavior (although it is a result of your behavior). A character with -127 notoriety and another with +127 notoriety will both be famous and respected, but in different ways. Most NPCs and players will not like an Evil player (negative notoriety), but will give him or her respect and goods out of fear. A player with +127 notoriety will also gain respect, but of a different nature.

Local and Global Notoriety

When you travel, your deeds (good or ill) do not necessarily follow you. Some deeds only affect your notoriety in the town where they occurred — when you go elsewhere, your new neighbors won't necessarily have heard of all of your past exploits.

Town Cryer

RELVINIAN: DAEMONS CAN DO OUR WORK

The eccentric mage known only as Relvinian has announced that his current project will free mankind forever from menial labor. From the steps of his laboratory, he described to a good-sized gathering what daemons can do for the human race. "With daemons doing the manual labor that takes up so much of everyone's day, people will be free to follow more cerebral paths," Relvinian said. "We will be able to better educate our society. Who knows what new heights we might attain!"

Daemons are usually associated with dark magic and other evil intentions. This would be the first attempt on record to bring them into a more positive light. Some experts are concerned about the implications of a creature borne of evil working daily with the citizens of Britannia. "I'm worried about our children. Our family values. What kind of a role model will these things be to our kids?" asked brother Andrew of Empath Abbey. "I mean kids will suddenly want to summon their own daemon to get out of making their beds, or going to the market. Children won't learn responsibility because here's this guardian of evil at their command. The next thing you know they'll be hexing each other, or sending their daemon out to exact revenge on Little William for

pulling a dog's tail."

Relvinian says that the fears of brother Andrew and others like him are completely unfounded. "I've created a spell that will summon and totally control a daemon and all its actions, but it can only be cast by a Grandmaster Mage such as myself. We will then assign the daemon to a household and place a schedule in its mind. The creature will have no choice but to perform the assigned tasks." In response to questions about not-so-well-intentioned mages who get possession of the spell, Relvinian replied, "The spell drains the caster a great deal. If one were to summon a daemon and charge it with malevolent tasks, it would be a simple thing to discover who the offending mage was and bring him or her to answer for the deed."

Other concerns were brought to light by a group calling themselves Britannian Species United. "Why must one group, in this case humans, control the minds or actions of another? We already have enough warring between the species of Britannia, must we have slavery, too?" asked a BSU spokesperson. "No creature should be able to control the mind of another, be they men, gargoyles or daemons. It just isn't right."

Relvinian goes Monday to further explain and demonstrate his theories to Lord British, who seems cautiously optimistic about the idea. "I think the potential is immense," The Ruler of Britannia said in conversation with Your Correspondent. "As you know, I have been actively promoting the eight Virtues throughout Britannia, and freedom from menial labor would be a great step toward the education of the populace as a whole, both in the Virtues and in the more standard curriculum of reading, writing and mathematics. I think Relvinian's ideas could possibly benefit the citizens of Britannia as much as the consolidation of the city-states, and thus the ending of their petty wars, did at the beginning of our current Enlightened Age. Sure there are a few bumps to smooth out, and I won't allow the plan to be adopted until the time that those problems are addressed, but I see promising things ahead." ▨

POINT ⟨⟩ ⟨⟩ COUNTERPOINT
DAEMONS AS MAIDS?

Guest columnists Brother Andrew the Wise from Empath Abbey, and Lord British, ruler of Britannia, have debated today's hot topic: Can daemons really do our work for us? Following is the transcript of their discussion.

Lord British: I think that daemons, when summoned as Relvinian plans, with no real thoughts of their own, are certainly capable of the manual labor that has hindered mankind for centuries. The ideal goal for us as humans is to improve our minds and our bodies, to grow mentally and spiritually. If we are no longer required to slave all day in the mines, or serve meals at the tavern, then our time can be better spent in more educational pursuits.

Brother Andrew: You have already touched on a few of my many points against this idea of Relivinian's. Whether the daemons are capable of the labor isn't the issue. If the work that we, as free-thinking humans, do is slavery, as you have just called it, then it will be even more so for the daemons. Slavery is wrong no matter who is doing it to whom.

LB: You miss the point, Andrew. The daemons won't have minds. They'll be like blank slates, waiting to be written upon.

BA: Says Relvinian. I have yet to see proof that they will be free of independent thought. I have full confidence that he can summon them, but if it was possible to erase their minds, wouldn't someone have done it long ago? Besides, does that make it right, the fact that the daemon's personality will be ripped from them?

LB: We have been working for centuries against these creatures of evil. There has never been any sign that they are other than mindless, malevolent monsters. They have no personality that we know of. Besides, the spiritual growth of the human race will continually bring us into contact with them. There's something to be said for weeding out the problem before it overwhelms us.

BA: Okay, let's talk about the spiritual growth of humans. Isn't physical labor a positive catalyst to growth? You know the phrase, "mentally and physically strong …" Should we take that away from the people?

LB: As I see it, this will be a marketable thing. If someone wants his or her own daemon, then buy one! Otherwise, no one will be forcing it on anyone. So if you are morally opposed to the idea, then don't buy a daemon. It's simple, really.

BA: But let's say your daemon is doing chores for you and he gets hungry. Not having a mind of his own, he just reacts and grabs the nearest thing at hand: my dog. Do I blame you? Can I take you to court for not feeding your daemon well enough so he wouldn't just eat at random? In fact, what if it were my kid? Can you put a block in its mind to not eat children?

LB: Those are some of the issues that Relvinian and I will discuss when we meet on Monday. We certainly have many things to iron out about legality issues, ownership issues, and what kind of training one can give his or her daemon. It'll be a lengthy process, but well worth it in the long run, you can be sure.

BA: Well, I guess we can only agree to disagree on this subject. ▣

Skills

STARTING TEMPLATES

Alchemist

(Alchemy, Resisting Spells, Taste Identification)

Jerimiah Remmint, student of the alchemical arts

Q: Why did you become an Alchemist?

I chose the alchemical arts for two simple reasons: I like magic, and I do not like combat. Mages are mercenaries. They strike me not so much as "adventurous" magic users, but rather as fighters who would rather not do battle up close. Myself, I study the craft itself — the way certain elements transcend to create undoubtedly extraordinary results. I seek to explain the inexplicable, if you will. I like to stay in town, and let the reagents come to me. I work with them, observe them and take note of the results. By and large I dispose of the resultant product in any way that seems the most prudent.

Q: Where is a good place to start?

I started my career in the town of Moonglow. It and Britain are the only two cities that I would even consider. They have a number of advantages, the greatest being that they both have adequate reagent shops, and claim a large population, many of whom are eager to buy the remnants of my studies.

Q: What advice would you give Novice Alchemists?

The first thing Alchemists needs must do is to become very familiar with all the wide varieties of reagents. They should have in their possession some random reagents, and if they are very lucky, these may transcend into some sought after potion. Healing potions are best. They should visit an Alchemist's shop and research the retail price of such a potion. They should be able to undercut a shop's price, since they have not acquired any overhead costs.

They should then go into an area heavily trafficked by adventuring Warriors, such as a smithy, and announce that they have a potion for sale, and they could also offer to identify any mysterious potions. The price does not have to be only gold — it could be in trade for some useful reagents, a few empty bottles, or anything else that seems useful.

They should avoid over-selling to the alchemy shops, if they can. It does not take too long for an eager Alchemist to glut the retail market with his own potions. It is always best to sell to adventurers, I've found.

Animal Trainer

(*Animal Lore, Animal Taming, Veterinary*)

Morello, Beast Master

Q: Why did you become an Animal Trainer?

I'm not a people person, you know what I mean? I don't like people, don't let anybody get control over me. I wanted to do something where I could go where I want, when I want, and I didn't have to worry about having some bark-chewing moron with an oversized knife coming and sticking a foot of steel in me. I get a couple of big furry bodyguards, and it's just as good as having a couple of soldiers with me. Plus, it's pretty good money. I can sell the critters as protectors to weaker folks. People like Alchemists like that, so they can go and get reagents without being stomped into the mud by some limping half-wit with a dagger.

Q: Where is a good place to start?

I started off in Yew, and that worked pretty good for me. It's a kind of spread out area, with lots of creatures nearby. Anyplace with woods nearby, I guess. And dogs. If there aren't any dogs around, you might as well just give up, 'cause you need dogs to practice on, and give you some initial income.

After I got some guard animals, I found a place with less people. That's just the way I am. Plus people tend to have a bit more money farther out. Fewer green-horns.

Q: What advice would you give Novice Trainers?

First off, I'd go around and tame the local animals. You know, cats and dogs and rabbits and stuff. Once you have an animal tamed, give it a name and get it to guard you. Don't forget to feed it every once in a while, especially right at first. When you have a couple of guard dogs, you should go out and try to train tougher and tougher animals. Work up to something like a panther or a bear, and tame it. Then bring it back into town and sell it to someone who needs a guard. When you get good with harts and panthers and bears, you can stick your neck out and try a polar bear or a giant spider.

Yeah, an Animal Trainer can tame monsters, if he don't get his head bit off. Or her head.

Something I do sometimes is go deer hunting with a panther, and sell the hide and meat.

Assassin

(Hiding, Poisoning, Taste Identification)

Butterwick, Urban Assassin

Q: Why did you become an Assassin?

There isn't any one reason I can point to. I adore a challenge, I simply thrive on adrenaline, and I have no desire to ever live anywhere but the city. Those are the three formative reasons. I knew it was a difficult career to break into, but that's never stopped me before. I've always loved being where I shouldn't be, doing what I shouldn't be doing, and this seemed like a good way of making money at it.

Q: Where's a good place to start?

Britain is good. Or Trinsic. Any place where there are enough people … especially an unebbing flow of new people … where a stealthy person might lose himself in the crowd. An Assassin isn't really someone who can survive on his own, and these cities also offer the benefits of a wide variety of shops where various "implements" can be discreetly purchased.

Q: What advice would you give Novice Assassins?

Know that this is a very difficult life to perfect. You are relatively weak, and working in a hostile environment — if you try to kill someone outright within the walls, you'll most likely be caught. As with anyone who might encounter an enemy in close quarters, you should ensure that you have adequate skill in Tactics.

The first thing a novice should do is go to the blacksmith shop and offer to test a client's food and poison one weapon for enough gold that you will be able to buy or make two more poison potions, not forgetting to include the cost of the vial in your offer. If you find someone who is sincerely interested in keeping you in business, you're set. Whenever you're not conducting business, practice hiding. And if possible, try to make friends with an alchemist. Otherwise you'll end up paying retail for your poisons, and that can be murder, you'll pardon the expression.

Another way to make money is to hang around the healers' places and offer to check food for poison. As you get more experienced, you can offer your services in poisoning food, gathering information for guilds, and following people outside the city walls to dispose of them.

Staying alive represents its own challenges for an Assassin. An Assassin survives on anonymity. When your negative notoriety gets too high, people will attack you on sight. An *Incognito* scroll can briefly mask your true identity and notoriety for a minute or two. For longer-term survival, consider performing *many* good deeds. Doing so can offset the occasional assassination, returning your notoriety to zero.

Bard

(*Musicianship, Peacemaking, Provocation*)

Flurry the Lute

Q: Why did you become a Bard?

Well now, 'tis the power of the music, isn't it? There's no other answer for it. 'Tis as plain as the nose on a pig that 'tis the gift of music what has *me*. It's stood me in good stead, though, and I cannot complain of it. It's saved me from the business end of a dagger many a time enough.

Also, I have to admit to a wee touch of wanderlust. As soon as I know the backside of every wall, why, I'm off through the woods. I'm a fair hand in an adventuring party, so I just make some friends and we're off to the next town.

Q: Where's a good place to start?

That would be Britain, and there's not a doubt about it. There's a music hall for practicing until you are a dab hand at the strings. Then you can join up with groups and travel.

Q: What advice would you give Novice Bards?

Now I can't say as it's an easy life if you're a loner. Also, don't try to Provoke people in town. It's illegal.

Practice, practice, practice. That's the only way to get skilled, and the better your Musicianship, the better your Peacemaking and Provocation. There's a conservatory in Britain, so go there. If you need money for something, the best you can do is go into the woods and Provoke the animals to fight each other. If you see a deer and three rabbits, for example, you can get the deer to kill the hares. (Now don't look like that, you know music isn't all waltzes and minuets.) Then you can sell the hides and meat for a little gold.

The real goal, though, is to get with a party and use your skills to keep troublemakers at bay. That's when you really start earning your wages. Just ask up front that a portion of the cash found be yours.

Blacksmith

(Arms Lore, Blacksmithy, Parrying)

Toman Ironarm

Q: Why did you become a Smith?

It's a good job. Especially if you like to stay active ... if you like to make things. I like to stay at home. I don't like killing things for sport. Looking for trouble, that is. I don't go out of town much ... I just like learning new things. Making new things.

Still, I'm not afraid to go outside the walls. Hammer work means a strong arm, and I can pound most people who would make trouble with me. Some other smiths, they like to go get their own ore. Usually they come back okay. But mostly, it's staying put and making things for folks.

Q: Where is a good place to start?

I'd say Minoc would be a fine place to start. It's got two forges, I hear. It's not so hustle-bustle as Britannia, but it's busy enough. There's ore nearby, so people can get it and bring it to you. Or you can mine it yourself if you have a mind to.

Q: What advice would you give Novice Smiths?

I'd make sure that before I came to town, I had as much Blacksmithy skills as I could get. That's important, because you make things for other people ... you don't want to sour the sword that someone else has paid for. The better you are when you start, the less mistakes you make. So as much Blacksmithy skills as possible.

Then I'd go to a Blacksmith's forge. I'd offer to anyone around that if they bring ore, I'll make them something. I would ask for more ore than the weapon uses, you understand. Maybe they want a blade that uses five ores, I'd ask for ten. I'd keep five. Sometimes asking for gold is okay ... if you need gold.

I'd start off with weapons. Weapons are fairly easy. I'd start on a cutlass, maybe, because it's much better than a dagger, but easy to make. When you get good, then try some easy armour. Armour is difficult. Also, if you try to fix something and fail, you'll make it worse.

Oh, and run away if you get in a fight. It's always better. Pound 'em only if you have to.

Bowyer

(Bowcraft/Fletching, Parrying, Archery)

Timony Fletcher

Q: Why did you become a Bowyer?

Well to tell you the truth it was because I couldn't quite make up my mind. Sometimes I wanted to be one of the townfolk, and make things for other people for my living, and never have to try to join a group of adventurers and face who knows what ... and sometimes I couldn't stand the thought of being stuck in town and never seeing what was going on in the far off places. So I figured, if I knew how to make arrows, that would be a good living in a town, and a good start as an adventurer.

Q: Where is a good place to start?

Now that's a question. Britain is good … Britain is always good … but maybe another good place would be Vesper. It's got lots of woods and trees near Vesper. That's mostly what you look for, you know. Trees and the like.

Q: What advice would you give Novice Bowyers?

Make up your mind. I didn't, and it made it a little harder to start. If you want to stay in town, you should have the highest possible skill in Bowcraft/Fletching, and change Archery to Lumberjacking, so you can get your own wood. I've always fancied a bit of Tinkering, but I haven't ever studied it much.

If you want to go wandering, you should be as good as possible in Archery. You won't really need Parrying, so concentrate instead on Tactics.

Anyway, the first thing you should do is make a bow. Then go out and hunt something, and get money for it. If you can get a hatchet, you can use it on trees to get logs. You can make arrow shafts and bows out of logs. You also need feathers, so hunting birds is good.

Healer

(Healing, Anatomy, Forensic Evaluation)

Aras Longfingers

Q: Why did you become a Healer?

It's a very powerful job. That's what originally attracted me. It works well inside the city walls, but is easily twice as useful out in the wilds. Any band who knows what it's doing will want to bring a Healer along, and there are very few places where you can't find business. I liked the freedom that gave me. Yes, I like helping people, but that's more of a side benefit, really.

Q: Where is a good place to start?

Britain is a good place. Lots of people running around, getting into fights, coming back from adventures. Trinsic has so many glory-hungry fighters crawling around it that it's a goldmine. Or it was last time I visited. I've gone more in the direction of traveling groups of adventurers.

Q: What advice would you give Novice Healers?

Hmmm. If they plan to go out with adventurers, it might be good if they did not put so much weight into the skill of Anatomy, and instead concentrated on Tracking as an alternative skill. When you combine that with Forensic Evaluation, you can look at the body of someone and know who killed it, or rifled it, and which way they went. That's an incredibly useful skill, especially if your friends don't like murderers.

The first thing I'd do would be to go to town entrances and offer to heal people for practice (and a little money or cloth). Smithy and healer shops are also good places. Don't worry about competing with the local retail healers, they're usually too busy resurrecting people to have time to cure wounds.

Also, whatever you do, don't go it alone outside of the city! You'll die friendless and lonely. Stay with groups of heavily armed fighters. They're your friends, they know you're their friend, and they will take care of you.

Mage

(*Magery, Inscription, Resisting Spells*)

Adrienne of Moonglow

Q: Why did you become a Mage?

I am compelled by my art to see the world as it truly is, shorn of the veils and screens of illusion which comfort those who have no desire for understanding. I have oft heard folk say that all Mages are mad. In truth, I believe it is the opposite that is true: we are, as it were, too sane to pass unmarked in the crowd of mad mundanity.

There are those, I will not call them Mages, but merely magic users, who use the arts by putting them to work in the market; it is almost like a prostitution. It is not wrong, I suppose, but certainly they are lured more by gold than by truth.

Q: Where is a good place to start?

The question of where to start is more complex than that of where to end. There is only one path to perfection, and that is in Moonglow's academic atmosphere, where all strive to pierce the ephemeral fog with which appearance blinds us. But it is not easy to get there.

Commercial centers where adventurous and gold-focused ilk abound Britain — Trinsic, and other like towns — are undoubtedly good place for Mages to begin their careers.

Q: What advice would you give Novice Mages?

Unfortunately for those who wish to apply themselves to the true art, it is not easy for a novice to make her way undefended to Moonglow's halls. They must first find companions to bring them there. These sort value spells such as *Heal*, *Magic Missile* and *Unlock*. Mages are valued for their skill at making and sharing scrolls, especially *Resurrect* and spells with "first strike" capabilities, such as *Fireball*. In return, I'm told they get any reagents and magical supplies that are found during the journey.

Ranger

(Tracking, Camping, Archery)

Braldt Ironeye

Q: Why did you become a Ranger?

Grew up in the woods, know the woods. Understand it, the way it breathes and grows. The way it moves.

Use Camping to make good, safe camps. Sleep isn't dangerous when you know what you're doing. Sleep can be deadly if you just lie down anywhere.

Don't like the city much. Too many people, pushing, running. Saying nothing with too many words.

Could have been a Warrior, but like to think too much. Could have been a Healer, but don't have the touch.

Q: Where is a good place to start?

Vesper is good. On the edge of forests, and near roads to Britain and Minoc. Good place to join parties if that's what you want.

Q: What advice would you give Novice Rangers?

Tracking is necessary. Show where creatures and people are, find them when you need them. For money, find monsters or other creatures for adventurers.

Forensic Evaluation is useful. You can find out who did something, then use Tracking to bring them to justice.

Archery brings you money if you need it. Track a creature, shoot it, then use your dagger to skin it and bring the skin, meat to market. Also good against enemies, monsters. Learn Bowcraft and Fletching, make your own arrows, don't have to buy them in town.

Always make a good camp. Saves lives.

Shepherd

(Herding, Animal Lore, Veterinary)

Crispin the Goatherd

Q: Why did you become a Shepherd?

It's not really something I do. It's what I am. I've always been with the animals, for as far back as I can remember. I like it. I enjoy eating simple foods in the open air, with the sunlight on my back and a breeze keeping me cool. People tend to make me a little nervous. Other people have so much to do, or say, and so little time to do it in. I feel like I'm getting in their way, like a stray dog. I try to keep to myself.

Q: Where is a good place to start?

I guess Britain would be the best place. There are some lovely fields to the north-west, and you can usually find some goats or sheep. I prefer sheep, myself, but to each his own. If you can't find a place to call your own, perhaps you could ask a tracker where to go. I've never done that, but they might help.

Q: What advice would you give Novice Shepherds?

I'm not a good person for asking questions, really. I can truly say that this is not the way for many people. They should really search their souls for what they want to do with their lives before deciding to herd. It's dangerous, and lonely, difficult to sustain and even more difficult to make a financial living.

They should be the very best Herder they can be. Your Herding ability should be as high as possible, otherwise what's the point?

If they want to make money, they could heal the tamed animals that people use as guards, I suppose. I've done that often, but I don't ask for much money. It wouldn't be fair to the animals. They could also shear the sheep, and sell the wool, but you can't do that every day, you know. Or they could slaughter some goats or sheep and sell the meat and hides.

I've often thought that the skill of Peacemaking would be useful in these troubled lands, but I haven't found an instrument yet. I will someday.

Thief

(Stealing, Snooping, Lockpicking)

Little Millet

Q: Why did you become a Thief?

I had some big friends that liked to go adventuring, and they asked me to go along to help out with some of the stuff that brute strength can't handle. I started when I was quite young, and it was a while before I realized that "Thief" has a lot of negative connotations. Everybody always seemed pretty glad to have me come along. They trusted me, and I think that was why I was pretty popular.

I'm not really big into picking pockets and breaking into people's houses, although I've done a lot of work breaking into guildhalls. Mostly I just concentrate on opening chests down in the dungeons, and going through the clothes of the recently departed.

Q: Where is a good place to start?

I started in Trinsic, which is good because of all the adventurers that go there. Britain is also a popular place to join a group. If you're more interested in the "involuntary liberation" of cash and goods, Magincia has a fairly rich populace. Still, until you're really good, don't pick pockets in the city. The guards really keep their eyes open for that kind of thing.

Q: What advice would you give Novice Thieves?

If they get caught red-handed, they'll be killed. If they try to snoop and fail, they'll be killed. If they get caught stealing in a house, and a lot of things have alarms on them, they'll be killed. It's a hard life, and a tough one to get good at.

If they don't want to join a band of adventurers, the best way to get practice might be to stay just outside the city gates and try to steal random objects out of backpacks. If they get caught, they can try to run inside the gates where they can't be killed. When they have enough skill, they can try their hand in crowded markets.

Of course, if they've got a significant stash and a good friend, they can buy a house and practice indoors without fear of the guards. But then, who among us has that kind of bankroll?

Worst comes to worst, they can always try to tide themselves over by catching a rabbit ....

Tinker

(*Tinkering, Item Identification, Lockpicking*)

Elas, Tinker and Wanderer

Q: Why did you become a Tinker?

Strangely enough, it was because I wanted to join an adventurer band. It's actually a good trade to have, because you have a natural inclination toward picking locks, but are more trustworthy than a thief. Tinkers also make tools which are good for selling in different towns, and it's always best to travel with some big thugs with swords when you go from place to place.

Q: Where is a good place to start?

Magincia and Jhelom are good places, because they both have Tinker shops. You can head over to the shop and watch what happens, and then put your hand to making some bits on your own.

Q: What advice would you give Novice Tinkers?

Well, now, if you want to make a fortune, it would be best to go to a seafaring town and sell sextants and other such useful implements. Also you could make carpentry tools to sell for cut rates to carpenters.

A bit of a steadier job would be to go adventuring, and polish up your Lockpicking ability.

The real goal for a professional Tinker, however, is to go to Minoc. It has the best Tinker shop, and it's where all the notable Tinkers go to earn their reputation.

Trader

(Arms Lore, Cartography, Item Identification)

Mikal Serity, Professional Peddler

Q: Why did you become a Trader?

Frankly, my first interest is really Cartography, but so few people understand a love of pure science. So I carry things from hither to yon, but most of my time and energy goes into creating maps of interesting areas, and selling them to hopeful adventurers.

I knew it was a dangerous trade, so I often find others who wish to travel with me for the promise of a map or two. They usually even provide the wherewithal for me to purchase blank maps, and I tend to make them a large-scale map, a medium scale one or three, and then a more detailed map of any one or two particular areas that interest them. I get what I want, they get what they want, everyone is happy.

Q: Where is a good place to start?

Britain is a marvelous place to begin the trading life. It has lots of people, shops to purchase everything you'll ever need, and no monsters to threaten a fledgling Trader, should he turn down the wrong alley.

Q: What advice would you give Novice Traders?

It wouldn't hurt to assess people's equipment, to get some early money flowing in. A good place for this is near the blacksmith's shop, since this is where adventurers tend to gravitate, especially after they come in from the dungeons.

A Trader is not an attractive member for a band of adventurers, which is too bad since maps tend to mean more to people who want to go to a certain place, rather than the people who are already there. Many people won't care for the opinion of an assessor, since they can just ask how much a shopkeeper will pay, and judge its worth according to the amount offered.

Moongates are a good way of getting to distant places, but you'll have to find some people who are interested in traveling with you, as a Trader is as good as unarmed in the woods.

It's a difficult life.

Warrior

(Arms Lore, Parrying, Tactics)

Demuel Longarm

Q: Why did you become a Warrior?

I got to thinkin', what it was in life that was important. I mean, my father, he's a good man and all, but he spent all his time in the pasture. He was a shepherd, you see. He didn't want much but to spend a life in peace, keeping his sheep safe, and his family fed and healthy. He didn't aspire to much fame or success. That was his way of saying he loved us — I see that now. But that's a difficult concept for a young lad to understand. I wanted him to give us money; I guess all kids do.

So I became a fighter. You can be more independent, don't have to deal much with people if you don't want to. You can get bags of gold, go on lots of adventures, and have a fighting chance at killing anyone who annoys you. That's why I became a Warrior.

Q: Where is a good place to start?

I got my start in Vesper, and I recommend it. It's got a good inn, called the Ironwood Inn, that's on the edge of a wilderness, so you can get up in the morning, go out into the woods and kill a couple of creatures, then make it back in time to sell the stuff at the market before lunch. There's a lot of monsters nearby, not to mention the cemetery. Always nasties crawling out of cemeteries. Good practice. Also, there's a dungeon nearby, once you get good.

Q: What advice would you give Novice Warriors?

Don't underestimate Tactics. Tactics is what actually keeps you alive.

If you want to make money, go out and start hunting small things, as soon as possible: deer and whatnot. Get the hide and meat and sell it at the market. Once you get a bit of practice with the sword, hire yourself out as a guard.

It's not the most interesting thing to be, right at the very start. In the long run, however, it's the most exciting job in the world.

Your ultimate goal, of course, is to make it to the bottom of a dungeon. That's where the good stuff is.

SKILLS

Alchemy

Skill 90%, Intelligence 8%, Dexterity 2%

Hendrika Crowbright — "Alchemy is the fountainhead of all other arts."

Standard Equipment

1 mortar & pestle
4 empty vials
4 random reagents
1 red robe

Method of creating potions

Select the *Alchemy* skill, then target a reagent.

Common Complementary Skills

Resisting Spells: Automatic

Taste Identification: Select the *Taste Identification* skill, then target an item (food, drink or potion).

Best Income

Selling potions, particularly health potions, to adventurers.

Identifying poisonous food/drink picked up in dungeons.

Best Towns

Britain, Moonglow

Potions	Reagent	Color	For more details, see **Potions**, p. 244.
Agility	Blood Moss	Blue	
Nightsight	Garlic	Black	
Explosion	Sulphurous Ash	Purple	
Healing	Ginseng	Yellow	
Poison	Nightshade	Green	
Refresh	Black Pearl	Red	
Sleep (Cure)	Spider Silk	Orange	
Strength	Mandrake	White	

Anatomy

Skill 50%, Intelligence 50%

Vimnock Rickers, Anatomist

It's, ah, the muscles, you see, and determining the tensile strength. Tensile is quickness, only sometimes it's strong. Depends on where it attaches, you see ....

Standard Equipment

1 robe

3 bandages

Method of Determining Something's Physical Capabilities

Select the *Anatomy* skill, then target a person or creature.

Best Use

Should only be used as a secondary skill. Use it to judge the danger in tackling an opponent, whether animal, monster or human.

Best Towns

Enemy infested woodland

Attribute/10	Strength	Dexterity
1-10	rather feeble	very clumsy
11-20	somewhat weak	somewhat uncoordinated
21-30	to be of normal strength	moderately dexterous
31-40	somewhat strong	somewhat agile
41-50	very strong	very agile
51-60	extremely strong	extremely agile
61-70	extraordinarily strong	extraordinarily agile
71-80	strong as an ox	moves like quicksilver
81-90	one of the strongest people you have ever seen	one of the fastest people you have ever seen
>90+	superhumanly strong	superhumanly agile

Figuring Strength/Speed

Animal Lore

Skill 50%, Intelligence 50%

Catarine De Calb, Animal Behaviorist

It is not so hard determining the thought and action patterns for creatures. I've done it all my life. You have to respect them. You have to respect their needs, and drives, and the environment in which they choose to live. Then you make your mind a blank, and let yourself melt … merge … mingle with the Trueness … the Realness … which is the creature. You ignore the itchy parts and concentrate on the deeper nature, that which makes a deer a deer … a wolf a wolf … an eagle an eagle. You go deeper, and as you fall, you rise higher. Past the trees … the hills … the clouds. One deer is all deer … one wolf all wolves … one eagle all eagles. You wrap yourself in the fur and feathers and you search out the hungers … the fears … the longings. You become all … the grass and the trees … the small flowers and the mountains. Then you take all that Truth and you hold it out in front of you. You see the lacework pattern of their souls, all interwoven. You take that lace and you carefully, carefully fold it over and over until it is a small packet you can hold in your hand. And then you open your eyes, and you understand.

Of course, I'll admit it's much easier if you can get a trace of their aura pattern first.

Standard Equipment

1 green robe

1 starting shepherd's crook

Method of Divining Creature Resource Information

Select *Animal Lore* skill and target animal or monster.

Best Use

This is best used as a temporary skill, until you feel confident about what makes animals act as they do. It is also a good secondary skill to Animal Taming — you can use it to judge a pet's current loyalty.

Best Towns

Creature-inhabited woodland

Animal Taming

Skill 80%, Strength 6%, Dexterity 2%, Intelligence 12%

Tagyerd Beastmaster

Yer gotta have their attention, first off.

Then yer gotta keep it.

Then yer gotta feed 'em.

Then they gotta know that they's allus got yer eye on 'em.

Then they stay good.

Standard Equipment

1 starting shepherd's crook

Method of Taming an Animal

Select the skill and target the animal, then stay near the animal for about 20 seconds.

Common Complementary Skills

Animal Lore: Select the skill, and target the animal.

Veterinary: Use bandage on animal.

Best Income

Selling trained animals to people as guards.

Having your trained animals attack other animals, and selling the proceeds.

Best Town

Yew

Archery

(See also Bowyer, p. 45)

Skill 90%, Dexterity 9%, Intelligence 1%

Combat Ability: Skill 45%, Tactics 45%, Dexterity 5.5%,
Intelligence 3.5%, Strength 1% (see *Tactics*, p. 93)

Ariella Featherleaf, Archer

Archery isn't for everyone. The bow is a peasant's tool, made from what lies at
hand: string and twigs and feathers. But I don't mind. You know the old joke ...
"why did the man run through the woods?" The answer is "because he broke his
sword."

Standard Equipment

1 starting bow

25 arrows

Method of Using Archery Skill

Automatic with use of bow or crossbow.

Common Complementary Skills

Bowcraft/Fletching: Use feather on shaft for arrow, use edged weapon on wood for
shaft or bow.

Parrying: Automatic

Note: If you plan to enter combat, consider changing Parrying to Tactics.

Best Income

Meat and hides from hunted creatures.

Archery is best if you are going to be part of a team. It gives you ability with a
good ranged weapon.

Best Towns

Britain has a good Bowyer's shop that you can use, and it's a great place for team-
ing up with adventurers.

Vesper is also good for its nearby woods.

Arms Lore

Skill 75%, Intelligence 9%, Strength 8%, Dexterity 8%

Tikyr the Trader

I wouldn't want to earn my bread with it, but it puts butter on the table.

Standard Equipment

1 random starting weapon

Method of Determining Armour Quality or Weapon Damage

Select skill, then target armour or weapon.

Common Complementary Skills

Cartography: Select the skill, target a map, then choose the scale.

Item Identification: Select the skill, then target the object.

Tactics: Automatic

Parrying: Automatic

Best Income

Determining the quality of "confiscated" weapons and armour.

Best Towns

Britain, or city with a large population of adventurers

Result	Armor Quality	Result	Weapon Damage
Gives almost no protection	1	Damage might scratch your opponent slightly	1
Gives very little protection	2	Would do minimal damage	2
Offers some protection against blows	3	Would do some damage	3-6
Serves as a sturdy protection	4	Would probably hurt your opponent a fair amount	7-10
Is a superior defense against attack	5	Would do quite a lot of damage	11-20
Offers excellent protection	6	Is a superior weapon	21-40
		Is extraordinarily deadly	41+

Begging

Skill 90%, Dexterity 5%, Intelligence 5%

Crazy Arliss

I prefer to call myself an arbitrary entrepreneur. I think of it as a kind of grassroots economic redistribution, good for the souls of others and for the financial health of the city at large. Originally I was going to save up and buy a boat, you know, be a ferryman for all these noble heroes rushing off to save the world, but then I thought, "what good am I if I don't put the money back in circulation?" No better than these rich folk who are barely generous enough to give me a bit of the overage. So I stopped setting the money aside.

Back in the lean years, I stayed in one place and let the business come to me. That had its good points. I could sit and contemplate my deep thoughts. Ponder on the finer things in life. Think about dinner. But then I got my limp perfected, and I'm more of a hither-and-yon type these days. More money, but more work too. Doesn't it always work out that way?

Standard Equipment

1 starting gnarled staff

Method of Begging

Select skill from list, target NPC.

Common Complementary Skills

Enticement: Select skill, target person or creature.

Musicianship: Select instrument.

Snooping: Double-left-click on someone's backpack.

Stealing: Select an item in a backpack you've *Snooped*.

Best Income

The generosity of non-player characters.

Best Towns

Any populated place

Blacksmithy

Skill 90%, Strength 7%, Dexterity 3%

Smiths' adage: One fire, one hammer.

Standard Equipment

1 random tool

1 brown apron

Method of Creating a New Item

Use hammer or tongs and select item you want to make from the list that appears. (Your inventory is automatically searched to see if you have enough metal to make the item.)

Method of Repairing Equipment

Use hammer or tongs and select Repair (the anvil icon). Then, select item to be repaired.

Common Complementary Skills

Parrying: Automatic

Arms Lore: Use skill on armour/weapons.

Mining: Use pick or shovel on mountainside or cave wall.

Best Income

Making weapons and armour for adventurers.

Best Towns

Minoc

Bowcraft/Fletching

Skill 80%, Dexterity 14%, Strength 3%, Intelligence 3%

Bowyer's Saying: Bad work kills business before aught else.

Standard Equipment

makings for 2 bows

shafts & feathers

Common Complementary Skills

	Use	On	To Produce
Arrowmaking	Arrow shaft	Feather	Arrow
	Feather	Arrow shaft	Arrow
	Feather	Bolt shaft	Crossbow bolt
	Edged Item	Wood	Arrow shaft, Bow, Crossbow bolt shaft Crossbow, Heavy crossbow

Lumberjacking: Use axe on wood.

Parrying: Automatic

Archery: Automatic

Best Income

Hunting

Make bows and arrows for others

Best Towns

Britain

Vesper

Camping

Skill 50%, Intelligence 18%, Dexterity 16%, Strength 16%

Luther, Tradesmaster

I would not say that I am an expert camper. Not at all, not at all. By profession I am a Trader, but I specialize in maps, and travel the realm making maps of the dangerous and unknown corners. Now, don't think that I recommend sleeping under an open sky! Not a bit of it! But there are times when passage is delayed, illness or injury strikes, or the way is harder than predicted.

Yes, yes, I make maps, but that doesn't mean I know where the Ettin tribes are active!

There are things in the darkness that follow and wait. I don't mean the dark of night, I mean the deep purple shadows that grow in the deep woods. The dappled brights and darks of the leafy tree branches hold invisible eyes. They know when you'll be weak and defenseless. Sleep will make you easy prey, just like a babe in the woods.

Guards are good. That's what they're paid for, I know, I know. And yes, animals, are a help. Nevertheless, give me a good campfire anytime.

Standard Equipment

5 kindlings

1 bedroll

Method of Setting Up Camp

Double-left-click on kindling to start a fire.

Note

You can have an instant logout in the vicinity of a fire, but there is a certain preparation time associated with starting the fire. To logout, be near the fire and use your bedroll. Campfires don't last forever, though, and will flicker a bit before going out. Be sure you've logged out before this happens.

Carpentry

Skill 75%, Strength 12.5%, Dexterity 7.5%, Intelligence 5%

Gray Veedo, cabinetmaker

I do it because I love the smell of wood, I love the feel of the tools. I like seeing my finished projects and knowing "that was done right." It makes a house something more than a box with people in it, and it gives friends a warm, welcoming place to gather.

Standard Equipment

1 carpentry tool

10 boards

1 brown apron

Method of Creating Items

Select a skill, then select board or log. Pick the item you wish to create from the list that appears.

Common Complementary Skills

Lumberjacking: Use hatchet or axe on source wood.

Best Income

Making furniture for people with houses. Chests are popular.

Best Towns

Any populated city

Carpentry tools

Dovetail Saw nails)	Draw	Froe	Hammer	Jointing Plane (and
	Inshave	Moulding Plane	Saw	Smoothing Plane
Scorp				

You can make the following items:

Armoire	Bookcase	Box (wooden)	Chair	Chest (wooden)	
Crate	Shelf	Small Crate	Stool	Throne	Table

Cartography

Skill 85%, Intelligence 12%, Dexterity 3%

Terrence Mapmaker

I've been a cartographer … that's a mapmaker, you know … for about two years now. Before that I was a kind of mercenary Healer, I guess you'd call it. I would go with bands of adventurers all over the world, finding dungeons and seeing how far down we could get before someone got so hurt I couldn't bring them back. Then we'd meet at the closest shrine, and go back home. I discovered I had a really good sense of direction, and would always know the way, and how far away things were. I drew some maps for fun, and got pretty good at it.

And the funny thing was, it got to where I just liked the traveling, seeing new places and new people. I still enjoy healing people, but it got to be … I don't know a good word … upsetting? … to get to know people, get to be friends, and then watch somebody come and slit them open. It got to where I didn't like that at all. So now I just go and make maps. There isn't as much prestige, but I can usually find people who will let me travel with them, and that's all I really want.

Standard Equipment

4 blank maps

1 sextant

Method of Making a Map

Select the skill and target a blank map. Choose the scale. Your location will be the center of the map.

Common Complementary Skills

Item Identification: Select the skill, target the item.

Arms Lore: Select the skill, target the armour/weapon.

Best Income

Making maps for adventurers.

Selling maps of popular areas (such as dungeons) to adventurers.

A map is needed to set course on a ship.

Best Towns

Britain, or any place with an active adventurer population.

Cooking

Skill 50%, Intelligence 30%, Dexterity 20%

Tarak, Chief Cook

"Raw food is animal food."

Standard Equipment

3 raw food items   1 flour sack
1 water pitcher   2 kindlings

Method of Preparing Food

Use an ingredient (or an oven) on an ingredient.

Best Income

Selling food to people whose health is diminished.

Best Towns

Cities with a large adventurer population

Places where battles are common

Notes

Cooked food has more food value than raw food.

Campfires and forges also serve as ovens.

Use an edged item on a fish, and you'll get three fish steaks.

Using a finished product means you'll eat it on the spot!

Recipes

Use	On	To Produce
water	flour	dough
flour	water	dough
oven	dough	bread
honey	dough	sweet dough
dough	honey	sweet dough
flour	sweet dough	cake mix
oven	cake mix	cake
oven	sweet dough	muffins
sweet dough	honey	cookie mix
oven	cookie mix	cookies
dough	fruit	fruit pie
dough	meat	meat pie
dough	vegetable	vegetable pie

Detecting Hidden

Skill 75%, Intelligence 20%, Dexterity 5%

Manetta, Swordsfighter

I'm pretty good at finding villains that hide in dark corners. It's not what I would call the most important skill I have, not like *Tactics* or *Healing*, but it's something I do well.

I got a lot of practice early on when I was looking for my ex-husband. He wasn't my ex-husband at the time … that was the whole point of looking for him. There's more than one way to end a relationship, if you know what I mean. That little weasel could hide in a drainpipe, and I got to be really good at recognizing when a shadow was a little too dark, or too wide, or too shadowy.

It comes in handy, but it isn't something that you can do all the time. You start looking in all the corners, and you'll bump into what's right in front of you. It's usually when you know there's someone you want to stick a knife into, and just can't put your hands on him right off. I hate it when that happens.

Standard Equipment

1 black cloak

Method of Revealing Hiders

Select the skill, and target an area. Any hiders in that specific location will be revealed to all people nearby.

Best Income

Best if used as a secondary skill.

Best Towns

Areas with thieves

Enticement

Skill 95%, Dexterity 2.5%, Intelligence 2.5%

Meredette, Wandering Bard

It's a silly little skill, and not a lot of people have it to any great extent. It's more like a parlor trick. Frankly I think it was designed to lure people closer to your tips cup, but I've never seen it work.

I started enticing people out of a purely egotistical notion that if I were going to be worth my salt as a Bard, I would need to have expertise in all the Bardic skills. I practiced how to walk the walk, talk the talk, and sing every last sappy song about lost love. So I would try my hand at enticing the natives every evening. Then it turned into a game, really. I promised myself I would buy drinks for the house if I ever found a man with blond hair and purple eyes. Like I said, it's a silly skill, but somebody's got to do it!

Standard Equipment

1 random musical instrument

Method of Luring Person Closer

Select the skill, then target the person or creature. (You must have a musical instrument.)

Best Income

Hunting

Luring creatures closer to adventure group.

Best Towns

Woodland

Notes

Your target will try to find the best way to approach you, not necessarily a direct line.

Evaluating Intellect

Skill 50%, Intelligence 50%

Troth, Evaluator

I'd try to explain, but you'd not understand.

Standard Equipment

None

Method of Evaluating Intellect

Select the skill, then target a person or creature.

Best Income

Best if used as a secondary skill.

Best Towns

Areas with monsters

Intelligence	Comment
1-9	slightly less intelligent than a rock
10-19	fairly stupid
20-29	not the brightest
30-39	about average
40-49	moderately intelligent
50-59	very intelligent
60-69	extremely intelligent
70-79	extraordinarily intelligent
80-89	like a formidable intellect, well beyond even the extraordinary
90-99	like a definite genius
100+	superhumanly intelligent in a manner you cannot comprehend

Evaluating Intellect

Fencing

Skill 90%, Dexterity 8%, Strength 2%

Ability in Combat: Skills 45%, Tactics 45%, Dexterity 5%, Intelligence 3%, Strength 2% (see *Tactics*, p. 93)

Astan, Ex-Fencer

Well, yeah, I was a fencer when I started the whole fighting thing. It seemed like a cool thing, very swash, very buckle. Tights and tunic, little mustache, curly hair. Jump on tables. I fenced using a chair once and the other guy took the chair and broke my jaw with it.

Let me explain something about fencing. It's all about taking a long piece of metal and poking holes in people with it. Little holes. And if the other guy's wearing armour, that's too bad for you, isn't it? And if he's got a longer sword, that's too bad. And if he gets in past the point of your blade, that's too bad. And what if he's some tough bruiser who doesn't care if he's got little holes in him? What if he's a fast little rat who whips around behind you? If you're lucky, you get your jaw broken.

So now I make exploding potions. Very swish, very boom. I recommend them.

Standard Equipment

1 spear

Method of Fighting

Put the weapon in your hand and enter war mode, then double-left-click on opponent.

Best Income

Fighting creatures

Exploring dungeons

Best Towns

Definitely not in a town!

Anywhere outside the city walls

Fishing

Skill 75%, Dexterity 22.5%, Strength 2.5%

Goodman Dunnet

I started fishing because I thought it would be a quick and easy way to make some money. I didn't have many skills back then. I figured I could always get enough to feed myself. Well, I went hungry the first few days, but I stuck it out. And then one day I understood the whole point.

The goal is not to catch a fish. It's *to* fish.

You stand on the bank of a river, or at the quiet edge of a bridge, and you look out at the water. You can feel your thoughts slow down, become all polished and smooth like a pebble. The best way I can describe it is that you begin to watch yourself think. A thought flows up, unwinds, and floats down.

And then you have a nice dinner, sell the rest of your catch, and wait until the next chance you can get away and watch the water flow past.

Standard Equipment

1 fishing pole

1 brown floppy hat

Method of Fishing

Use fishing pole on water.

Best Income

Selling fish in town.

Selling fish to injured parties.

Note

Use string on stick to make fishing pole.

Forensic Evaluation

Skill 75%, Intelligence 25%

Midrah, Professional Examiner

Some people tell me, as if they expected to be telling a man how his very own profession is accomplished, that there is an "underground" magic that allows me to divine the individual attacker of any corpse I encounter.

This is not so. There is nothing occult about my announcements. They are based on facts, which is something of which these "informed" people have no acquaintance. A pox on them.

I know things. I know about the imprint of shoes, the angle of the sun, the leaf overturned in the woods and of small hairs caught on nails. The victims scratch furrows in their attackers' flesh, and leave remnants under their nails. Their retinas retain the dying image. The lines on their hands mark their killer by name. I am able to acquire all these facts and weave them into an answer. It is mere logic.

Okay, okay, so I use magic when I'm stumped. If I admitted it, they'd make me join a guild.

Standard Equipment

Nothing

Method of Examining a Corpse

Select skill, then target corpse.

Common Complementary Skills

Tracking: Select skill, pick target.

Healing: Use bandage on person.

Best Income

Helping find the killer of a guildmember

Finding a murderering thief, killing him (with or without help), taking his spoils.

Healing

Skill 80%, Intelligence 14%, Dexterity 6%

The Healer's miracle: "clean bandages, wholesome food"

Standard Equipment

5 bandages

1 pair of scissors

Method of healing

Use bandage on person.

Common Complementary Skills

Anatomy: Select skill, target person.

Forensic Evaluation: Select skill, target person.

Tracking: Select skill, pick target.

Best Income

Healing fighters, either as a business or as part of a group.

Best Towns

Britain

Trinsic

Any city populated with adventurers

Notes

The amount of healing done is commensurate with the skill.

Make bandages by using scissors on cloth.

Herding

Skill 75%, Dexterity 11.5%, Intelligence 7.5%, Strength 6%

Mayderry Two-River

"A sheep has more wool than it needs, and thus placidly teaches more of sharing than ever a human might learn."

Standard Equipment

1 starting shepherd's crook

Method of Herding Animals

Select your sheperd's crook, then target the animal.

Common Complementary Skills

Animal Lore: Select skill, target creature.

Veterinary: Use bandage on creature.

Musicianship: Automatic

Peacemaking: Select skill, target creature.

Best Income

Meat and hides

Veterinarian work

Best Towns

Britain

Note

This is a difficult profession, with few rewards.

Hiding

Skill 75%, Dexterity 20%, Intelligence 5%

Zilred, profession undefined

Yes. Um, yes. Wait a sec … okay, now let me tell you something. Hiding is not a profession, okay? It's a professional flourish. It's style. It's like long robes on a Mage. Like the apron on a Smith. Very panache.

Anybody can go up and stab someone in the back. If nobody's around to see you do it, you think "good job," right? But if the victim just keels over on a busy street, now that's a class act.

But it's not just killing, you know. Wait! Shhhh …!

It's not just killing. It's being where no one thinks you can be. It's knowing things no one else knows. Brute strength is easy, but subtlety is a real trick. Sub-tle. Staying alone in a crowd. Being wise when everyone else is foolish. Being deep as the ocean, as deep as death.

Being a shadow at noon, at dusk, at midnight.

Shhhhhhhhhhhhh …

Standard Equipment

1 black cloak

Method of Hiding

Select the skill, the rest is automatic.

Best Income

Not being killed and having all your money taken.

Eavesdropping on guilds for information to sell to other guilds.

Best Towns

Any town with dangerous people

Inscription

Skill 90%, Intelligence 10%

Tad the Limner

The art of making scrolls for a Mage is similar to the art of kneading for a Baker. It's an essential. Get it wrong and nothing good will come of it.

I've made a study of scrollwork, although this is not likely to impress anyone but the most devoted of scholars. Every Mage's style is different, either in lettering or in materials. I can safely say that the more skilled Mages have the more esoteric scrolls. The success of a scroll does not seem to reside in the penmanship or the quality of ink. Blood, although popular to certain people, carries no more power or assurance than berry juice.

It seems, instead, to be that the act of writing a scroll is a sort of magic in itself. Writing the scroll is casting the spell and binding it at the same time.

That is the source of my academic pursuit. Where, exactly, is the magic stored? How is the power quelled into submission, by the mundane act of touching ink to paper? It is a humble pursuit, but one which promises great power in the conclusion. Perhaps I will find another Method of spellcasting! We shall see.

Standard Equipment

2 blank scrolls

1 small blank book (to take notes)

Method of Inscribing Text

Select skill, target a blank scroll, select a spell from the list. (The list includes all spells that you can cast and for which you have sufficient reagents. Reagents are expended when Inscribing the scroll.)

To copy a spell from a scroll onto a spellbook, drag the scroll onto the book. *Inscription* is not necessary to do this.

Common Complementary Skills

Magery: Cast a spell

Resisting Spells: Automatic

Best Income

Best if used as a secondary income.

Item Identification

Skill 75%, Intelligence 25%

Druc the Daring

I think that every craftsman should have skill in *Item Identification*. Traders and any other merchant types who go out on their own, especially. When you're far from a town as fine and busy as Britain, you get to miss the little amenities, and everybody ought to do their share.

Now me, I'd like to know if the plate armour I'd just picked up in a dungeon is worth my taking off my leather jerkin, or if it's going to come to pieces in the first battle. I've heard tales of fighters who finally got a sword they thought would be worthy of their deeds, only to see it bend like a willow the first time it parried an axeblade. That's not the kind of story you tell from first hand experience, if you know what I mean. I'd pay good gold to know if I could trust my gear!

Standard Equipment

1 starting gnarled staff

Method of Identifying an Object

Select skill, then target item.

Best Income

Usually best if used as a secondary skill, but there are scattered opportunities to make a living identifying magic items.

Best Towns

Towns with few shops

Notes

Since a shopkeeper, when asked, will offer a price which is indicative of an object's value, this skill is less useful that it would appear. Only in places without such shops would the skill be financially viable.

Depending on the ability of the user, the evaluation might be off by up to 50% or so.

Lockpicking

Skill 75%, Dexterity 20%, Intelligence 5%

Trenton the Tinker

It's no simple thing, picking a lock. It looks it, but it ain't. If a fellow was to take a lockpick and just poke it around in a lock, why, the first good twist and it would snap like a twig. And then you've done all bad and no good. A broke pick, and now a broke lock.

I'll give you the clue. To unlock a lock, you've got to build a lock. It's the pins, you see. You can't move the little pins around like you was stirrin' a pot. You've got to get them all in a line and marching in order. A Tinker like me, we've seen a lock from the inside, and know how they work. A Thief, he knows how it works too, only it's from practice and poking and playing. He gets to know how the pins work from spending the kind of time with them that gives him more than just a casual knowledge. It's a thing no lazy Thief can master … nor a stupid one, neither.

Standard Equipment

5 lockpicks

Method of Picking a Lock

Use a lockpick, then target a locked object.

Common Complementary Skills

Stealing: Drag item from other person's backpack into yours.

Snooping: Select skill, target backpack.

Tinkering: Use Tinkers' tools on items.

Item Identification: Select skill, target item.

Best Income

Opening locked chests in dungeons.

Best Towns

Dangerous in town, could be caught stealing.

Best out of town.

Lumberjacking

Skill 80%, Strength 18%, Dexterity 2%

Aelfwine

I have betimes been accused by ignorant city folk of "cutting down" trees for their wood. Even if such a thing were possible, it would be a disgraceful act. The function of the lumberjack is to harvest the bounty of the wood, not to destroy it. I gather useable wood from living trees (taking care always to do no harm) and from fallen logs.

Standard Equipment

1 starting hatchet

Method of Lumberjacking

Use hatchet or axe on source of wood.

Common Complementary Skills

Bowcraft/Fletching: Select skill, target wood.

Carpentry: Select skill, target wood.

Best Income

Reduce overhead on other craft skills.

Sell kindling to provisioners.

Best Towns

Britain

Vesper

Mace Fighting

Skill 90%, Strength 8%, Dexterity 2%

Ability in combat: Skill 45%, *Tactics* 45%, Strength 5%, Intelligence 3%, Dexterity 2% (see *Tactics*, p. 93)

Jedd of Jhelom

If you ask me, the only real man's weapon is the mace. Well, I suppose the axe is all right too, if you want to do things the easy way, but I don't hold with none of that mincing swordplay or cowardly archery — yeah, you heard me right, blade-boy, I said "mincing." You don't like it, come talk to me in the pit. Interested? Didn't think so.

Anyway, nothing like the jar of a full forearm swing and the sound of a crunching skull to make you feel like a real Warrior.

Standard Equipment

1 starting mace

Method of Mace Fighting

Automatic whenever mace is used in combat.

Common Complementary Skills

Parrying: Used automatically in combat when holding a shield.

Tactics: Used automatically in combat.

Best Income

Adventuring

Best Towns

Jhelom

Trinsic

Magery

Skill 85%, Intelligence 15%

Xedric, Master Mage

"Magic is hard, and successful Mages are as rare as dragon teeth."

Standard Equipment

1 spell book

5 random reagents

3 random First Circle scrolls

Method of Using Magery

Automatic whenever a spell is cast.

Common Complementary Skills

Inscription: Select skill, target blank scroll, select spell from list.

Resist Spells: Automatic

Best Income

Create and sell scrolls.

Adventuring

Best Towns

Britain

Moonglow

Note

See **The Secrets of Magic** (p. 215) for a full explanation of Magery and spellcasting.

Mining

Skill 80%, Strength 14%, Dexterity 6%

Tobias of Minoc

I don't know anybody who's just a miner, although I suppose you could make a living at it. Almost all the miners I know are really Blacksmiths, and almost all the Blacksmiths I know do their own mining, or at least can do their own mining if they need to.

You have to know how to take care of yourself if you're going to mine for yourself, for ore is always found far beyond the city walls, and no guard will hear you if you cry out. The mining sites themselves are pretty safe, because the miners look out for one another, but brigands and thieves like to haunt the routes between the mines and the forges, preying on anyone who's foolish enough to travel alone.

Standard Equipment

1 starting pickaxe

1 shovel

Method of Mining

Double-left-click on pick or shovel, target mountainside or cave wall.

Double-left-click on ore, then target forge to produce ingots.

Common Complementary Skills

Blacksmithy: Select skill, double-click on raw material, select item to make.

Tinkering: Select skill, double-click on raw material, select item to make.

Best Income

Eliminate overhead for *Blacksmithy*.

Sell ore to Smiths.

Best Towns

Minoc

Jhelom

Musicianship

Skill 90%, Dexterity 8%, Intelligence 2%

Rhianna Songbird

"The proof of the Bard is in the playing." That's the simple truth of it. People look to Bards as a source of gossip, or as a sort of lesser Mage with the power to cause others mischief, but every true Bard knows that the real foundation of the thing is always firmly bound into the music. If you can't play the music, all else is simply delusion. People make much of the vaunted powers of the Bard, but in truth the power resides in the music. A single missed note, a briefly untuned string and all your efforts to sway the minds of others will go for naught.

Standard Equipment

1 random musical instrument

Method of Making Music

Select instrument

Common Complementary Skills

Enticement: Select skill, select instrument, target person or creature.

Peacemaking: Select skill, select instrument, target person or creature.

Provocation: Select skill, select instrument, target person or creature.

Best Income

Adventuring as a Bard

Hunting with *Enticement* and *Provocation*

Best Towns

Britain

Ocllo

Parrying

Skill 90%, Strength 3%, Dexterity 4%, Intelligence 3%

Captain Emil d'Leon

In its most precise definition, parrying is the act of turning an attacking weapon with one's own weapon. However, when the Arms Masters of Britannia speak of the art of *Parrying,* they are referring to the Warrior's techniques of evasion and defense with a shield, channeling blows to those locations where they can do no harm. I have known many foolish young Warriors who have channeled all their efforts into learning to inflict harm, and little into the more subtle techniques of defense. I know no old Warriors who pursue that philosophy.

Standard Equipment

1 wooden shield

Method of Parrying

If holding a shield, checked automatically when attacked.

Common Complementary Skills

Tactics: Automatic

All weapon skills: Automatic

Best Income

Any combat-related activity.

Best Towns

Trinsic

Jhelom

Peacemaking

Skill 95%, Dexterity 2.5%, Intelligence 2.5%

Germyn Hightone

There are those who follow the Bardic calling (it shames me to confess it) who relish more the mischief they can do through *Enticement* or *Provocation,* than the good they can do through peacemaking. For though no magic is strong enough to change the human heart, it is often enough to simply cause those who contend against one another to stop a moment and consider the wisdom of their course.

Those who scorn the gentle art of the peacemaker are foolish, furthermore, for they reject a means to great profit, for the master of this art may walk in peace where the mightiest of champions would be torn asunder, and may gather the bounty of such perilous regions with relative impunity.

Standard Equipment

1 random musical instrument

Method of Peacemaking

Select skill, target individual or creature in combat. (You must have a musical instrument.)

Common Complementary Skills

Musicianship: Select skill, target instrument.

Provocation: Select skill, target one or more creatures or individuals.

Best Income

Scavenging in hostile areas.

Best Towns

Britain

Trinsic

Poisoning

Skill 80%, Intelligence 16%, Dexterity 4%

Alonzo Quietus

They say that the Poisoner's art lacks honor, but two great armored asses chopping each other to bits, that's honorable as anything can be. I say, if somebody needs to remove someone else, do it the quiet way, the clean way, my way. That's what I call honorable.

Anyway, it's not as though the only use for poison is, er, the resolution of inter-personal disagreements. Can a simple farmer be expected to drive off a bear or a harpy or some similar monstrosity all on his own with his pitchfork? Of course not, but leave out some of my special meat, and such pests never bother honest folk no more.

Standard Equipment

2 poison potions

Method of Poisoning

Select skill, select vial of poison, target food or drink.

Select skill, select vial of poison, target weapon. It is then poisoned for a while.

Common Complementary Skills

Alchemy: Select skill, target reagent, target bottle.

Taste Identification: Select skill, target item.

Best Income

Assassination

Trapping

Best Towns

Magincia

Nujel'm

Provocation

Skill 95%, Dexterity 4%, Intelligence 1%

Benin, Apprentice Bard

You get taught that *Provocation* is wrong, you know, and something that no self-respecting musician would ever do. But I've got news for you ... Bards tend to travel, and it's a cruel mean world out there. You either keep up or get kicked aside.

Really, just think about it. How often do you find money just lying in the road, free for taking? Never! If you need gold, the best way for me to get it is to trade something. Now my choices are: I could sell my lute, or try to beat a rabbit to death with it, or play a tune that would compel some passing stag to skewer a hare, and then sell the pelt. Only one road can I take, and still remain a musician, and that's the one I'll take, thank you very much.

Standard Equipment

1 random musical instrument

Method of encouraging others to fight

Select skill, target individual or creature. (You must have a musical instrument.)

Common Complementary Skills

Peacemaking: Select skill, target individual or creature.

Musicianship: Select instrument.

Best Income

Adventuring as a Bard with a group.

Selling hide and meat from animals provoked to kill each other.

Best Towns

Britain, for its music hall (*Provocation* is better the more skilled your *Musicianship*)

Buccaneer's Den, because it has no guards on patrol

Note

Provocation is illegal, and will be promptly punished within any city walls.

Resisting Spells

Skill 50%, Intelligence 50%

Master Runyon, Mage for Hire

Resisting Spells is a standard precaution in my occupation. It takes a bit of time and attention to mature this skill, but I would no more be without it than a Warrior would enter battle bare of armor.

It is a subtle sensation, when it takes effect. In fact, it feels most like a gentle spring breeze, brief and cool to the skin … only instead of blowing *across* you, it feels as though it is blowing *outward*. Quite an innocuous feeling, actually.

Of course, now that I am experienced in occult battles, I must say the sensation triggers the same immediate reaction as the sound of an arrow whizzing by my ear: a quick counterstrike.

Standard Equipment

1 spellbook

Method of Resisting Magic

Automatic

Common Complementary Skills

Alchemy: Select skill, target reagent, target bottle.

Taste Identification: Select skill, target item.

Best Income

Best if used as a secondary skill.

Best Towns

Any place with hostile magical occupants

Snooping

Skill 75%, Dexterity 25%

Arman DeAdder

Snooping! Snooping is what little old ladies do through their son's sock drawers! Perhaps you are referring to the honorable endeavor of gathering intelligence, hmmm?

I would say it is a harmless and sometime necessary practice. The true masters claim to be able to identify all the contents in someone's pack by simply looking at it, although I doubt their veracity. I think instead they are so quick that no one sees them peek under the flap. It is a difficult thing to become thoroughly skilled in, and should not be practiced within the city walls.

Standard Equipment

4 lockpicks

Method of Peeking into Someone's Backpack or Container

Double-click on someone, then double-click on their backpack/container.

Common Complementary Skills

Stealing: Drag item from other person's backpack into your own.

Lockpicking: Double-click on lockpick, then target lock.

Best Income

Best if used in conjunction with *Stealing*.

Best Towns

Buccaneer's Den, because it has no guards. Very dangerous using it in a town with a vigilant guard.

Note

It is illegal to be caught snooping within the city walls. If you get caught, guards come. If you fail twice in a row, guards come. It's generally not worth it inside the town proper.

Spirit Speak

Skill 50%, Intelligence 50%

Zaharian the Healer

Almost anyone can hear the speech of the dead. They speak in vowels, or I should say vowel, since they almost never achieve actual diphthongs. Only the practiced medium, however, can understand what the spirit is actually trying to communicate. I'll warn you now, it is not an art to be pursued by the faint of heart. Ghosts have much anger to express, and once you can hear the consonants, the language is usually quite shocking.

Still, if you venture off into dangerous territories, it is better for several, if not all, of the members to be able to understand the words of the departed. Should no one have a *Resurrection* spell, meeting places and times can be arranged in order that the deceased may be able to rejoin his friends, reclaim his equipment, and set off for another day's battle and adventure.

Standard Equipment

1 black cloak

Method of hearing the Speech of Ghosts

Select skill to understand the speech of any nearby ghosts.

Best Income

Best if used as a secondary skill.

Note

Most often used to understand the speech of your recently departed comrades.

The duration is dependent upon the user's skill and intelligence.

Stealing

Skill 90%, Dexterity 10%

Toran Woodshield, Captain of the Guard

I made a vow to keep my town free of bloodshed, free of crime and free of the civic tarnish that comes from living in a place of fear. If I have to kill every man, woman and child three times over to accomplish that, I'll think no more of it than of washing my hands before breakfast.

Standard Equipment

4 lockpicks

Method of Acquiring Goods

If you've already Snooped, select the skill, then select an item in the backpack or container you've revealed.

or

Select the skill, then select a person on the screen (not the person's display). Success gives you a random item from that person's belongings.

Common Complementary Skills

Snooping: Double-click on someone's backpack.

Lockpicking: Select a lockpick, then target a lock.

Best Income

Participating in a band of adventurers.

Other people's money.

Best Towns

Outside the cities

Buccaneer's Den, because it has no guards

Note

If you plan to join an adventuring group and fight at all, *Tactics* is a good skill to develop, and so is *Parrying*.

Swordsmanship

Skill 90%, Strength 5%, Dexterity 5%

Ability in Combat: Skill 45%, *Tactics* 45%, Strength 3.5%, Dexterity 3.5%, Intelligence 3% (see *Tactics*, p. 93)

Padrig the Swift

Anyone can swing a sword. A true swordsfighter is one who practices the swing.

Standard Equipment

1 starting long sword

Method of Fighting

Put the weapon in your hand and enter war mode, then double-left-click on opponent.

Common Complementary Skills

Parrying: Automatic

Tactics: Automatic

Arms Lore: Select skill, target weapon.

Best Income

Adventuring with groups into dungeons.

Alternative professions, such as bodyguard or highwayman.

Best Towns

Vesper

Britain

Trinsic

Tactics

Skill 90%, Intelligence 6%, Strength 2%, Dexterity 2%

Kel Joertzs, Senior Arms Master

Don't underestimate the importance of *Tactics*!

That's what I tell all my students. You can be the best swordsman in the world, and if you don't know tactics you won't last five minutes in a real fight! Sure, it's easy standing next to a practice dummy, slapping away at it with your sword or whatever like a some peasant beating a carpet, but if you don't know where to be — and where not to be — it's you what's going to be the practice dummy.

Get your Tactics ability up!

Standard Equipment

None

Method of Using Tactics in Battle

Automatic. Your actual ability with any weapon is the average of your skill with that weapon and your *Tactics* skill. A high *Tactics* skill can greatly improve your chance to hit with any weapon. A low *Tactics* skill can seriously hurt your chances to succeed in combat.

Common Complementary Skills

Arms Lore: Select skill, then target specific weapon.

Parrying: Automatic

Various weapons skills: Put the weapon in your hand and enter war mode, then double-left-click on opponent.

Best Income

Best if used as a secondary skill.

Tailoring

Skill 75%, Dexterity 19%, Intelligence 5%, Strength 1%

Tad the Tailor

Clothes are identity and confidence. They are the disguise the naked beast dons to fool the world.

Standard Equipment

1 sewing kit

4 folded cloths

Method of Making Cloth and Clothes

Use tools on raw material to create sewing goods. Sew these to create clothes.

Best Income

Selling clothes to adventurers, at lower rates than retail shops.

Best Towns

Magincia and Nujel'm have a richer population, thus tend to pay more for their clothing

Clothes Making

Use	On	To Produce
Spinning wheel	Wool	Yarn
Spinning wheel	Cotton	Thread
Knife	Hide	Pile of Hides
Sewing kit	Hide	Leather clothing
Loom	Thread	Cloth
Loom	Yarn	Cloth
Dye	Cloth	Hued cloth
Dye	Yarn	Hued yarn
Sewing kit	Cloth	Clothing
Spinning wheel	Pile of hemp	Rope

Taste Identification

Skill 50%, Intelligence 40%, Strength 10%

Lucius Snuffler

"The whole secret is not saying 'yick'."

Standard Equipment

3 random potions

Method of Taste-Testing an Item

Select skill, then target the food or drink.

Common Complementary Skills

Alchemy: Select skill, target a reagent, then target a bottle.

Resisting Spells: Automatic

Hiding: Select skill, the rest is automatic.

Poisoning: Select the skill, target the potion, then target the item to be poisoned.

Best Income

Identifying poisoned food for adventurers (usually people who have been poisoned by something they ate, and want to know if anything else is bad).

Best if used as a secondary skill.

Best Towns

Britain, or any town with a large adventurer population

Tinkering

Skill 90%, Intelligence 6%, Strength 2%, Dexterity 2%

O'Halligan, Tinker: "My world is smaller and more straightforward than yours."

Standard Equipment

1 set of Tinker parts 1 set of Tinker tools 1 brown apron

Tools That a Tinker Can Make

Butcher Knife	Dovetail Saw	Draw Knife	Froe
Hammer	Inshave	Jointing Plane	Moulding Plane
Saw	Scissors	Scorp	Sewing Kit
Shovel	Sledge Hammer	Smith's Hammer	Smoothing Plane
Tongs			

Method of Making Things

Use tools on raw materials, then use tools on newly created items to create more complex items.

Common Complementary Skills

Item Identification: Select skill, target item to be identified.

Lockpicking: Select lockpick, target lock.

Best Income

Creating and selling tools

Joining an adventure group

Best Towns

Minoc — it has a Tinker's shop and plentiful ore nearby

Use	On	To Produce
Tinker's Tool	Wood/Ore	Tool (from list above)
Gears	Sticks	Axle with Gears
Sticks	Gears	Axle with Gears
Spring	Axle with Gears	Clock Parts
Hinge	Axle with Gears	Sextant Parts
Axle with Gears	Spring	Clock Parts
Axle with Gears	Hinge	Sextant Parts
Clock Parts	Clock Frame	Clock
Clock Frame	Clock Parts	Clock
Sextant Parts		Sextant

Tinkering

Tracking

Skill 75%, Dexterity 12.5%, Intelligence 12.5%

Myberd the Ranger

I was a tracker since my childhood years. I'd go into the woods and try to follow tracks, pick up signs, find creatures I'd never seen before. My best advice is to remember that a good tracker should expect to be tracked, and be prepared to be found.

Standard Equipment

1 starting skinning knife

1 pair brown boots

Method of Tracking

Select skill, then pick creature/person to track from list.

Common Complementary Skills

Camping: Select skill, target kindling to start fire.

Archery: Use bow or crossbow.

Best Income

Being an adventurer.

Guiding people through woods.

Tracking creatures and people for adventurers.

Tracking creatures and selling their hides and meat.

Best Towns

Vesper

Skara Brae

Any city near a forest

Veterinary

Skill 80%, Intelligence 12%, Strength 4%, Dexterity 4%

Jenna Pinchear, Vet

Well frankly I don't like people enough to go out of my way for them. Most of the thugs who wander into town minus a quart of blood were trying to take it out of some other slack-jawed idiot. Let's face it, there's not a lot of people around here who mind their own business, am I right?

It's the dumb animals that are the only innocent bystanders, as far as I can tell. Horses get slaughtered in battle, wildlife gets hunted for meat where there's more than enough vegetables for everyone, and bears and panthers get spell-tricked into taking the brunt of a battle for some myopic Trader who doesn't want to pay a guard's wages. And you want to know why I don't get rich patching Warriors up? I like to see them limp, that's why!

Standard Equipment

5 bandages

1 pair of scissors

Method of Healing Animals

Use bandage on animal.

Best Income

Heal the mounts of adventurers.

Best Towns

Any town with a lot of adventurers passing through.

Common Complementary Skills

Animal Lore: Select skill, target animal.

Musicianship: Select instrument.

Peacemaking: Select skill, target individual or creature.

Tracking: Select skill, then select creature/person to track from list.

Note

The amount of healing done is commensurate with the skill.

Make bandages by using scissors on cloth.

Wrestling

Skill 90%, Strength 5%, Dexterity 5%

Ability in combat: Skill 45%, *Tactics* 45%, Strength 3.5%, Dexterity 3.5%, Intelligence 3% (see *Tactics*, p. 93)

Brock Barrelhead

Well, you gotta have a good offense. Somebody shoots a coupla arrows into you, it's almost too late. You gotta get 'em after the first one, maybe sooner. Just tackle 'em and try to rupture an internal organ, maybe break some bones that they use a lot.

If you want to be a wrestler, you gotta know *Tactics*. Almost every barmaid is gonna have more steel than you, and so you gotta be able to get around them, or past their guard, or just plain not rush them from head on. So yeah, *Tactics* is a good thing. *Parrying* is good too, if you feel like holding a shield, just 'cause every shot that don't land is enough time for you to get yours in.

And armour, that's useful. The less damage you take reaching an Archer is all the more time you'll have to relocate his arrows into his spare quiver, if you know what I mean.

And last, you gotta be mean. Arrows are for little girls, and swords are for puppies. Fists are for fighters.

Standard Equipment

1 pair leather gloves

Method of Fighting

Enter war-mode, then double-left-click on opponent.

Common Complementary Skills

Tactics: Automatic

Parrying: Automatic

Best Income

Adventuring

Guarding travelers.

Best Towns

Trinsic, or any place with a Warriors' Guild

Useable Items

The world of *Ultima Online* is a fully interactive world in many respects, and nearly everything in the game can be carried or used to make something else. (Chairs, tables and other large items, of course, are exceptions.)

To use some items, such as doors, chests and food items, you simply double-left-click on them. Other items must be combined in specific ways to make something else. For example, you can use a weapon to kill a bull, then use a knife to skin it. By taking the hide to a tanner and then to an armourer, you can obtain a piece of leather armour.

This section lists usable items in the game and explains how to combine items to use them or make salable goods. The use is generally performed by double-left-clicking on the item. In cases where you must use the item on something else, the second item is listed as well.

Item List

Food

Apple	Cookies (pan)	Lettuce	Pumpkins
Bacon (slab/slice) *	Corn	Limes	Ribs * (cooked)
Bananas	Dates	Melons	Roast pig
Bird * (cooked)	Donuts	Milk	Sausages
Bread (French)	Eggs * (fried)	Muffins	Soup
Bread (loaf)	Fish steaks * (cooked)	Mushrooms	Spam
Cabbage	Food	Onions	Sprouts
Cake	Gourds	Peaches	Squash
Cantaloupe	Grapes	Pears	Stew
Carrots	Ham	Peas	Tomatoes
Cheese	Honeydew melons	Pies (baked)	Turnips
Chicken leg *	Leg of lamb *	Pizza	Watermelons
Coconuts	Lemons	Potatoes	

Combinations

Use	On	To Get	Use	On	To Get
Flour (sack)	Water	Dough * (Bread)	Dough	Fruit	Fruit Pie *
Dough	Honey	Sweet Dough * (Muffins)	Sweet Dough	Flour	Cake Mix * (Cake)
Sweet Dough	Honey	Cookie Mix *	Edged Item	Fish	3 Fish Steaks *
Dough	Meat	Meat Pie *	Dough	Vegetables	Vegetable Pie *

* Cooked Foods

Use a Campfire, Oven or Forge on any of the raw foods with an * to get a cooked food.

Containers (Liquid) / Drinks

You can pour liquids into the following containers. When this is done, the name of the container changes to reflect what it contains. For example, a mug filled with ale becomes a mug of ale. When it is empty, it once again becomes a mug (empty).

Containers:	Bottle	Flask	Glass	Goblet	Jug
	Mug (Ceramic, Pewter, Skull)				
Drinks:	Ale	Cider	Liquor	Water	Wine

Use	On	To Get
Container	Drink	Filled Container

Double-left-click on a container to drink its contents.

Containers (Storage)

Double-left-click on a container to display a view of its contents. Place items into containers by dragging them into this display view.

Portable Containers:	Backpack	Bag	Chest (small)	Pouch
	Mug (Ceramic, Pewter, Skull)			
Fixed Containers:	Armoire	Barrel	Bookcase	Chest (Gold, Steel, Wood)
	Crate	Chest of Drawers		

To unlock a storage container, use its key, or use a Lockpick (and *Lockpicking* skill).

Edged Items

Edged items include:

Axe	Broadsword	Butcher Knife	Cleaver	Cutlass	Dagger
Double Axe	Executioner's Axe	Hatchet	Katana	Kryss	Large Battle Axe
Longsword	Scimitar	Skinning Knife	Two-Handed Axe	Viking Sword	War Axe

Uses of edged items:
Use on target to attack
Use on sheep to obtain wool
Use on dead alligator, cow, deer, goat, horse to get hide
Use on dead bird (chicken, crow, eagle, tropical bird, harpy, magpie, raven) to get feathers
Use on dead fish to get fish steaks
Use on carcass to skin an animal
Use on corpse to obtain meat

Furniture

Bed	Bench	Chair	Shelf	Stool	Table
Throne					

Field Crops

Cotton	Use plant to obtain basket of Cotton
Hay	Feed animals
Wheat	Use plant to harvest Wheat
	Grind into Flour
Flax	Use plant to obtain RettedFflax

Fruit Crops

Fruit Trees	Pick fruit (Apples, Peaches, Pears) from ground near tree
Grapevines	Use Grapevines to pick Grapes

Reagents

Reagents can only be found in certain areas. Use them to cast spells and create potions.

Black Pearl	Blood Moss	Garlic	Ginseng	Mandrake Root	Nightshade
Spider's Silk	Sulphurous Ash				

Potions

To use a potion, drink it. Once you drink a potion, the flask disappears.

Using a Sulphurous Ash potion brings up a targeting cursor, which allows you to "throw" the potion at a specified location or person.

Black Pearl	Refresh (reduces fatigue)
Blood Moss	Agility (improves Dexterity temporarily)
Garlic	Nightsight (gives night vision)
Ginseng	Heal (restores hit points)
Mandrake	Strength (improves Strength temporarily)
Nightshade	Poison (causes poisoning)
Spider's Silk	Sleep (causes deep curative sleep)
Sulphurous Ash	Explosion (causes explosion)

Books and Bulletin Boards

Bulletin board	Use to post or reply to messages
Books (readable)	Use a book to read it
Books (writable)	Use a book to write in it
	If book is writable, previous contents can be erased

Scrolls

Scroll	Use *Inscribe* skill on a blank scroll to create a spell scroll (also requires that spell's reagents)
	Use to cast the spell inscribed on it
	Drag onto spellbook to copy spell inscribed on it into spellbook

Miscellaneous Items

Ankh	Use on yourself to heal wounds, fatigue and/or mana loss
Bedroll	Log out near an active Campfire
Clock	Use to get time of day (in game time, not real time)
Curtains	Use to open or close them
Dye Set/Dyeing Tub	Use with Cloth to dye Clothing
Flour Mill	Use on wheat to make flour
Kindling	Use *Camping* skill on kindling (prior to logging out)
Map	Use to set sailing course for a ship
Millstone	Use on Wheat to make Flour
Moongate	Use to teleport (see **Moongate Travel**, p. 32)
Oil Flask	Use on location/target (throws oil flask)
Oil Flask	Use to refill Lantern or Lamp
Sextant	Use to get current compass coordinates
Shrine	Use on your character's ghost to resurrect
Spyglass	Use to identify phases of the moons

Items Used with Skills

Your skill level determines your chance of success in using these items.

Blacksmithy

Ore	Use on Forge to make Metal
Smith's Hammer or Tongs	Use on Ore with Anvil and Forge to make Metal
	Use on Metal to make a metal item (select item to forge from list that appears)
	(list includes all metal armour and weapons)
	Use on damaged weapon/armour near an Anvil and a Forge to repair item
	(successful repair improves item's condition by 1-5 points; failure reduces it by the same)

Carpentry

Carpentry tools include:

Dovetail Saw	Hammer	Moulding Plane	Scorp
Draw Knife	Inshave	Nails	Smoothing Plane
Froe	Jointing Plane	Saw	

When you use carpentry tools on wood, a screen appears. Select an item to build:

Armoire	Bench	Bookcase	Box	Chair
Chest	Crate	Shelf	Stool	Table
Throne				

Lockpicking

Use a Lockpick and target a locked object. Objects that can be locked include:

Chests	Crates	Doors

Musicianship

Playing a musical instrument will result in either a pleasing sound or a "bad sound," depending on how successful you are.

Drums	Harp	Lute	Mandolin	Tambourine

Tailoring

Wool, Spinning Wheel	Use together to make Yarn
Cotton, Spinning Wheel	Use together to spin Thread
Retted Flax, Spinning Wheel	Use together to spin Thread
Thread, Loom	Use together to make Cloth
Yarn, Loom	Use together to make Cloth
Scissors, Cloth	Use together to make Bandages
Bandage	Use on player/NPC/animal to heal wounds
Leather	Use on Sewing Kit to make clothing
Cloth	Use on Sewing Kit to make clothing

Clothes made from a Sewing Kit used on Leather:

Leather Bustier	Leather Gloves	Leather Gorget	Leather Leggings	Leather Shorts	Leather Skirt
Leather Sleeves	Leather Tunic	One Piece	Studded Gloves	Studded Gorget	Studded Leggings
Studded Sleeves	Studded Tunic				

Clothes made from a Sewing Kit used on Cloth:

Bandana	Cloak	Cloth Coif	Cloth Leggings	Cloth Tunic	Fancy Pants
Fancy Shirt	Ful Apron	Gold Belt	Half Apron	Kilt	Poor Shirt
Sash	Shirt	Skirt	Skullcap		

Tinkering

Target the specified item to make the Tinkered item:

All Tinker's Tools	Use on wood or metal to make tools or tinkered items*
Gear, Stick	Use together to make an Axle with Gears
Spring	Use on Axle with Gears to make Clock Parts
Hinge	Use on an Axle with Gears to make Sextant Parts
Axle	Use with Gears on Springs to make Clock Parts
Clock Parts	Use with Clock Frame to make a Clock
Sextant Parts	Use to make a Sextant

Tools made from metal:

Butcher Knife	Dovetail Saw	Draw Knife	Froe	Hammer	Inshave
Saw	Scissors	Scorp	Sewing Kit	Shovel	Smith's Hammer
Sledge Hammer	Tongs				

Tools made from wood:

Jointing Plane	Moulding Plane	Smoothing Plane

Town Cryer

DAEMONS LOOSE IN CASTLE BRITANNIA. FIFTEEN MISSING, PRESUMED DEAD.

Disaster struck Castle Britannia yesterday as several daemons, summoned by the mage Relvinian, went on a killing rampage throughout the great fortress.

Relvinian had been invited to the castle to discuss with Lord British his theories of a daemon workforce for Britannia and to demonstrate his improved summoning spell. He claimed that the spell would bring a daemon under the complete control of the caster, wiping its mind and preparing it for instructions which would compel it to any assigned task. When he cast the spell in the Great Hall, however, his theories went up in smoke.

"I don't know what happened," one incredulous bystander exclaimed. "I saw a daemon appear, it looked around at us, and then more showed up out of nowhere! They just started throwing fire at everyone."

A Britannian noble added, "All I remember is that huge daemon, looking down on us. Oh, and a cat. There was a cat hissing at it. I don't remember where the cat came from. Then everyone started running."

Members of the Guild of Mages stayed in the Great Hall and attempted to dispel the daemons, but only managed to spread them throughout the castle. "One ran into the kitchen. I saw a magic-wielder charge in after it, and then I heard a lot of noise. I don't know what happened after that, but they're still looking for the kitchen staff, the mage, and the daemon," said Torrie Flynn, a valet to Lord British.

The castle guards were mobilized and sent throughout the maze of halls in teams of five with one accompanying mage for each group. As of this writing, no recent word has been reported as to the current status of the daemons or the guards. The castle, however has been evacuated of all non-defensive personnel, and fifteen, including the kitchen staff, are currently unaccounted for.

"It's a travesty," according to brother Andrew of Empath Abbey. "I was afraid something terrible would come of Relvinian's tamperings, but I never imagined it would be like this. Those things have been loose in the castle for more than twelve hours now. I can only hope that the creation has cost its creator as much as it has cost the citizens of Britain."

Turnius, guildmaster for the Guild of Arcane Arts, said he will be calling a special hearing of the guild to look into the revocation of Relvinian's status in that organization. "This was just irresponsible and reprehensible! We cannot have this kind of thing going unchecked. Someone should have been reviewing Relvinian's research, and it's now my job to figure out who failed to do so and what we can do about it."

Lord British was safely escorted from the Great Hall and is directing rescue missions with his personal guard from the old keep, where he can better view the ongoing situation. ▣

ASK DEATHDEALER

Jorgan the Conqueror has written to me from Vesper. He asks if he should accept a well-paying position as a guard for a merchant in Magincia, or go with some of his buddies on a scheduled foray into the legendary dungeon Deceit.

Take the job in Magincia. If you're a yellow, leather-skirted wanna-be, that is.

Be serious, Jorg! "Let's see — do I want to protect some egotistically over-inflated rich arrogant idiot from losing his money to some right-minded thief, or do I want to go on a kick-butt adventure with some friends and possibly get

(Continued on next page)

ASK DEATHDEALER (cont.)

more gold than I ever dreamed of, or possibly die? Choices, choices."

GIVE ME A BREAK! Are we warriors for the money? NO! We're warriors so we can get out there and mix it up with the leanest and meanest of the world. Death's just an annoyance to us! Working for some rich moron is just likely to bore you to death, AND you'll wind up fat and rusty. You won't swing a sword for weeks, except at some stuffed dummy.

My advice is to blow off the cushy job and go kill some critters that need killin'! You'll get more out of it. And face it — if you survive Deceit, you can charge that same goon of a merchant DOUBLE what he's offering now, if you decide you want to take it easy later. Think about it. ▨

All opinions expressed in this column are my own, nobody else's, and take it or leave it, I don't care, just don't call me a liar. Ever.

TRINSIC GUARDS: EXCESSIVE FORCE?

The crew of "The Skewered Titan" accused the guards of Trinsic of excessive force in the fatal beating of their captain, Marco Macintire. They claim that Captain Macintire was merely playing a prank on an old friend when three guards rushed onto the scene and hacked the sailor to death with their halberds. "It was horrible," said One-Eye Fitzhugh, the vessel's first mate. "He was just showin' his new cutlass to old … uh … what'shisname there, and the guards came runnin' in and killed him. There weren't no need to do that! That guy's been friends with the crew for years, he knew the Captain wasn't really serious." "Yeah, an' they're jus' about impossible to kill, them guards!" said fellow sailor, Jake the Mauler.

Guards say they were summoned by citizens to the scene in front of the Peg Leg Inn where Cap. Macintire was brutally attacking Roger the Fisher. Roger, according to most reports, was curled up in a fetal position on the road as the captain cut him again and again with a large, new cutlass. "It is my job to keep Britannia safe," said Maldrid, one of the three guards involved in the incident. Drakwin and Norman, the other two guards on the scene, echoed Maldrid's words.

Bystanders were convinced that justice had been done. "They're a bunch of pirates! That's all they are," said a wandering adventurer who asked to remain anonymous. "They were beatin' up the fisherman just for fun. They know the rules as well as anyone. You don't attack people in town. Period. They got what was coming!"

"My friends? I, uh, guess so. Yeah, that pirate was just showing me his sword, that's all. I swear it! I mean sailor. Not pirate. Don't tell 'em where I am!" Roger the Fisher said, recovering in a healer's home south of Britain.

Cap. Macintire will be buried at sea with a wake to follow on board his last command. ▨

ANNOUNCEMENT

Come one, come all to the gates of Lord British's fine estate to hear the great Ophidian Dragon sing until his Majesty emerges. The songs will be of popular choosings, and all Britannians are invited to gather for a night of soulful ballads. Search for the purple-caped Scholar named "Ophidian Dragon" at our Majesty's castle at half-past eight each evening.

CLASSIFIEDS

ROGUE SEEKING WORK for gold, armour, weapons or goods. Can pick pockets, steal, lockpick, and hide with ease. No murdering of others, although stealing OK. Prefer Guild of Thieves, but all welcome to answer.

KINDRED CREW WANTED. Small group of privateers seek sailors, warriors and magi to crew ships. We offer fine benefits, and a family-run business. Prefer to avoid senseless killing. Please contact Mckenna.

SAILORS WANTED. APG (Pirates' Guild) seeking experienced sailors to join mighty guild. If you are experienced pirating sailing, navigation, or combat, contact our recruitment center for the ship nearest you. Wages paid weekly, with a % loot per mission.

WANTED: DEAD — ZODIAC. Low-class thief, who's struck deals with dark forces to gain invisibility. Temple of Circe will pay a reward for proof the cretin is dead and return of stolen goods.

Economics

RESOURCE SYSTEM

Resource Bank

Ultima Online has a bountiful (though finite) supply of crops, minerals, livestock and other natural resources. The balance of these resources in the world are based on regional "resource banks," or predetermined sets of resources in a certain area. Each region has its own resource bank, an "account" that keeps track of how many units of each resource exist. As resources are consumed in the world, the "bank" is adjusted.

Note: The game's magic system is also based on a limited resource bank.

What Affects Resource Banks

Many factors can adjust the units of a particular resource in a region. The most obvious is supply — if all the trees are cut down, there are no more trees until the forest has time to naturally regenerate itself. Other factors are not so visible:

- All regions start out with different resource banks. This means that some areas might be rich in iron ore deposits, while other areas are perfect for raising crops and livestock.

- The total sum of resources in the world is increased slightly each time a new character is created.

- Players can stash resources and purposefully deplete the resource bank.

- When an item in the world is destroyed, its base resource is added back into the resource bank where the item originated.

  Example: A metal sword is made in Trinsic from iron ore. Its owner fights in Jhelom, where the sword is destroyed in battle.

  It regenerates as units of metal ore, which are placed back into Trinsic's resource bank.

- As resources are consumed, the resource bank is adjusted to reflect how many resources are in the world, as well as how many resources are left to allocate in the world.

  Example: A farmer plants 20 acres of corn.

  The number of "corn" resources in the bank drops, since these resources are in the world, rather than in the bank. In the bank, the resource is "unplanted crops." In the game world, the presence of the corn resource affects the supply of corn in that area.

Resource System and the World

Even though it's invisible to players, the resource bank is the major dynamic entity that watches over and manages events in the world. The operation of the bank can be summed up as follows:

- ♀ The game's economy is based on the availability of raw materials.

- ♀ Raw materials are tracked by region.

- ♀ The game evaluates, region by region, the world.

- ♀ The game identifies areas with surpluses.

- ♀ The game alters the existing inhabitants (NPCs) or adds creatures/monsters to reduce the surplus.

  Example Trinsic has many general laborers, and an abundant supply of wheat and flour.

  Result Several general laborers take up baking and open shops.

  Example Sheep are over-reproducing in an area, and the farmers don't have enough grassy fields to feed them.

  Result Dragons move into the area with a surplus of sheep.

- ♀ The resource bank cannot add to or change its resource types.

- ♀ If resources in an area need to be adjusted, the game will add keywords to the NPC conversations to initiate actions.

  Example Farmers in an area raise sheep and grain crops. Rabbits in the area constantly eat the crops, and a local dragon eats sheep and deer in the forest.

  Result Now, if a player asks the townsfolk about how things are going, the folk will complain about the rabbits eating their crops. If players then go "harvest" the rabbits, the NPCS will be pleased. And as an added bonus, the players raise their notoriety rating, earning gold or goods in the process.

Resource Types

The world has many types of resources. Some are "living" resources, such as chickens, pigs and other forms of meat that serve as food staples for carnivores. Other resources are production-oriented and are used to produce goods. One example is iron ore, which can be mined and smelted into iron goods.

SHOPS

Britannia's trade centers operate on the free-market principle. Whatever you desire, chances are you can find what you need among the shops in each town. Upgrading your potion collection or augmenting your hard-earned armour with a sturdy shield is often as easy as travelling to the nearest town and asking a few questions.

To discover where certain goods are sold in a town, talk to NPCs. Most of them are quite familiar with trade shops and such, and they'll be more than happy to give you general directions (west, north, etc.). You can locate shops that currently exist on the town maps (pp. 248-281).

Once you do find a shop, you'll need to be specific about what you want. Not all shops carry the same goods all of the time, especially if demand is high. Prices vary as well — to find the best deal, you may have to visit several towns.

Buying

In keeping with Britannia's stringent work ethics, all NPC-run shops in Britannia are open night and day. (A game day is 2 hours in real time, meaning that 12 game days pass for each 24 hours of real time.) Shopkeepers respond to "Buy" and "Sell," as well as to certain keywords (listed in **Non-Player Character Descriptions**, pp. 162-177). If you're trying to find something, just ask for it.

Selling

Shopkeepers will only buy items that are in their "buy" list (see **Non-Player Character Descriptions**, pp. 162-177), and only if they have enough money. To offer goods to a shopkeeper, tell the shopkeeper what you'd like to sell. Be sure to use the word "Sell" somewhere in your sentence.

Occasionally, if you offer an NPC shopkeeper a valuable or needed item, he or she may reward you with something non-monetary, such as a scroll. Otherwise, the shopkeeper may just buy the item for a specific number of pieces of gold. The price offered is not fixed — it changes according to supply and demand.

If the shopkeeper desires the item, the Sale scroll will pop up with the shopkeeper's offer. You can then either accept or decline the offer. To accept the offer, confirm the sale by left-clicking ACCEPT. The money automatically transfers into your backpack, adding to your current supply of gold coins.

Shop Inventory

All NPC shops start out with a standard collection of goods, although the list varies by shop type. An alchemy shop will deal solely in flasks, potions and similar items, while a bakery will offer raw cooking materials and baked goods.

Additionally, all shopkeepers buy some items from players on the side. The item must be in their list of preferred items to buy, however (see the **Sell** and **Buy** entries for each shopkeeper in the **NPC Descriptions**, pp. 162-177). If you have extra bolts of cloth, you may be able to convince a tailor to purchase them.

Risky Business

Starting up a business may seem like an easy task, but in reality, NPC business is as risky as real business. By nature, some shop types are more prosperous that others. How much capital a shop has depends on what the shop sells, and how much its items cost to produce. Armourers that make leather goods will have less money than one that makes metal goods — leather is less profitable than metal. Shopkeepers can go bankrupt if they run out of money needed to restock.

Shopkeepers have a lot of control over what they carry as well. They operate on the rules of supply and demand, just as any business-conscious Britannian would. If an item is popular, they'll keep restocking their shelves with it. If they're carrying a hundred extra flasks and not selling any, they'll try to get rid of the excess.

Specialties

Shops can also specialize in certain items. For example, a weaponsmith may specialize in blunt weapons — she buys the metal and forges it into hammers, maces, and other items she wishes to sell. This doesn't mean, however, that you can't sell a razor-sharp sword to a blunt weaponsmith. Shopkeepers are always looking for good deals on raw materials. The weaponsmith might buy your sword, then turn around and melt it down into several smaller, blunt weapons.

Some shopkeepers might purchase certain items from players and sell them, even though they don't specialize in that particular good. A leather armourer, for instance, may have a couple of suits of plate armour in stock that he's bought from other adventurers. Although he doesn't typically sell plate, he'll probably hang onto the armour awhile and sell it to another player.

Specialty shopowners will buy all items in their normal buy list (see the **Sell** and **Buy** entries for each shopkeeper in the **NPC Descriptions**, beginning on p. 162). They'll tend to pay more for things they don't normally carry and also charge more during resale, since they don't keep these items in stock. This can be a good way to make a little extra cash on the side — buying items cheaply from one source, then turning around and selling them to a specialty shop for a profit.

PRICES

Cost Adjustments

One of the first things you'll notice when you start purchasing goods is that supplies and costs are not static. In the game's free market, prices are determined by a number of fluctuating factors. What you pay for a shield in one town will probably differ from what you'd pay in another town. Effectiveness, material properties, material availability and magical charges all affect an item's cost.

Material makes a large difference in price. Something made out of wood is usually going to cost less then something made out of metal. The basic cost for metal items is 5 gold pieces per resource (unit value for an ingot of metal), while wooden items cost 1 gold piece per board.

The effectiveness of an item affects price as well. A magical shield is going to cost more than a standard shield because it has more defensive power. Similarly, you'll pay more for a quality durable good than for a less expensive, less durable good.

Here are some general guidelines on pricing:

♀ Food prices are based on the food value, or how much that item will fill you up in food units.

♀ House prices are based on size and architectural elements (boards, stones, etc.).

♀ Ship prices are based on size — i.e., the number of boards used.

♀ Wooden, metal and cloth items are priced based on size and materials, at a current rate of 5 gold pieces/unit for metal, and 1 gold/unit for wood and cloth.

♀ Armour prices start out at material cost, and are increased according to how effective the armour is.

♀ Weapon prices start out at material cost, and are increased according to how much damage the weapon can deliver, the amount of material required for manufacturing, and how much protection it offers to the wielder. Price is also affected by extra attack speed (if the weapon is lightweight), durability and the quantity of magic charges (which normally decrease each time a magical weapon is used).

♀ Magical item prices are based on the quantity of magical ability the item has, currently ranging in cost between 500 and 50,000 gold pieces.

Magical points wear off differently for different item types. Wands, for example, consume one charge per use. Shields lose magical charges when they get hit, and other items have time limits imposed on their magical abilities.

Prices and Resources

All items have a base price, which is then adjusted according to how many relevant natural resources exist in that region. For example, if iron ore is plentiful in one region, all iron goods will be available in nearby towns for an attractive price. But, in an iron ore-poor area, the price of iron goods will be significantly higher.

If all the iron ore in an area is mined, it won't be as plentiful, and iron prices will rise. Although some resources regenerate naturally, the rate is not fast enough to provide a never-ending supply of ore or any other natural resource.

This is merely one instance of how the game is affected by player actions. Like the real world, all the towns are affected by the rules of supply and demand. Therefore, it is impossible to provide a concrete list of prices for items in the game.

The rest of this section discusses how items are priced according to different factors in the game — availability, notoriety, etc. For more information about how game resources work, see **Resource System**, p. 108.

Economic Modifications

After the basic cost is determined, other factors come into play as well.

Rare Items. First, there is the age-old problem of supply and demand. The shopkeepers in *Ultima Online* are of the greedy sort, and they'll overcharge any and all Britannians for a rare item. Just consider it a general rule that the smaller the quantity of an item in a particular town, the more expensive the item becomes.

Availability of raw materials. The economic situation of a region also has some bearing on how much an item costs from town to town. (See **Resource Bank**, p. 108, for a full explanation of how resources are allocated in the game.) If metal resources are at an all-time low, then buyers of swords, plate armour and other metallic goods are going to see a rise in price.

Availability within other shops. If an item is common, prices for that item will drop to balance the supply and demand. Oversupply can be caused by several things. If someone comes into town and sells a wagonload of swords to various shops, the price of swords will drop. Conversely, if someone buys up every ear of corn in town, the price of corn will skyrocket.

However, just because a resource is present doesn't mean it affects price. For instance, a miner brings a wagonload of iron ore into town and parks it. At that moment, the ore simply exists as the property of whoever brought it into town. Once this ore is sold to blacksmiths, however, it begins affecting the price of iron in that area. In other words, only items in shops are part of the supply and demand calculation.

Notoriety Pricing

In the game, notoriety affects more than just your reputation — it can determine how much you'll have to pay for certain goods. If you have negative notoriety, prices will be higher. If you have positive notoriety, they'll be lower. Other people (especially NPCs) will notice your notoriety and respond accordingly.

Negative Notoriety. Dastardly deeds can cause your notoriety to fall. Negative notoriety can increase the price of an item you're buying from 1% to 25%, depending on your current notoriety rating. Unless you enjoy evil deeds and have money to spare, it's in your best economic interest to pursue positive notoriety.

Positive Notoriety. Just as good karma accompanies good deeds, unselfish actions can raise your notoriety. In turn, you get a positive rating, and anywhere from a 1% to 25% discount on prices.

See **Notoriety**, p. 34, for information on what actions can affect your notoriety.

Guild Discounts

Today's professional societies surely stem from the guilds and trade associations that exist in Britannia. Game guilds are more than a way to make contacts and drop a few names around town — they're also a great way to save money in shops.

If you're in the Warriors' Guild, for instance, you'll get a 10% discount if you buy your weapons from a shopkeeper affiliated with that guild. Check the signs outside the shops. If the color scheme matches that of your guild, ask the shopkeeper if you can receive a guild discount. Some shops don't have signs — go in and ask the shopkeeper if they belong to a guild.

See **Game Guilds** next page, and the color poster for details on specific guilds.

How Much Does It Cost?

The easiest way to figure out how much an item costs is to ask the shopkeeper. But, say you don't trust the shopkeeper, or you're finalizing a verbal deal with a player on the street. If you don't want to lose out to a deceitful trader, learn the *Item Identification* skill. Once you master it, you can use it to determine the regional cost of the item you're considering buying. On the other hand, *Item Identification* won't take into account variables that modify prices at a specific shop, such as overstock of an item. Appraised prices can also vary from region to region.

Automatic Drafting

If you're one of Britannia's wealthier citizens and you want to purchase an item that costs upward of 2000 gold pieces, don't lug bag after bag of gold down to the shop. Instead, just visit the shop and tell the shopkeeper you'd like to buy the item — the shopkeeper will then deduct the total from your bank account.

GUILDS

In the game, groups of players can band together in a group called a *guild* for the sake of furthering their principles, fostering an occupational community or numerous other goals. Some guilds are of the serious, occupational sort, such as the Warriors' Guild. Others are geared more toward social gatherings.

Ultima Online has two types of guilds — *game guilds* (trade guilds run by NPCs) and *player guilds* (created and managed by players). Anyone can join a game guild by finding the NPC guildmaster and paying a membership fee. Joining player guilds is a bit more difficult — you must contact the player guildmaster to gain permission to join.

The first section of this chapter discusses **Game Guilds**. The second section covers a broad spectrum of major **Player Guilds**. Although only 24 appear here, player guilds number into the thousands and are created and disbanded each day — check the web site (WWW.ULTIMAONLINE.COM) for the most current list.

Game Guilds

By joining a game guild, you can receive discounts at certain shops. Merchants affiliated with a certain guild display the guild's coat of arms on a sign in front of their shops. Members of that particular guild receive a 10% discount at that shop. The exception is the Thieves' Guild — instead of a discount, membership renders guild members immune to NPC thieves and beggars.

Most main trade guilds have branches that represent local or specialty divisions. These sub-guilds use the same colors (green and white, for example), but their coat-of-arms design varies slightly (such as vertical vs. horizontal stripes). All sub-guilds offer discounts to members of all branches of the guild. (See the color poster for coats of arms for each guild and sub-guild.)

Joining/Leaving a Game Guild

You can join nearly any game guild, as long as you pay the 500-gold piece membership fee. (A couple are not currently accepting new members.) This ensures lifetime membership in that guild. However, you must pay again if you ever decide to change guilds.

♀   If you say the word "guild" or "guilds" to an NPC Guildmaster, he or she will offer you membership in that particular guild.

♀   If you say "join" or "member" to a Guildmaster of an NPC guild, you will automatically join that guild, if you don't already belong to another guild.

♀   If you wish to withdraw your guild membership, say "resign" or "quit" to that Guildmaster.

Joining/Leaving a Player Guild

Player guilds are controlled independently, and ORIGIN exerts little control over them. Unlike game guilds, player guilds don't provide shop discounts (unless players in the same guild agree to trade goods at lower prices).

To join a particular player guild, you must find its guildmaster. This can be quite a task in some cases. Your best bet is to ask around or post a notice on the town bulletin board. Some players create guild halls that you can visit. If you can't find the guildmaster, visit the *Guild Hall* on the *Ultima Online* web site (**www.owo.com**) and use the guild search engine to track down guilds by category, name, guildmaster or location. Then, you can contact the Guildmaster via e-mail.

To leave a guild, e-mail the guildmaster and ask to cancel your membership.

Game Guilds By City

To find a guild you want to join, you may have to travel to different towns — not every guild has a chapter in every town. Currently, no permanent guild halls exist for the Society of Clothiers and the Guild of Healers. However, you might encounter a guildmaster at any of their shops throughout Britannia.

Britain
(G1) Warriors' Guild [SW]
(G2) The Sorcerer's Delight: Shop, Library & Guild [N]
(G3) Mining Cooperative [NW]
(G4) Merchants' Association [C]
(G5) Order of Engineers [W]
(G7) Guild of Cavalry and Horse [NE]

Buccaneer's Den
(G1) Pirate's Den (Society of Thieves) [SW]

Jhelom
(G1) Brothers in Arms Warriors' Guild [NW]

Magincia
(G1) Mining Cooperative [W]
(G2) Fishermen's Guild & Supplies [S]
(G3) Merchants' Association [S]

Minoc
(G1) The New World Order (Warriors' Guild) [N]
(G2) The Golden Pick Axe (Mining Cooperative) [N]
(G3) The Matewan (Mining Cooperative) [C]

Moonglow
(G1) Encyclopedia Magicka (Guild of Mages) [C]
(G3) Guild of Arcane Arts [C]
(G4) Merchants' Association [C]
(G5) Masters of Illusion [E]
(G6) Guild of Sorcery [SE]

NuJel'm
(G1) Merchant's Association [S]

Ocllo
(G1) Guild of Sorcery [NW]
(G2) Bardic Collegium [N]

Serpent's Hold
(G1) Warriors' Guild [E]

Skara Brae
(G1) League of Rangers [NW]

Trinsic
(G1) Order of Engineers [NW]
(G2) Brotherhood of Trinsic (Warriors' Guild) [N]
(G3) Paladins' Guild [NE]
(G4) Sons of the Sea (Guild of Fishermen) [SE]

Vesper
(G1) Guild of Fishermen [E]
(G2) Society of Thieves [S]
(G3) The Champions of Light (Warriors' Guild) [C]

Game Guilds by Type

For a complete listing of guilds and their color emblems and subguilds, see the pull-out poster included with this book.

General Membership. The prominent occupation for the group — i.e., alchemist, paladin, healer, etc. The occupations listed here indicate what types of shopkeepers will give you discounts. Not all guilds are currently open for membership. At this time, the Guild of Barbers, Society of Cooks and Society of Smiths are closed to new membership. However, note that the Society of Weaponsmiths (a subguild of the Society of Smiths) extends membership discount privileges to the Warriors' Guild.

Subguilds. Specialty branches of a main guild or association. Sub-guilds offer discounts to members of all branches of the main guild.

Guild of Arcane Arts

General Membership	Alchemists, mages
Subguilds	Guild of Mages
	Guild of Sorcery
	Masters of Illusion

Guild of Barbers *(Not currently accepting new members)*

General Membership	Barbers, hairstylists
Subguilds	None

Society of Clothiers

General Membership	Tailors, weavers
Subguilds	Tailor's Hall

Bardic Collegium

General Membership	Bards, musicians, storytellers, performers
Subguilds	None

Society of Cooks and Chefs *(Not currently accepting new members)*

General Membership	Cooks, chefs
Subguilds	None

Order of Engineers

General Membership	Tinkers, engineers
Subguilds	None

Guild of Healers

General Membership	Healers
Subguilds	Healers' Guild
	Lord British's Healers of Virtue

Maritime Guild

General Membership	Fishermen, sailors, mapmakers, shipwrights
Subguilds	Guild of Fishermen
	Sailors' Maritime Association
	Seamen's Chapter
	Society of Shipwrights

Merchants' Association

General Membership	Merchants, innkeepers, tavernkeepers, jewelers, provisioners
Subguilds	Merchants' Guild
	Guild of Provisioners
	Traders' Guild
	Barterers' Guild

Mining Cooperative

General Membership	Miners
Subguilds	None

League of Rangers

General Membership	Bowyers, animal trainers, rangers
Subguilds	None

Society of Smiths *(Not currently accepting new members)*

General Membership	Blacksmiths, weaponsmiths
Subguilds	Armourers' Guild
	Blacksmiths' Guild
	Guild of Armaments
	Society of Weaponsmiths

Society of Thieves

General Membership	Beggars, thieves, assassins, brigands
Subguilds	Federation of Rogues and Beggars
	Guild of Assassins
	Society of Thieves

Warriors' Guild

General Membership	Fighters (mercenaries, warriors), weapons trainers, soldiers, guard, paladins (Weaponsmiths also commonly belong to this guild)
Subguilds	Association of Warriors
	Fighters and Footmen
	Guild of Cavalry and Horse

Players' Guilds

Britannia has countless guilds created by players. Anyone can create a guild, as long as you register the guild and it is deemed appropriate by ORIGIN. The only requirement is that the guildmaster have an e-mail address, web page and emblem.

Player guilds differ from game guilds in that a player (instead of an NPC) guildmaster runs them. Player guilds rarely give you any shop discounts, but they can be good for companionship and human contacts, and protection if you need it.

The following list of player guilds, collected somewhat at random, represent the broad spectrum of player guilds. We cannot guarantee that any one will still be active in a month. However, new guilds are constantly forming. For an up-to-date list, check the guild registry on the *Ultima Online* web site (**www.owo.com**).

All Girls Guild

Web Address   http://www.geocities.com/TimesSquare/2468/
Guildmaster   Infinitee: infinitee@geocities.com

Although the name suggests otherwise, these law-abiding citizens of the realm in fact allow males to walk among them. A strong bond ties these maidens of virtue together with their brothers, forming a family of kindred souls. Their membership is of utmost importance, and they go to great lengths to protect their kin.

The Band

Web Address   http://gogan.landlords.com/theband/
Guildmaster   http://gogan.landlords.com/theband/forms/f_contact.html

Seek companions? Look no further than The Band. Although not a political organization, this guild is a tightly knit family. What it lacks politically, it makes up for in spirit and fellowship. Members walk the land in honest pursuit of the virtues.

The Bane of Chaos

Web Address   http://baneofchaos.uo.org/
Guildmaster   Nicodemus: jshaft@o2.net

The Bane of Chaos is a guild of spiritual believers. Divided into many groups, each group worships a different totem. Probing into their devote worship, many say that this worship renders unexplainable effects. In all honesty, there appears to be inspiration gleaned from their totems and a unity that many other guilds lack.

Totems are a concept unique to this guild. Each division of The Bane of Chaos is represented by a different totem. These totems are the spiritual embodiments of each division's most sacred characteristics. They provide inspiration, unity and a connection to the ethereal world. Each member must strive to attain a bond with that member's totem, for only then can he or she truly be powerful.

Blades of Justice

Web Address   http://www.geocities.com/TimesSquare/Alley/1435/

Guildmaster   http://home1.gte.net/segurson/BoJ/contact.html

The Blades of Justice is a knightly order of warriors most pure and stout upholders of Lord British's sacred laws. These knights of virtue pursue the ideals of Justice in all that they do. It has been argued that the Blades of Justice care more for justice than Lord British's own guard. Comrades in arms, comrades in belief, this guild is strongly united.

The Black Hand

Web Address   http://www.globility.com/~paull/

Guildmaster   Orion: pnch09b@prodigy.com

In all ages, there have been those seeking to satisfy none other than themselves. In this day and age, the Black Hand embodies this belief. This guild's only purpose is to gain power through any means. Compassion has no sway in these cold souls unless it gives them what they need. A harsh outlook upon the realm binds this guild together, for their loyalties are only to themselves, and when useful, to their brothers.

The Bookies

Web Address   http://bookies.uo.org/

Guildmaster   Vanin: bookies@uo.org

The realm of Brittania is a dangerous one, yet it can also be extremely enriching. To those who prefer to taunt danger and live on the edge, The Bookies are a welcome sight. The Bookies lay odds for many contests, often paying off a high reward to the winner. Spectators can bet on the match through the Bookies, increasing their own wealth.

Britannian Thespian League

Web Address   http://www.geocities.com/TimesSquare/5604/thespian.html

Guildmaster   Draconi: draconi@geocities.com

Many actors of Britannia have come together to form the Britannian Thespian League. This traveling troupe performs all over the known realm, spreading both culture and entertainment. Their plays of drama, suspense and humor bring many an audience enjoyment. Rather than running away to join the gypsies, many would counsel joining the Thespian League.

Order of Balance

Web Address   http://www.westworld.com/~guardian/uol

Guildmaster   http://www.wgn.net/~guardian/uol/gateway.html

Order and Chaos hold diametrically opposed views. In Order and Law, everything is predictable, everything is in its proper place and everything is clearly defined. In Chaos and Freedom, nothing is predictable, everything can do what it would and none is as it seems.

In Britannia, there are those who seek each extreme. The Order of Balance strives to complement one with the other to form the ideal medium. The Order of Balance comprises of many divisions (including an all-female one), each a unique entity with its own vision.

Brotherhood of Crimson Knights

Web Address   http://home.earthlink.net/~abktalon/index/Crimson.htm

Guildmaster   BCK Talon: abktalon@mail.earthlink.net

Duty, Valor and Honor form the triad upon which this guild is based. A brotherhood of knights who champion the cause of good in the lands, these knights strive for influence in the realm. Unafraid to back up their words of honor with action, they seek to leave their mark on Britannia.

The Burning Heart

Web Address   http://www.diac.com/~damont

Guildmaster   Daylar: Daylar@hotmail.com

The Burning Heart, with truth as its guide, pursues with devotion the virtues Lord British has put into place. Utterly loyal to Lord British, these virtuous adventurers scour the land to defeat evil and prevent the corruption of truth. In their quest, they rely on both unity and friendship.

Clan Woad

Web Address   http://www.telalink.net/~duncan/

Guildmaster   Kerowynn: wayaadis@inreach.com

A close-knit group of amusing antics and obscure beliefs, the members of this guild are free souls, seeking information to pass unto their brethren. Freedom is their way, as is their friendship to one another. They are wary of strangers and seldom let more into their fold. To quote their favorite saying, "Paint yourself blue and start taking heads!"

Companions of the Dawn

Web Address   http://www.geocities.com/TimesSquare/Alley/2587/

Guildmaster   Mecandes: companions@usa.net

Companions of the Dawn is a small group of loyal companions whose backgrounds are as varied as the stars in the night sky. Creative talent resides within the ranks of this guild and gives off a plethora of artistic energy. Formed among a band of friends, the guild's only bonds are friendship among its members and a driving desire to explore the world.

Disciples of Exodus

Web Address   http://silcon.com/~world/aura/doe/

Guildmaster   Valles: valles@silcon.com

Acquiring information is the key goal for the Disciples of Exodus, who journey the land seeking out the unknown and recording it for their own use. They seek freedom and feel that Lord British's forcing of the Virtues upon the citizenry is the miscreant deed of a tyrant. Their ways are old — as old as the shattering of the realm — and thus, they gather information not only for its own sake, but because it is what they have always done. Any aspiring adventurer can join their ranks, so long as he or she carries a field journal.

Duir Sidhe

Web Address   http://www.geocities.com/TimesSquare/Alley/5686/

Guildmaster   http://www.geocities.com/TimesSquare/Alley/5686/join.htm

A reclusive enclave that is self-sufficient, the Duir Sidhe are druids of an ancient belief. They strive to protect the land, and beyond that, to seek out the delicate balance between life and death. Many of the druids study the arts of alchemy and the ways of Spirit Speaking. Rumors of druids walking the nights with the unseen are common, for it is said they speak with the dead.

Guild of Free Traders

Web Address   http://www.europa.com/~strad/freetrader/welcome.html

Guildmaster   Stradius Plexar: strad@europa.com

To fatten your coffers, seek out a Free Trader in the realm. The ways of a merchant can be quite profitable. The Guild of Free Traders is for merchants who go it alone, yet wish to be part of a larger group. With the combined resources of others, these traders have a greater range of items to sell and greater resources with which to procure rare objects.

Guild of the Lost Eighth

Web Address   http://webhome.idirect.com/~ook/tgotl8th.html

Guildmaster   http://webhome.idirect.com/~ook/join.html

No one can alone embody all eight Virtues, for we all have at least one Vice. Members of Guild of the Lost Eighth excel in all Virtues but one — each member has a fatal flaw exactly opposed to one of the Virtues. Perhaps a member embodies all virtues but humility, so rather than being humble, he is extremely proud. Many speculate that members purposefully oppose the one Virtue that they lack.

League of Pirates

Web Address   http://matrix.binary.net/sirvival/lop/

Guildmaster   http://matrix.binary.net/sirvival/lop/join.htm

The League of Pirates needs little definition, they sail the seas striking terror into those they raid. Joy is found in the bottom of a barrel, with a bloodied scimitar in hand and loot bursting from a chest. Yet even the lawless have a code unto themselves — among their ranks, they say there is no surer a friend than a fellow pirate.

Lords of the Night

Web Address   http://night.org/

Guildmaster   http://night.org/join.html

The night is their time to spread fear and uncertainty. Little is known about them, for they are a mysterious lot. It is rumored that they sacrifice children, but I lend no credence to such tales. They are the keepers of the night and enforce its rules.

The Nobility

Web Address   http://www.netlink.com.au/~istuart/

Guildmaster   Berek: ahughes@inreach.com

Followers of Order, this democratic guild strives for prosperity and are only satisfied with the best. Members of the Nobility live well within the laws of the realm, and stealing is a deed unknown to them. Only in desperation might one of the Nobility steal, and would later recompensate the value of any goods stolen.

The Obsidian Circle

Web Address   http://www.primenet.com/~paradox/guild.html

Guildmaster   http://www.primenet.com/%7Eparadox/apply.html

There is but one goal for those in The Obsidian Circle — power. They don't employ obvious and violent methods practiced by others, but gather their power quietly through allies and friendships. They view money as the root of power.

Sosarian Socialist Party

Web Address   http://www.magincia.org

Guildmaster   http://www.magincia.org/forms/join.htm

The cry of the worker to rise up and resist the tyranny of Lord British rings loud and clear wherever a member of the Sosarian Socialist Party passes by. This guild's belief that the virtues are nothing but a means to keep the population placated and dutifully producing stir emotions in those with whom they speak. The SSP wishes to bestow freedom on all workers and strive for a more socialist society.

Syndicate

Web Address   http://www.erols.com/seanst/synd/iiiguild.html

Guildmaster   http://www.erols.com/seanst/synd/joinsynd.html

You might be wondering about the existence of the underworld guilds. Well, my friend, many have been absorbed by a larger organization, the Syndicate. The Syndicate is a unification of many smaller guilds, having pooled their strengths and formed a overshadowing entity. Each chapter focuses on a single aspect of the underworld and combines its efforts with other chapters for maximum effect. It is the Syndicate's goal to control all underworld dealings in Britannia.

Unified Magistracy

Web Address   http://www2.uwindsor.ca/~beaudoi/um/

Guildmaster   http://www2.uwindsor.ca/%7Ebeaudoi/um/membship.htm

No one is above justice, and the Unified Magistracy seeks to unite Britannia under the laws set forth by Universal Law. They believe that only through a Just society can the Chaos abounding in the realm be stopped. The Unified Magistracy seeks to set up courts in all cities, where those who break the law shall be dealt with.

Venerable Ones

Web Address   http://www.tiac.net/users/hollyoak/venerable/main.htm

Guildmaster   http://web0.tiac.net/users/hollyoak/venerable/join.htm

A fun-loving, adventuring troupe, the Venerable Ones hold companionship dear. Maturity is the key in this guild, for all the members are expected to act responsibly in the arms of society. A spoken word is often times better than a sword drawn in haste, and the members of the Venerable Ones excel at this. To adventure in good company is what the Venerable Ones strive for.

KEYWORDS

Trying to find out exactly what you need to know from an NPC stranger can occasionally prove difficult. To assist you, this chapter lists NPC keywords — recognizable words you can use in everyday conversations with NPCs. The lists are divided by **General** (applicable to all NPCs) and **City** keywords. **Occupation** keywords are listed with each NPC description, starting on p. 162. Keep in mind that these lists are subject to expand and change over time.

Usage Guidelines

To help you interpret these listings, here are some general guidelines:

⚲ **Bold words** must be typed by themselves (i.e., not in a sentence), and must be spelled exactly as the word is in the list. Capitalization does not matter, however.

⚲ **Multiple-word entries** (such as "green potion") will only elicit the desired response if you type both words consecutively, without any other words in between them. For example, "green" by itself will not draw an NPC into an in-depth conversation, and "potion" will probably result in general directions to a magic shop. "Green potion," however, will evoke a totally different answer.

⚲ Keywords ending with " **'s** "(primarily city names) trigger the same response whether you place the apostrophe before or after the "s," or if you leave it out entirely. Asking an NPC about "Buccaneer's Den," "Buccaneers' Den" or "Buccaneers Den" will get the same response. (Here, however, the keyword is only listed once, and with the apostrophe before the "s.")

⚲ Some words listed are **partially spelled** to allow for multiple word endings. In the more obscure cases, a sample word follows in parentheses to help you understand the general meaning of the root word. An example is "thiev," which allows NPCs to respond to "thieving," "thievery" and "thieves." Similarly, "alchem" lets you ask about "alchemy" and "alchemists."

⚲ **<any>** between two words indicates that you can insert additional words between the keywords. Either "What job do you like to do?" or "What do wild ettins like to do in their free time?" will result in the same response, because the NPC responds to "What .... do .... do?"

All NPCs have general keywords (given in the first entry). Similarly, people in a given town will respond to certain keywords for that region. Most keyword responses, however, are based on occupation, as well as your notoriety. If you're well-liked, the response will usually be more polite, and perhaps even more helpful. (Responses are not listed here due to space constraints.)

General (All NPCs)

avatar	blackthorn	britannia	buccaneer's den	bye	cove
capital	farewell	go away	greetings	hasta la vista	hello
hi	Jhelom	job	king	leave me alone	
lord british	magincia	moonglow	name	new magincia	nujel'm
ocllo	occupation	profession	ruler	serpent's hold	shrine
skara brae	see ya	take a hike	trinsic	vesper	virtue
yew	yo	what <any> do <any> do			

Hiring

You can hire NPCs with the following keywords:

hire	hireling	hiring	mercenary	servant	work

Needs

Use the following keywords to identify an NPCs current needs you can help fulfill.

Are you <any> well	How art thou	How <any> you	thou fare thou need	thou require
thou want	what is wrong	what's wrong	you fare	you lac	you need
you needing	you require	you want		

Cities

The following keywords work with NPCs in specific cities.

Britain

alchemist	ankh	armour	artisan	baker	bank
bard	bay	blacksmith	blackthorn's castle	blue boar	boats
bowyer	bread	bridge	brittany	brittany river	butcher
camp	carpenter	cartographer	castle	cat's lair	cemetery
city wall	clothes	clothiers	conservatory	crypt	customs
customs house	cypress bridge	death	dummies	dummy	ethereal
ethereal goods	farmers	farms	fighter	fletcher	gate
graves	graveyard	great bridge	great northern	guild	
guard house	guardhouse	gung farmer	healer	incantations	inn
incantations and enchantments	I'm lost	jewel	lb (weight; pound)	leather	
lighthouse	mage	mage guild	mage shop	mage tower	magic
mage's bridge	mage's shop	magic shop	main gate	mapmaker	map
mausoleum	mechanician	miners	mining guild	minstrel	moat
musician	narrows	narrows neck	northside	northern bridge	neck
oaken oar	ocean	old keep	orc	paws	poor gate
provision	resurrect	river	river's gate	sage advice	ships
salty dog	shipwright	skeleton	smith	sorcerer's delight	stables
steal	sweet dreams	tanner	tavern	temple	theater
theatre	thief	thieves	training dummy	troubadour	train
undead	unicorn horn	vet	virtue's pass	wall	warrior
waterfront	wayfarer's inn	weaponeer	weapons trainer	weaponsmith	
where am I	woodworker	where is			

Buccaneer's Den

ale	bath	drink	fur	heal	hide	inn	provisioner
smith	supplies	tanner	tavern	woodworker			

Cove

armor	armour	dock	fort	heal	lighthouse	orc

Jhelom

ale	amber	amethyst	armor	armorer	armour
armourer	axe	baker	bakery	blacksmith	carpenter
cartographer	cemetery	citrine	city hall	clothes	clothier
diamond	dock	drink	drinduel	dueling pit	emerald
farmer	fighter's guild	fish	fisher's guild	food	gem
gold	grave	guard	guard house	guard tower	guard-inn
house	hammer	healer	healing	horse	inn
jeweler	jewler	library	mace	mage	map
mapmaker	pit	provision	ranch	rubies	ruby
sapphire	scorpion's tail	shipwright	silver	sleep	supplies
supply	sword	tailor	tavern	theater	theatre
thieves guild	tinker	tourmaline	town hall	warehouse	weapon

Magincia

allies	architecture	artist	artwork	baker	cartogra-pher
council	craft	dock	fish market	Healer	history
house of parliament	Inn	item of protection	jeweler	kidnap	lyceum
mage	mage guild	mage shop	magic guild	magic	Magic Shop
map	mapmaker	merchant's guild	mining guild	mine	nujel'm
parliament	pirate	politic	provisioner	pride	ransom
ship wright	shipwright	tailor	tavern	temple	town square
tinkerwarehouse	youth				

Minoc

armor (or armour	blacksmith	butcher	clock	concert	drink
fighters	guild	heal	hides	house	mine
miners	music	provisioner	smith	stable	supply
tanner	tavern	tent	tinker	woodworker	warrior

Moonglow

apprentice	armour	artist's guild	baker	butcher	cemetery
city hall	docks	farm	food	fruit	gadget
graveyard	healer	herb	inn	lycaeum	mage
mage's guild	mag \<any\> student	mag \<any\> teacher	meat	produce	professor
provisioner	reagent	scholar	supplies	tailor	teleporter
teach \<any\> mag	telescope	town hall	woodworker	zoo	

NuJel'm

arbor	bank	bard's guild	blacksmith	bowyer	casino
cemetery	chess	clothier	concert	custom \<any\> house	conservatory
customs	food	gamble	gaming	gazebo	graves
graveyard	inn	jail	jeweler	jewelry	mall
manor	mansion	merchant's guild	market	mystical spirit	palace
patio	pergola	restful slumber	silver bow	slave auction	slave market
supplies	tailor	tanner	tavern	wager	weaponsmith

Serpent's Hold

armor (or armour	blacksmith	butcher	healer	inn	keep
provisioner	stable	supplies	tailor	tavern	tinker

Skara Brae

alchem	ale	animal	armor (or armour)	blacksmith	beekeeper
bow	bowyer	butcher	cartographer	carver	city hall
cloth	clothier	farm	farmer	food	fruit
heal	honey	inn	mage	magic	map
mapmaker	meat	provision	ranger's guild	ranger	shipwright
smith	supplies	tavern	theater	theatre	town hall
trainer	vegetable	weapon	wood	woodcarver	

Trinsic

armour	baker	barrack	butcher	constable	engineer
engineer's guild	fishermen's guild	fishermen's shop	guard	guild	healer
inn	jeweler	mage	mayor	monast	provision
paladin's guild	shop <any> fish	stable	supplies	tailor	tavern
tinker	train	weapon			

Vesper

alchemist	armor (or armour)	art	bakery	bard <any> guild	bank
beekeeper	blacksmith	bowyer	bury <any> dead	butcher	cemetery
cartographer	city hall	crypt	customs	farm	fish
fighter's guild	grave	healer	inn	jewel	mage
magicians' guild	magic <any> hall	map	mapmaker	miners' guild	meat
mortuary	museum	paint	produce	provisioner	reagent
seamen's guild	ship wright	shipwright	smith	sorcerery	sorcerer
supplies	tailor	tailor	tanner	thieves' guild	tavern
tinker	town hall	warriors' guild	wood		

Wind

eat	food	forest	healer	inn	lab	library	magic
mushroom	provisioner	reagent	scholar	supplies	tailor	wood	

Yew

abbey	baker	bowyer	butcher	cemetery	court	empath	farm
flour	food	gaol	healer	jail	market	meat	mill
prison	produce	storehouse	wine	woodworker			

Countryside (outside cities)

appreciate	bedroll	britanny bay	bye	camp	cave
chow	ciao	colony	concerns	covetous	deceit
despise	destard	dungeon	Dupre	earn <any> money	gold
fare <any> well	get <any> money	good <any> see <any> thee		greetings	hello
how <any> quit <any>?		how <any> you	hythloth	is <any> kindling	lolo
knights	log off	logoff	love	many lands	moon
make <any> money	many realms	moongates	order of the silver Serpent	one realm of many	
other lands	other realm	lord robere	robere	see <any> ya	shame
see <any> you	Shamino	shrines <any> truth	thank thee	thank you	thank ye
thanks	thou <any> live	treasure	troubles	virtues	weather
what is your	what town am I in	what's your	what <any> town is this	what's thy	wrong
who are you	where <any> thou <any> live		where <any> thou <any> work		
where <any> am <any>	you <any> live				

Town Cryer

TWENTY-THREE DEAD IN MINOC TRAGEDY

Yesterday in Minoc a half-dozen crazed ettins stormed through town, uprooting trees and bashing heads at random. It was utter chaos as the town guard rushed in, but were beaten back time and again.

"I couldn't believe it," said Minoc resident, Olaff Verhoven. "I was sittin' on my front porch, enjoyin' the breeze when I see a tree land on the provisioner's shop. Then I saw those brutes and dove for it. They were mad as all get out, and I wanted no part of 'em."

Artemus, captain of the town guard, questioned the effectiveness of the guards' training. "We did all we could do, and it just wasn't enough. They went berserk. I've dealt with ettins before and it was nothing like this."

When asked what could have caused such a tragedy, Artemus replied, "I think it was the kids. A few days ago a gang came into town stirring up trouble. They managed to ambush a young ettin and put his heads on a couple of

pikes in the middle of town. I have a feeling that young one was part of the clan that attacked us. Of course, those kids were the first to leave town when the other ettins showed up."

The mayor of Minoc is asking for all who can to assist in the cleaning and repair of the town, and donations are being accepted at the local tavern for the victims' families. There will be a memorial service on Friday for those lost in the tragedy. ▨

BRITAIN GUARDS STILL SEARCHING FOR ROGUE MAGE

The Britain guard will be sweeping through the city tonight, searching for the mage known as Relvinian. The Grandmaster Mage has been missing since the disaster at Castle Britannia in which he failed to adequately control several daemons he had summoned. The daemons then went on a murderous spree throughout the castle, killing at least five, with ten more missing and presumed dead.

Lord British's guards fought their way through Castle Britannia in an effort to end destruction and locate the instigator of this tragedy, but found no sign of Relvinian. His residence in Britain was then searched, uncovering no clue as to his whereabouts. A house-to-house search of Britain and the outlying farms has begun.

"He has to be around somewhere," said Martin, a town guard. "People don't just disappear for good. Not even mages."

Relvinian has not been seen since the killings began, but Lord British is sure he will return to take responsibility for his actions.

"He misjudged his powers, that's all. He's not a killer. Relvinian is a visionary who attached himself to a more or less dangerous idea. I still think his plan might have merit, but it certainly must be closely analyzed before any further harm is done."

Relvinian believed he could summon daemons to undertake labor-intensive jobs for the citizens of Britannia. He claimed that a spell that he had created could control

the daemons' thoughts, making it possible to place a schedule of labor activities in their heads.

Some, such as brother Andrew of Empath Abbey, warned Lord British about the inherent dangers of summoning creatures of the dark for "fun and profit." But the monarch chose to ignore the warnings. "Given what's occurred, I would hate to say I told you so," Andrew told reporters. "You can never trust creatures born of evil. My two-year-old niece could tell you that. Relvinian should have known better. I want the Guild of Arcane Arts to ensure he never practices magic in Britannia again."

If anyone knows of Relvinian's whereabouts, please contact the guild or the town guard. ▨

ASK DEATHDEALER

Today's letter is from Sven in Moonglow. Why's a warrior want to live in Moonglow? You got me. Go ask Sven.

Anyway, so he asks us to "compare and contrast the standard battle axe and the broadsword." He wants to know which I would prefer in a given fight. As I never really considered the fact that one might be more suited to kill certain things than the other, I decided to assemble a committee and conduct some tests. I chose Rikki Bearkiller, Hatchet Maxx, Deathblow Smith (no relation), myself and Magnus Stargazer for my committee. Rikki and Hatchet worked with battleaxes and Deathblow and I tested the broadswords. Magnus kept us alive — most of the time, at least, but we'll get to that later.

Our equipment was your standard dungeon-delving fare: rope, food, torches, healing potions, healing scrolls and pieces of spare armor. Our goal was to test the weapons, so I won't go into the armor we used. (The only relevance our armor would have to this study would be its effect on our ability to handle our weapons. Given our tester's experience, any such effect was minor.) The weapons themselves were a double-headed battle axe, a single-headed axe, and two of your standard, run o' the mill broadswords, all purchased new from the Strength and Steel Armory in Britain.

We set off in the morning, arriving at Covetous about mid-day. We were able to perform our first battery of tests before we even entered the dungeon, for there were a bunch of orcs ambling around just outside the entrance.

Rikki's double-axe immediately took the arm off one of them, while it took two good swings of my broadsword before my test-case's head rolled on the ground. Hatchet and Deathblow swung three times each before they managed to separate torsos from trunks. Test completed, we compared notes and headed inside.

An ettin lumbered up inside the first room and again we set to work gathering data. The weight of the axes seemed to really take major bites out of the ettin's hide. The swords did some damage, but in the long run I think I would have preferred an axe in this case. Hatchet almost ended his testing early as the ettin's club came down on his head. Before he hit the ground, though, Magnus used one of our scrolls, and Hatchet stumbled off, whole but dazed.

The ettin had raised quite a stir, so when we had finished our work with her, creatures were lining up in the hall to participate in our test. We experimented with mongbats, gargoyles, a headless and two more ettins. We had gathered quite a lot of data by the time the last ettin fell. Magnus then announced that he had one scroll left and the potions were gone, so we decided that it was about time to call it quits. As we were gathering our equipment to leave, a ball of fire came screaming into the room and lit Deathblow up like a torch in a closet. Rikki let out a string of curses that would make a sailor blush, and Magnus just pointed down the hall muttering the word "dragon" over and over again. (Hey, whattaya expect of a guy with a last name of Stargazer?)

Rikki, Hatchet and I managed to put Deathblow out by beating him against the dirt floor, and we dragged him and Magnus back out of the cave. I ain't ashamed to tell you, we got far away from there before we stopped moving. Deathblow had expired by then, and we set about trying to find a healer that could resurrect him.

After the healer brought Deathblow back and he had calmed down a bit (he gets really riled when he dies for even a few minutes), the four of us compared notes once again and came up with an answer for Sven in Moonglow. The final verdict is: Use an axe on thicker-skinned opponents, but use a sword on smaller beasts, when speed is a more important consideration. The weight of the axe helps with a good solid swing, much like a hammer, but the swords tend to be better balanced and quicker in the long run.

So there you have it, Sven, I hope this helps. ▨

All opinions expressed in this column are my own, nobody else's, and take it or leave it, I don't care, just don't call me a liar. Ever.

Creatures and NPCs

CREATURE AND NON-PLAYER BEHAVIOR

One of the most in-depth systems in the game is the artificial intelligence design for creatures (animals and monsters) and NPCs. All of them interact in *Ultima Online*, and each has survival needs, desires and fears. As in the real world, man is the supreme predator. Additionally, what they do — and what human players do — affects the world. This complex behavior system is based on a hierarchy of drives for all inhabitants of the world.

The next few sections describe the intricacies of creature and NPC behaviors. **Creature Descriptions** begin on p. 137 and **Non-Player Character Descriptions** begin on p. 162.

Drives

All creatures and NPCs have behaviors and priorities based on three drives — **food**, **shelter** and **desires**.

Food Items required for survival, such as food and water

Shelter Locations that provide some degree of comfort, such as homes or caves

Desires Luxuries not required for survival, such as gold or honey

Creature and NPC searches nearly always proceed from food to shelter to desires. Survival is always the most urgent element, however — if anything threatens survival, that takes precedence.

Not everything has complex drives. Rabbits happily live in a grass field, eating grass. For that matter, not everything must have a specified shelter —some NPCs are nomads without a permanent shelter.

Here are some examples:

Dragons	*Rabbits*	*NPC Townspeople*	*NPC Nomads*
Eat meat	*Eat grass/crops*	*Eat meat*	*Eat meat*
Live in caves	*Live in grass*	*Live in the village*	*No permanent home*
Desire gold	*Desire crops*	*Desire wool, gold, notoriety, similar NPCs, etc.*	*Desire gold, similar NPCs, etc.*

Rules of Behavior

Food

Many plants are sources of food — grass, grain, wheat, carrots, apples, etc. In addition, all people and animals are meat sources for carnivores.

"It's Not Big Enough"

When NPCs and creatures search for food, they generally ignore anything smaller than a single bite. A dragon that eats in 5-unit bites won't bother with crows that are only 2 meat units. This rule is violated, however, if the carnivore is starving.

"Can That Eat Me?"

Most NPCs are smart enough not to try killing a dragon for food. It's bigger, it's more powerful, and it's likely to win. Creatures follow this same basic rule — if they see something that desires them as food, they tend to avoid the predator.

"I Can't Get to It!"

NPCs and grounded creatures won't waste their time trying to get to something that's obstructed or out of reach. For instance, a wolf realizes he's grounded and probably won't spend precious hunting time chasing a bird flying overhead.

"Splitting the Pack"

This rule pertains more to creatures than NPCs. If a group of creatures need more food than an area can supply, the group will split into two packs. The strongest member stays and takes one half of the group, while the second strongest member splits off with the other half of the group (randomly chosen) and migrates to a new region with enough food resources.

"What Should I Eat?"

NPCs and creatures in Britannia follow a set of guidelines when they're hungry. They want to eat, and they want to eat as much as they can, as safely as they can. Here are the basic rules they use to determine what the food of choice will be:

- Most inhabitants of Britannia prefer their meat already dead. No NPC wants to risk life and limb hunting evasive game in the wilderness, and most creatures would rather eat a freshly prepared carcass than kill something themselves.

- The larger the quantity of food, the better. This is especially true with a group of creatures — the preferred food source is one that feeds the entire group.

- The closer the food source, the better.

- If the food source provides other resources as well (like hides, which comes from some animals that produce meat), it is more appealing.

- Once the search for food is finished, the NPC or creature will eat the food or, if it's smart enough, take the food back to its home or lair.

Shelter

Most creatures seek out suitable shelter for their permanent homes. Once they find it, they're settled for the duration of the game and won't move unless they die, they're driven out, or their home is destroyed.

Other creatures are more nomadic and will take shelter wherever they happen to be when that drive occurs. Later, when they desire shelter again, they may return to the previous shelter or seek out a new one.

Here are the rules for living space:

"Where Should I Live?"

If no home currently exists, he/she/it will look for a location that has the largest amount of space available (grass, cave space, housing space, etc.). Creatures look for grassy areas, forests, caves or whatever their natural habitat happens to be.

Once they find suitable shelter, they claim it as their home. However, the area must be large enough to satisfy their needs. For example, sheep consider grassy areas as shelter. They also eat grass, however, which reduces the size of this shelter until it is insufficient, and they have to move to another grassy area.

"Should I Move or Should I Stay?"

Most NPCs and creatures prefer permanent homes. However, if an NPC or creature has a home but discovers a similar shelter that offers more free space or other advantages, a move may take place. If the NPC has a stash of food, gold or other items, it will begin moving its possessions to the new location.

For example, if a wandering dragon happens across a larger cave currently occupied by a lone adventurer and a large pile of gold bigger than the dragon's current hoard, it may attempt to kill the human and take over the cave space. Once that happens, the dragon will return to its previous quarters to transfer its hoard.

"Nothing Here ..."

If a homeless NPC or creature can't find suitable shelter in a certain area, it will migrate to a new area and seek out an area with enough free space and nearby food resources.

Desires

Several types of desires exist. Some are constant, meaning that the need never goes away. For example, an NPC female might fall in love with a male player and persistently follow him wherever he goes. Or, a thief remains constantly on the lookout for anyone carrying 100 gold pieces. Other desires are satiable, meaning that the NPC remains satisfied for some time, then seeks to fulfill his or her desires once more.

"Kill the Invaders"

This rule is slightly different from the normal shelter rule. Instead of a desire, it is usually a response to an action by some other creature, NPC or human player.

If one creature or NPC tries to move into another's home, a fight may commence. For example, a wolf will attack a bear that tries to claim its corner of the forest. Both desire to live in the forest, and both consume local meat resources. However, a fight will probably not occur, if a rabbit moves into a sheep's grassy area. Both are herbivores, and one or both will probably just migrate to a nearby grassy knoll.

"Protect the Hoard"

If a creature or NPC's home is invaded by anyone that wants something from within the shelter, the homeowner will display aggression toward the invader.

"Find a Master"

Examples of this activity include an NPC following a player, or the formation of a pack of creatures. Most creatures and NPCs desire to be around others of their type. Within such a group, the most powerful creature or person is often considered the leader or master. Others in the pack follow the master.

With creatures, pack behavior occurs only if there is enough food in the area to feed the entire group. If not, the group will either never form, or will split in two.

The "Find a Master" rule has interesting implications for NPCs. NPCs desire to be around other NPCs and human players, but instead of forming packs, they choose areas of the city to live in and role models, and they can fall in love.

"Am I in Love?"

(NPCs only) If an NPC desires another NPC or a human player, the desire will remain unsatisfied until the other NPC has a reciprocal desire. If the person admired is similarly desired by other NPCs, and does not return the attention, the love-stricken NPC constantly follows his or her object of desire.

"Hmm ... I Could Use That!"

Sometimes a creature with high intelligence or an NPC finds something it desires that can be moved. If the creature or NPC has a home and can carry the item, it will be taken home and added to the personal possessions.

This can apply to food as well as items — if the creature or NPC is not hungry when it runs across something tasty, the food can be taken back home and stored.

"I'm Bored!"

Both creatures and NPCs can get bored. If they have some desire that has been satisfied several times — such as the desire for gold coins, or for the company of a particular person, they may seek an alternative instead.

Productions and Aversions

Besides the basic food, shelter and desire drives, two other forces affect creatures and NPCs. They are **productions** (resources contributed by that creature or NPC) and **aversions** (anything that causes fear in an creature or NPC). These two things help drive decision-making and behavior patterns.

Productions

Productions are resources that a creature or NPC can contribute to the region's resources. This can also apply to some objects. These resources are either fixed (such as meat) or consumable and renewable (such as wool on a sheep, or trees in a forest).

For example, a tree produces up to 5 units of wood. If the tree is cut, it will eventually renew itself and grow back. Thus, wood is a renewable resource that can be consumed without being destroyed. A tree also represents 5 units of forest that can be used as shelter.

Similarly, grass serves both as food and shelter for some creatures. After a grassy area has been eaten, it no longer serves as shelter for grassland creatures.

Aversions

Aversions are items, creatures or NPCs that cause a negative reaction — usually fear, but occasionally hatred (leading to attack) or dissatisfaction and unease (these latter being more typical of humans). Aversions essentially are the reverse of drives.

CREATURE DESCRIPTIONS

Ranges of numbers. If the value listed is a range (for example, 15-38), that stat will vary from creature to creature (or NPC to NPC) between the two numbers.

Alignment is only mentioned if the creature or NPC is not neutral.

Damage (creatures) lists the base damage the creature can inflict with one blow.

Natural armor (creatures) lists the "armor" protection the creature's skin provides.

Strength, **Dexterity**, **Intelligence**, **Hit Points**, **Stamina** and **Mana** are on the same scale and mean the same thing as the corresponding player stats.

Skills. Of course, not every alligator has had a chance to matriculate at Bendar's School of Unarmed Combat. However, when you are attempting to attack, capture or resist a creature, these skill values represent the creature's natural abilities brought to bear against you.

Spell Circle. (monsters, NPCs) the highest circle from which this monster or NPC can cast spells.

Food is what the creature or NPC eats. The first number is the number of food units it takes to fill the creature. The number in parentheses is how many units it can consume in a single bite. For example, an ogre (*Food:* Meat 15 (3)) eats meat, becomes full after consuming 15 units, and takes bites of 3 units at a time.

Shelter is the type of natural habitat the creature/NPC seeks out as its home. The letter in parentheses indicates whether that habitat is considered to be *permanent* (P) or *temporary* (T) shelter. For example, alligators (Shelter: Swamps (P); Water (T); Caves (T)) seek permanent shelter in swamps. If no swamps are immediately available, an alligator will seek out temporary shelter in a cave or body of water.

Desires are preferences, not survival necessities. The desire is either *satiable* (S) — the desire can be met, but reoccurs — or *constant* (C).

Resources are units of usable resources that the creature or NPC represents. For example, a sheep is both a meat resource and a wool resource. The number preceding the resource describes the number of units generated.

We didn't feel it necessary to repeat this throughout the NPC stats, but all humans represent 8 units of meat to carnivores adventurous enough to stalk them.

Aversions are things that this creature or NPC fears or hates.

Sell/Buy lists (NPCs) are explained on p. 162.

Keywords (NPCs) are explained on pp. 125 and 162.

AS WITH ALL OTHER SPECIFICS IN THIS BOOK, GIVEN THE NATURE OF THIS GAME, THESE DESCRIPTIONS AND STATS ARE SUBJECT TO CHANGE.

Animals

Alligator

Damage	2-14	Natural Armor	12		
Skill to Tame	60	Alignment	Evil		
Strength	66-80	Hit Points	66-80		
Dexterity	6-15	Mana	0		
Intelligence	11-20	Stamina	36-45		
Parrying	27-63	Resist. Spells	25-40		
Tactics	40-60	Wrestling	40-60		
Food	Meat 5 (1)				
Shelter	Swamps (P)	Water (T)	Caves (T)		
Desires	Dead logs (C)				
Resources	4 Meat	10 Leather			
Aversions	Civilization	Humans	Carnivores (3+ bites)		

Bear (Black/Brown)

Damage	2-12/3-11	Natural Armor	8/10
Skill to Tame	50 (Black) / 55 (Brown)		
Strength	66-80	Hit Points	66-80
Dexterity	46-55	Stamina	46-55
Intelligence	11-14	Mana	0
(Black) Parrying	25-45	Resist. Spells	20-40
(Brn) Parrying	37-55	Resist. Spells	25-35
Tactics	40-60	Wrestling	40-60
Food	Fish 5 (1)	Fruit 5 (1)	Meat 15 (3)
	Honey 5 (1)		
Shelter	Forests (P)	Caves (P)	
Desires	Honey (C)		
Resources	9 Meat	5 Fur	
Aversions	Traps	Civilization	

Bear (Grizzly)

Damage	3-12	Natural Armor	10
Skill to Tame	70		
Strength	116-135	Hit Points	116-135
Dexterity	71-85	Stamina	71-85
Intelligence	6-20	Mana	0
Parrying	70-85	Resist. Spells	35-50
Tactics	70-100	Wrestling	50-65
Food	Fish 6 (1)	Fruit 5 (1)	Meat 15 (3)
	Honey 5 (1)		
Shelter	Forests (P)	Caves (P)	Mountains (P)
Desires	Honey (C)		
Resources	10 Meat	8 Fur	
Aversions	Traps	Civilization	

Bear (Polar)

Damage	3-12	Natural Armor	7	
Skill to Tame	50			
Strength	11-255	Hit Points	11-255	
Dexterity	71-85	Stamina	71-85	
Intelligence	16-30	Mana	0	
Parrying	70-85	Resist. Spells	35-50	
Tactics	70-100	Wrestling	60-90	
Food	Fish 6 (1)	Fruit 5 (1)	Meat 15 (3)	
Shelter	Snow (P)	Caves (P)	Mountains (P)	
Desires	Snow (C)			
Resources	11 Meat	8 Fur		
Aversions	Traps	Civilization		

Cat

Damage	1	Natural Armor	4
Skill to Tame	20		
Strength	10-18	Hit Points	11-17
Dexterity	26-45	Stamina	40-70
Intelligence	6-30	Mana	0
Parrying	22-45	Resist. Spells	15-30
Tactics	91-180	Wrestling	9-19
Food	Meat 5 (1)	Fish 5 (1)	
Shelter	Houses (P)	1 Human (P)	
Desires	1 Human (S)	1 Window (C)	
Resources	2 Meat		
Aversions	None		

Cattle (Cow)

Damage	1-4	Natural Armor	2-12
Skill to Tame	30		
Strength	32-46	Hit Points	35-75
Dexterity	16-25	Stamina	22-26
Intelligence	2-10	Mana	0
Parrying	12-25	Resist. Spells	7-15
Tactics	17-35	Wrestling	17-35
Food	Grass 588 (64)	Grain 25 (5)	Hay 25 (5)
Shelter	Grass (P)	Stables (P)	
Desires	Cows (C)		
Resources	40 Meat	5 Leather	
Aversions	Traps	Carnivores (3+ bites)	

Cattle (Bull)

Damage	1-6	Natural Armor	14
Skill to Tame	80		
Strength	67-81	Hit Points	75-115
Dexterity	46-55	Stamina	62-66
Intelligence	37-45	Mana	0
Parrying	32-45	Resist. Spells	76-15
Tactics	67-85	Wrestling	40-57
Food	Grain 25 (1)	Hay 25 (1)	Grass 588 (64)
Shelter	Grass (P)	Stables (P)	
Desires	Bulls (C)		
Resources	50 Meat	Leather	
Aversions	Traps	Carnivores (3+ bites)	

Cougar

Damage	2-10	Natural Armor	6
Skill to Tame	55		
Strength	46-60	Hit Points	46-60
Dexterity	6-155	Stamina	6-155
Intelligence	16-30	Mana	0
Parrying	55-65	Resist. Spells	15-30
Tactics	45-60	Wrestling	45-60
Food	Meat 15 (3)		
Shelter	Caves (P)	Mountains (T)	Forests (T)
Desires	Cougars (C)	Foliage (C)	
Resources	4 Meat	6 Fur	
Aversions	Traps	Civilization	Water

Deer (Doe)

Damage	1-8	Natural Armor	5
Skill to Tame	40		
Strength	11-21	Hit Points	21-39
Dexterity	37-47	Stamina	31-43
Intelligence	7-17	Mana	0
Parrying	27-14	Resist. Spells	5-17
Tactics	9-21	Wrestling	6-18
Food	Crops 25 (1)	Fruit 25 (1)	Grass 576 (64)
Shelter	Forests (P)		
Desires	Deer (C)	Foliage (C)	
Resources	25 Meat	5 Leather	
Aversions	Traps	Civilization	Carnivores (3+ bites)

Deer (Stag)

Damage	2-8	Natural Armor	10
Skill to Tame	70		
Strength	31-41	Hit Points	31-49
Dexterity	47-57	Stamina	51-63
Intelligence	27-37	Mana	0
Parrying	48-22	Resist. Spells	68-24
Tactics	9-27	Wrestling	9-27
Food	Crops 25 (1)	Fruit 13 (1)	Grass 575 (64)
Shelter	Forests (P)		
Desires	Deer (C)	Foliage (S)	
Resources	30 Meat	5 Leather	
Aversions	Traps	Civilization	Carnivores (3+ bites)

Dog

Damage	1-4	Natural Armor	3
Skill to Tame	3		
Strength	11-21	Hit Points	18-27
Dexterity	28-43	Stamina	31-49
Intelligence	29-37	Mana	0
Parrying	18-43	Resist. Spells	12-37
Tactics	9-21	Wrestling	9-21
Food	Meat 5 (1)		
Shelter	Houses (P)	2 Humans (P)	
Desires	Humans (S)	3 Dogs (C)	
Resources	3 Meat		
Aversions	Traps		

Dolphin

Damage	1-4	Natural Armor	2-12
Strength	11-19	Hit Points	11-19
Dexterity	56-65	Stamina	50-100
Intelligence	6-10	Mana	0
Parrying	55-65	Resist. Spells	5-10
Tactics	9-19	Wrestling	9-19
Food	Fish 5 (1)	Water 576 (64)	
Shelter	Water (P)		
Desires	Ships (C)	Dolphins (C)	
Resources	4 Meat		
Aversions	Traps	Coastline	

Goat

Damage	1-3	Natural Armor	3
Skill to Tame	30		
Strength	11-19	Hit Points	6-24
Dexterity	27-37	Stamina	30-40
Intelligence	7-15	Mana	0
Parrying	15-27	Resist. Spells	5-15
Tactics	9-19	Wrestling	10-20
Food	Fruit 5 (1)	Leather 5 (1)	Grass 576 (64)
	Garbage 5 (1)		
Shelter	Grass (P)	Stables (P)	
Desires	Humans (S)	Goats (C)	
Resources	14 Meat		
Aversions	Traps	Carnivores (3+ bites)	

Mountain Goat

Damage	1-5	Natural Armor	2-6
Skill to Tame	20		
Strength	12-24	Hit Points	12-24
Dexterity	46-55	Stamina	46-55
Intelligence	6-10	Mana	0
Parrying	45-55	Resist. Spells	5-10
Tactics	9-24	Wrestling	9-24
Food	Forests 5 (1)	Fruit 5 (1)	Grass 576 (64)
	Leather 5 (1)		
Shelter	Grass (P)	Mountains (P)	
Desires	Mountain goats (C)		
Resources	16 Meat	10 Leather	
Aversions	Traps	Civilization	Carnivores (3+ bites)

Gorilla

Damage	2-12	Natural Armor	14
Skill to Tame	5		
Strength	43-55	Hit Points	12-24
Dexterity	26-35	Stamina	26-35
Intelligence	26-40	Mana	0
Parrying	31-130	Resist. Spells	51-20
Tactics	33-180	Wrestling	33-180
Food	Crops 25 (1)	Fruit 25 (1)	Mushrooms 25 (1)
	Grain 25 (1)	Insects 25 (1)	
Shelter	Foliage (P)	Jungle (P)	
Desires	Jungle (C)	Gorillas (C)	
Resources	6 Meat		
Aversions	Traps	Civilization	

Horse

Damage	2-10	Natural Armor	7	
Skill to Tame	45			
Strength	14-70	Hit Points	12-39	
Dexterity	26-35	Stamina	26-35	
Intelligence	6-10	Mana	0	
Parrying	15-25	Resist. Spells	5-10	
Tactics	9-24	Wrestling	9-24	
Food	Crops 55 (1)	Fruit 55 (1)	Grain 55 (1)	
	Grass 576 (64)			
Shelter	Stables (P)	1 Human (P)		
Desires	Horses (C)	Humans (C)		
Resources	15 Meat	10 Leather	Transportation	
Aversions	Traps	Carnivores (3+ bites)		

Llama

Damage	1-5	Natural Armor	2-6	
Skill to Tame	50			
Strength	11-19	Hit Points	11-19	
Dexterity	26-35	Stamina	26-35	
Intelligence	6-10	Mana	0	
Parrying	25-35	Resist. Spells	5-10	
Tactics	9-19	Wrestling	9-19	
Food	Crops 5 (1)	Fruit 5 (1)	Grain 5 (1)	
	Hay 5 (1)	Grass 576 (64)		
Shelter	Stables (P)	Human (P)		
Resources	7 Meat	8 Fur		
Aversions	Traps	Eerie items and places		

Panther

Damage	2-12	Natural Armor	2-6	
Skill to Tame	65			
Strength	51-65	Hit Points	61-75	
Dexterity	76-85	Stamina	6-155	
Intelligence	16-30	Mana	0	
Parrying	55-65	Resist. Spells	15-30	
Tactics	50-65	Wrestling	50-65	
Food	Meat 15 (3)			
Shelter	Caves (P)	Jungle (T)	Grass (T)	
Desires	Panthers (C)	Foliage (C)		
Resources	4 Meat	6 Fur		
Aversions	Traps	Civilization	Water	

Pig

Damage	1-3	Natural Armor	4
Skill to Tame	30		
Strength	12-24	Hit Points	15-25
Dexterity	12-24	Stamina	25-35
Intelligence	26-33	Mana	0
Parrying	9-24	Resist. Spells	15-23
Tactics	9-24	Wrestling	9-24
Food	Fruit 55 (1)	Crops 55 (1)	Grain 55 (1)
	Garbage 55 (1)		
Shelter	Wood (C)	Dirt (C)	Stables (C)
Desires	Pigs (C)		
Resources	6 Meat		
Aversions	Traps		

Boar

Damage	1-4	Natural Armor	5
Skill to Tame	45		
Strength	21-31	Hit Points	31-49
Dexterity	37-47	Stamina	41-53
Intelligence	17-27	Mana	0
Parrying	4-22	Resist. Spells	7-25
Tactics	11-29	Wrestling	11-29
Food, Shelter, Desires and Aversions		Same as pig	
Resources	11 Meat		

Rabbit

Damage	1-2	Natural Armor	2-5
Skill to Tame	5		
Strength	6-10	Hit Points	4-8
Dexterity	26-38	Stamina	40-70
Intelligence	6-14	Mana	0
Parrying	25-38	Resist. Spells	5-14
Tactics	5-10	Wrestling	5-10
Food	Crops 55 (1)	Forests 55 (1)	Grass 576 (64)
Shelter	Grass (P)	Wood (P)	Foliage (P)
Desires	Rabbits (C)	Crops (C)	Dirt (C)
Resources	2 Meat		
Aversions	Traps	Civilization	Carnivores (2+ bites)

Jackrabbit

Jackrabbits are the same as other rabbits, with these exceptions:

Damage	1-2	Natural Armor 4
Food	Crops 55 (1)	Grass 576 (64)
Shelter	Grass (P)	
Desires	Crops (C)	Jackrabbits (C)
Aversions	Traps	

Rat

Damage	1-4	Natural Armor	5
Skill to Tame	20		
Strength	11-17	Hit Points	9-17
Dexterity	16-25	Stamina	40-70
Intelligence	6-10	Mana	0
Parrying	15-25	Resist. Spells	5-10
Tactics	9-17	Wrestling	9-17
Food	Food 5 (1)	Garbage 25 (1)	
Shelter	Docks (T)	Civilization (P)	Garbage (P)
	Eerie locations (P)		
Desires	Rats (C)	Darkness (C)	
Resources	2 Meat		
Aversions	Traps	Light	Humans
	Carnivores		

Sewer Rat

Damage	1-3	Natural Armor	1-3
Alignment	Evil		
Strength	11-19	Hit Points	11-19
Dexterity	36-45	Stamina	36-45
Intelligence	6-10	Mana	0
Parrying	35-45	Resist. Spells	5-10
Tactics	5-10	Wrestling	5-10
Food	Fruit 5 (1)	Crops 5 (1)	Mushrooms 5 (1)
	Honey 5 (1)	Leather 5 (1)	Fish 5 (1)
	Garbage 5 (1)		
Shelter	Dungeons (P)	Caves (P)	Eerie locations (P)
Desires	Garbage (C)	Darkness (C)	Sewer rats (C)
Resources	3 Meat		
Aversions	Traps	Civilization	Light

Sheep

Damage	1-3	Natural Armor	1-3
Skill to Tame	30		
Strength	11-19	Hit Points	11-19
Dexterity	26-35	Stamina	26-35
Intelligence	6-10	Mana	0
Parrying	15-25	Resist. Spells	5-10
Tactics	9-19	Wrestling	9-19
Food	Crops 5 (1)	Grain 5 (1)	Grass 576 (64)
Shelter	Grass (P)	Stables (P)	1 Human (T)
Desires	Sheep (C)	Humans (T)	
Resources	20 Meat	30 Cloth	
		(from wool; regrows 5 units/game day)	
Aversions	Traps	Carnivores (3+ bites)	

Snake (Small)

Damage	1-4	Natural Armor	7	
Skill to Tame	70	Alignment	Evil	
Strength	12-24	Hit Points	12-24	
Dexterity	16-25	Stamina	16-25	
Intelligence	6-10	Mana	0	
Parrying	15-25	Resist. Spells	5-10	
Tactics	9-24	Wrestling	9-24	
Food	None			
Shelter	Caves (P)	Dungeons (P)	Desert (P)	
Desires	Gold (S)			
Resources	1 Meat			
Aversions	Traps			

Snow Leopard

Damage	2-10	Natural Armor	12	
Skill to Tame	65			
Strength	46-60	Hit Points	46-60	
Dexterity	6-155	Stamina	6-155	
Intelligence	16-30	Mana	0	
Parrying	55-65	Resist. Spells	15-25	
Tactics	45-60	Wrestling	40-50	
Food	Meat 15 (3)			
Shelter	Caves (P)	Snow (P)	Mountains (T)	
Desires	Snow (C)	Snow leopards (C)		
Resources	4 Meat	6 Fur		
Aversions	Traps	Civilization	Water	

Walrus

Damage	3-6	Natural Armor	2-12	
Skill to Tame	50			
Strength	11-19	Hit Points	11-19	
Dexterity	46-55	Stamina	46-55	
Intelligence	6-10	Mana	0	
Parrying	45-55	Resist. Spells	5-10	
Tactics	92-190	Wrestling	9-19	
Food	Fish 45 (1)			
Shelter	Water (P)	Snow (P)		
Desires	Ships (C)	Walruses (C)		
Resources	23 Meat			
Aversions	Traps	Civilization		

Wolf

Grey Wolf

Damage	2-8	Natural Armor	9	
Skill to Tame	65			
Strength	46-60	Hit Points	46-60	
Dexterity	46-55	Stamina	46-55	
Intelligence	21-35	Mana	0	
Parrying	45-55	Resist. Spells	20-35	
Tactics	45-60	Wrestling	45-60	
Food	Meat 15 (3)			
Shelter	Forests (P)	Caves (P)	Mountains (P)	
Desires	Wolves (C)			
Resources	3 Meat			
Aversions	Traps	Civilization		

Timber Wolf

Damage	2-8	Natural Armor	7
Skill to Tame	40		
Strength	46-60	Hit Points	46-60
Dexterity	46-55	Stamina	46-55
Intelligence	11-25	Mana	0
Parrying	32-45	Resist. Spells	17-35
Tactics	20-40		
Food	Meat 15 (3)		
Shelter	Forests (P)	Caves (P)	
Desires	Wolves (C)		
Resources	3 Meat		
Aversions	Traps	Civilization	

White Wolf

Damage	2-8	Natural Armor	7
Skill to Tame	75		
Strength	46-60	Hit Points	46-60
Dexterity	46-55	Stamina	46-55
Intelligence	21-35	Mana	0
Parrying	45-55	Resist. Spells	20-35
Tactics	45-60	Wrestling	45-60
Food	Meat 15 (3)		
Shelter	Snow (P)	Caves (P)	
Desires	Wolves (C)	Snow (C)	
Resources	3 Meat		
Aversions	Traps	Civilization	

BIRD

Damage	1	Natural Armor	0	
Skill to Tame	10	Movement	Flying	
Strength	1-4	Hit Points	3-6	
Dexterity	26-35	Stamina	50-100	
Intelligence	1-4	Mana	0	
Parrying	25-35	Resist. Spells	5-10	
Tactics	5-10	Wrestling	10-15	
Food	Crops 3 (1)	Fruit 6 (1)	Grain 3 (1)	
	Insects 6 (1)	Mushrooms 6 (1)		
Shelter	Foliage (P)	Grass (T)		
Desires	Forests (C)	Birds (C)		
Resources	2 Meat	12 Feathers		
Aversions	Traps	Carnivores	Humans	

TROPICAL BIRD

Damage	1	Natural Armor	1
Skill to Tame	10	Movement	Flying
Strength	6-10	Hit Points	3-6
Dexterity	26-35	Stamina	50-100
Intelligence	6-10	Mana	0
Parrying	15-25	Resist. Spells	5-10
Tactics	5-10	Wrestling	5-10
Food	Crops 55 (1)	Fruit 55 (1)	Insects 55 (1)
	Grain 55 (1)	Mushrooms 55 (1)	
Shelter	Foliage (P)	Jungle (P)	
Desires	Tropical birds (C)		
Resources	2 Meat	12 Feathers	
Aversions	Traps	Carnivores	Humans

CROW

Damage	1	Natural Armor	1
Skill to Tame	15	Movement	Flying
Strength	11-17	Hit Points	5-15
Dexterity	26-35	Stamina	50-100
Intelligence	6-10	Mana	0
Parrying	25-35	Resist. Spells	5-10
Tactics	9-17	Wrestling	9-17
Food	Crops 25 (1)	Fruit 25 (1)	Grain 25 (1)
Shelter	Crops (P)	Wheat (P)	Scarecrows (T)
Desires	Crows (C)	Crops (C)	
Resources	2 Meat	12 Feathers	
Aversions	Traps	Carnivores	Humans

RAVEN

Damage	1	Natural Armor	3
Skill to Tame	19	Movement	Flying
Strength	11-17	Hit Points	5-15
Dexterity	26-35	Stamina	50-100
Intelligence	6-10	Mana	0
Parrying	10-35	Resist. Spells	5-10
Tactics	8-17	Wrestling	8-17
Food	Crops 15 (1)	Fruit 15 (1)	Grain 15 (3)
Shelter	Eerie locations (P)		
Desires	Ravens (C)		
Resources	2 Meat	12 Feathers	
Aversions	Traps	Carnivores	

MAGPIE

Magpies are the same as crows, with these exceptions:

Food	Crops 25 (1)	Fruit 25 (1)	Grain 25 (1)
	Foliage 64 (1)		
Shelter	Foliage (P)		
Desires	Magpies (C)	Gold (C)	Jewels (C)
Aversions	Traps	Carnivores	Humans

Chicken

Damage	1	Natural Armor	1
Skill to Tame	20		
Strength	6-10	Hit Points	2-8
Dexterity	16-25	Stamina	30-60
Intelligence	1-6	Mana	0
Parrying	15-25	Resist. Spells	4-9
Tactics	5-10	Wrestling	5-10

Food	Grain 5 (1)	
Shelter	Chicken nest	
Desires	Chickens (C)	
Resources	2 Meat	5 Feathers
Aversions	Carnivores (2+ bites)	

Eagle

Damage	2-8	Natural Armor	9
Skill to Tame	35	Movement	Flying
Strength	21-27	Hit Points	20-60
Dexterity	26-40	Stamina	50-100
Intelligence	8-20	Mana	0
Parrying	25-40	Resist. Spells	5-20
Tactics	8-27	Wrestling	10-20

Food	Fruit 5 (1)	Meat 5 (1)	Fish 5 (1)
Shelter	Foliage (P)	Mountains (P)	
Desires	None		
Resources	2 Meat	12 Feathers	
Aversions	Traps	Civilization	Carnivores (2+ bites) (becomes aggressive)

Monsters

Air Elemental

Damage	5-13	Natural Armor	19
Alignment	Evil		
Strength	116-135	Hit Points	116-135
Dexterity	6-155	Stamina	6-155
Intelligence	61-75	Mana	61-75
Magery	60-750	Parrying	55-65
Resist. Spells	60-75	Tactics	60-80
Wrestling	60-80		
Spell Circle	3-7		
Food	None		
Shelter	Mountains (P)		
Desires	Mountains (C)		
Resources	None		
Aversions	Traps		

Corpser

Damage	3-6	Natural Armor	9
Alignment	Chaotic		
Strength	46-60	Hit Points	46-60
Dexterity	16-25	Stamina	21-35
Intelligence	16-20	Mana	0
Parrying	15-250	Resist. Spells	15-20
Tactics	45-60	Wrestling	45-60
Food	Meat 24 (3)		
Shelter	Jungle (P)	Swamps (P)	Forests (P)
Desires	Foliage (C)		
Resources	Eeriness		
Aversions	Traps	Civilization	

Daemon

Damage	30*	Natural Armor	3-18
Movement	Flying	Alignment	Evil
Strength	166-185	Hit Points	166-185
Dexterity	66-75	Stamina	66-75
Intelligence	91-105	Mana	91-105
Magery	70-80	Parrying	65-165
Resist. Spells	70-80	Tactics	70-80
Wrestling	60-80		
Spell Circle	7-8		

Food	None	
Shelter	Dungeons (P)	Caves (P)
Desires	Daemons (C)	Gold (C)
Resources	None	
Aversions	Traps	Civilization

*Daemons can wield a weapon; damage varies by weapon.

Dragon

Damage	4-24	Natural Armor	30
Skill to Tame	99	Movement	Flying
Strength	186-205	Hit Points	600-1000
Dexterity	56-65	Stamina	56-65
Intelligence	125-155	Mana	150-250
Parrying	55-65	Resist. Spells	99-100
Tactics	97-100	Wrestling	90-93
Spell Circle	6		

Food	Meat 80 (3)	
Shelter	Caves (P)	Dungeons (P)
Desires	Gold (C)	
Resources	99 Meat	8 Dragon blood
Aversions	Traps	Civilization

Drake

Damage	4-24	Natural Armor	28
Skill to Tame	100	Movement	Flying
Strength	91-110	Hit Points	300-700
Dexterity	23-32	Stamina	23-32
Intelligence	91-120	Mana	76-175
Parrying	60-70	Resist. Spells	60-75
Tactics	60-63	Wrestling	60-70
Spell Circle	4		

Food	Meat 25 (3)	
Shelter	Caves (P)	Dungeons (P)
Desires	Gold (C)	
Resources	50 Meat	8 Dragon blood
Aversions	Traps	Civilization

Earth Elemental

Damage	3-18	Natural Armor	15
Alignment	Evil		
Strength	116-135	Hit Points	116-135
Dexterity	6-155	Stamina	6-155
Intelligence	61-75	Mana	61-75
Parrying	40-52	Resist. Spells	30-75
Tactics	60-100	Wrestling	40-80
Food	None		
Shelter	Mountains (P)	Caves (P)	Dirt (P)
Desires	Caves (C)		
Resources	8 Magic		
Aversions	Traps		

Ettin

Damage	2-18*	Natural Armor	17
Alignment	Evil		
Strength	126-145	Hit Points	156-175
Dexterity	46-55	Stamina	46-55
Intelligence	21-35	Mana	0
Parrying	40-50	Resist. Spells	30-45
Tactics	40-60	Wrestling	40-50
Food	Meat 15 (3)		
Shelter	Forests (P)	Mountains (P)	
Desires	Ettins (C)	Gold (C)	
Resources	20 Meat		
Aversions	Traps	Civilization	

*Ettins can wield weapons; damage varies by weapon.

Fire Elemental

Damage	4-12	Natural Armor	19
Alignment	Evil		
Strength	116-135	Hit Points	116-135
Dexterity	6-155	Stamina	6-155
Intelligence	61-75	Mana	61-75
Magery	60-75	Parrying	55-65
Resist. Spells	60-75	Tactics	80-100
Wrestling	70-100		
Spell Circle	3-5		
Food	None		
Shelter	Lava (P)		
Desires	Lava (C)		
Resources	8 Magic		
Aversions	None		

Gargoyle

Damage	3-18	Natural Armor	15
Movement	Flying	Alignment	Evil
Strength	136-155	Hit Points	136-155
Dexterity	66-75	Stamina	66-75
Intelligence	71-85	Mana	71-85
Magery	70-85	Parrying	35-45
Resist. Spells	70-85	Tactics	50-70
Wrestling	40-80		
Spell Circle	4-8		

Food	Meat 15 (3)	
Shelter	Caves (P)	Dungeons (P)
Desires	Gargoyles (C)	Gold (C)
Resources	8 Meat	
Aversions	Traps	Civilization

Gazer

Damage	3-12	Natural Armor	19
Alignment	Evil		
Strength	86-105	Hit Points	86-105
Dexterity	46-55	Stamina	46-55
Intelligence	41-55	Mana	41-55
Magery	40-55	Parrying	45-55
Resist. Spells	40-55	Tactics	40-60
Wrestling	40-60		
Spell Circle	3-5		

Food	None	
Shelter	Caves (P)	Dungeons (P)
Desires	Gold (C)	
Resources	8 Meat	
Aversions	Traps	Civilization

Ghoul, Ghost or Spectre

Damage	6-12	Natural Armor	12
Alignment	Evil		
Strength	56-70	Hit Points	56-70
Dexterity	66-75	Stamina	66-75
Intelligence	26-40	Mana	26-40
Parrying	35-45	Resist. Spells	25-40
Tactics	35-50	Wrestling	35-45

Food	None	
Shelter	Eerie locations (P)	Dungeons (P)
Desires	Gold (C)	
Resources	None	
Aversions	Traps	

Harpy

Damage	3-9	Natural Armor	10
Movement	Flying	Alignment	Evil
Strength	86-100	Hit Points	86-100
Dexterity	76-95	Stamina	76-95
Intelligence	41-55	Mana	41-55
Parrying	75-90	Resist. Spells	40-55
Tactics	70-100	Wrestling	60-90

Food	Meat 5 (1)	
Shelter	Forests (P)	Mountains (P)
Desires	Gold (C)	Harpies (C)
Resources	9 Meat	
Aversions	Traps	Civilization

Headless

Damage	3-12	Natural Armor	9
Alignment	Evil		
Strength	26-40	Hit Points	26-40
Dexterity	36-45	Stamina	36-45
Intelligence	16-20	Mana	16-20
Parrying	35-45	Resist. Spells	15-20
Tactics	25-40	Wrestling	25-40

Food	None	
Shelter	Mountains (P)	Dungeons (P)
Desires	Gold (C)	Headless (C)
Resources	8 Meat	
Aversions	Traps	Civilization

Liche

Damage	15-25	Natural Armor	25
Alignment	Evil		
Strength	96-115	Hit Points	96-115
Dexterity	6-155	Stamina	6-155
Intelligence	156-175	Mana	156-175
Magery	50-60	Parrying	45-55
Resist. Spells	60-80	Tactics	60-80

Food	None		
Shelter	Dungeons (P)	Caves (P)	Eerie locations (P)
Desires	Gold (C)		
Resources	Eeriness		
Aversions	Traps		

Lizard Man

Damage	3-9*	Natural Armor	12
Alignment	Evil		
Strength	76-95	Hit Points	76-95
Dexterity	66-75	Stamina	66-75
Intelligence	26-40	Mana	0
Parrying	55-65	Resist. Spells	25-40
Tactics	55-70	Wrestling	50-60
Food	Meat 15 (3)		
Shelter	Dungeons (P)	Swamps (C)	
Desires	Gold (C)	Lizard Men (C)	
Resources	6 Meat		
Aversions	Traps	Carnivores (3+ bites)	

*Lizard Men can carry weapons; damage varies by weapon.

Mongbat (Arboreal)

Damage	1-2	Natural Armor	2-10
Movement	Flying	Alignment	Evil
Strength	6-10	Hit Points	4-8
Dexterity	26-38	Stamina	40-70
Intelligence	6-14	Mana	0
Parrying	25-38	Resist. Spells	5-14
Tactics	5-10	Wrestling	5-10
Food	Meat 5 (1)		
Shelter	Forests (P)	Jungle (P)	Eerie locations (C)
	Swamps (P)		
Desires	Gold (C)		
Resources	3 Meat		
Aversions	Traps		

Mongbat (Subterranean)

Damage	3-9	Natural Armor	10
Movement	Flying	Alignment	Evil
Strength	46-60	Hit Points	36-50
Dexterity	6-15	Stamina	6-15
Intelligence	16-30	Mana	16-30
Parrying	50-60	Resist. Spells	15-30
Tactics	35-50	Wrestling	20-35
Food	Meat 9 (3)		
Shelter	Caves (P)	Dungeons (P)	Eerie locations (C)
Desires	Gold (C)		
Resources	3 Meat		
Aversions	Traps	Civilization	

Ogre

Damage	16	Natural Armor	5-15
Alignment	Evil		
Strength	146-165	Hit Points	146-165
Dexterity	36-45	Stamina	36-45
Intelligence	36-50	Mana	0
Parrying	35-45	Resist. Spells	35-50
Tactics	60-70	Wrestling	70-80

Food	Meat 15 (3)	
Shelter	Forests (P)	Mountains (P)
Desires	Gold (C)	Ogres (C)
Resources	10 Meat	
Aversions	Traps	Civilization

*Ogres can carry weapons; damage varies by weapon.

Orc

Damage	3-9*	Natural Armor	11
Alignment	Evil		
Strength	76-95	Hit Points	86-100
Dexterity	61-75	Stamina	71-85
Intelligence	26-40	Mana	71-85
Magery	30-45	Parrying	30-45
Resist. Spells	30-45	Tactics	45-60
Wrestling	40-60		
Spell Circle	2-3		

Food	Meat 15 (3)		
Shelter	Orc camps (P)	Caves (P)	Dungeons (P)
Desires	Orcs (C)	Orc captain (C)	Gold (C)
Resources	9 Meat		
Aversions	Traps		

Orc Captain

Damage	2-16*	Natural Armor	15
Alignment	Evil		
Strength	91-105	Hit Points	11-250
Dexterity	91-105	Stamina	11-250
Intelligence	61-75	Mana	86-100
Magery	60-75	Parrying	60-75
Resist. Spells	70-85	Tactics	75-90
Spell Circle	2-3		

Food	Meat 15 (3)		
Shelter	Caves (P)	Dungeons (P)	Orc camps (P)
Desires	Gold (C)	Orc followers (C)	
Resources	9 Meat	Orc camp (attracts followers)	
Aversions	Traps		

*Orcs can carry weapons; damage varies by weapon.

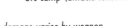

Rat (Giant Rat)

Damage	2-8	Natural Armor	8
Skill to Tame	45	Alignment	Evil
Strength	12-24	Hit Points	12-24
Dexterity	36-45	Stamina	36-45
Intelligence	6-10	Mana	0
Parrying	35-45	Resist. Spells	5-10
Tactics	9-24	Wrestling	9-24

Food	Meat 9 (3)
Shelter	Dungeons (T) Darkness (P) Eerie locations (P)
Desires	Rats (C) Eerie items and places (C)
Resources	3 Meat
Aversions	Traps

Rat Man

Damage	3-6*	Natural Armor	14
Alignment	Evil		
Strength	46-60	Hit Points	41-50
Dexterity	6-15	Stamina	6-15
Intelligence	26-40	Mana	26-40
Parrying	40-50	Resist. Spells	25-40
Tactics	40-55	Wrestling	40-55

Food	Meat 45 (1)
Shelter	Caves (P) Dungeons (P) Swamps (C)
	Desert (C)
Desires	Rat Men (C) Gold (C)
Resources	6 Meat
Aversions	Traps

* Rat men can acarry weapons; damage varies by weapon.

Reaper

Damage	5-15	Natural Armor	12
Alignment	Chaotic		
Strength	46-60	Hit Points	46-60
Dexterity	6-155	Stamina	0
Intelligence	26-40	Mana	0
Magery	30-40	Parrying	55-65
Resist. Spells	25-40	Tactics	45-60
Wrestling	40-50		
Spell Circle	1-2		

Food	Meat 15 (3)
Shelter	Jungle (P) Swamps (P) Forests (P)
Desires	Foliage (C)
Resources	Eeriness
Aversions	Traps

Scorpion (Giant Scorpion)

Damage	3-12	Natural Armor	12	
Skill to Tame	60	Alignment	Evil	
Strength	63-75	Hit Points	12-24	
Dexterity	66-75	Stamina	151-160	
Intelligence	6-10	Mana	0	
Parrying	60-70	Resist. Spells	30-35	
Tactics	60-75	Wrestling	5-20	
Food	Meat 15 (3)			
Shelter	Dungeons (P)	Caves (P)	Desert (P)	
Desires	Gold (C)			
Resources	8 Meat			
Aversions	Traps	Civilization		

Sea Serpent

Damage	2-12	Natural Armor	4-12
Strength	166-185	Hit Points	166-185
Dexterity	6-155	Stamina	6-155
Intelligence	51-65	Mana	51-65
Parrying	55-65	Resist. Spells	50-65
Tactics	50-60	Wrestling	50-60
Food	Meat 25 (1)		
Shelter	Water (P)		
Desires	Ships (C)		
Resources	50 Meat	8 Serpent scales	
Aversions	Traps	Coastline	

Serpent (Giant Serpent)

Damage	2-16	Natural Armor	4-24
Strength	176-195	Hit Points	176-195
Dexterity	46-60	Stamina	46-55
Intelligence	6-155	Mana	26-40
Parrying	45-60	Resist. Spells	25-40
Tactics	65-70	Wrestling	40-60
Food	Meat 6 (3)		
Shelter	Forests (P)	Jungle (P)	
Desires	Foliage (C)		
Resources	50 Meat	8 Scales	
Aversions	Traps	Civilization	

Silver Serpent

Damage	1-8	Natural Armor	9
Skill to Tame	60		
Strength	61-80	Hit Points	26-45
Dexterity	51-65	Stamina	46-55
Intelligence	11-20	Mana	26-40
Parrying	45-60	Resist. Spells	25-40
Tactics	41-90	Wrestling	40-55
Food	None		
Shelter	Forests (P)	Jungle (P)	
Desires	Foliage (C)		
Resources	1 Meat		
Aversions	Traps	Civilization	

Skeleton

Damage	2-8*	Natural Armor	8
Alignment	Evil		
Strength	46-60	Hit Points	46-60
Dexterity	46-55	Stamina	46-55
Intelligence	6-20	Mana	0
Parrying	45-55	Resist. Spells	51-20
Tactics	45-60	Wrestling	45-55
Food	None		
Shelter	Eerie locations (T)		
Desires	Eerie items and places (C)		
Resources	Eeriness	8 Bones	
Aversions	Traps		

* Skeletons can wield various weapons; damage varies by weapon.

Slime

Damage	1-5	Natural Armor	1-4
Skill to Tame	40	Alignment	Evil
Strength	12-24	Hit Points	18-30
Dexterity	16-21	Stamina	16-21
Intelligence	6-10	Mana	6-10
Parrying	15-21	Resist. Spells	5-10
Tactics	9-24	Wrestling	9-24
Food	Cloth 55 (1)	Meat 35 (1)	Leather 55 (1)
	Metal 55 (1)		
Shelter	Caves (P)	Dungeons (P)	
Desires	Gold (C)		
Resources	Eeriness		
Aversions	Traps		

Spider (Giant Spider)

Damage	2-14	Natural Armor	6	
Skill to Tame	70	Alignment	Evil	
Strength	66-80	Hit Points	66-80	
Dexterity	66-75	Stamina	66-75	
Intelligence	26-40	Mana	26-40	
Parrying	35-45	Resist. Spells	25-40	
Tactics	35-50	Wrestling	50-65	
Food	Meat 15 (3)			
Shelter	Web (P)	Caves (P)	Dungeons (P)	
Desires	Eerie items and places (C)			
Resources	8 Spider silk	Eeriness		
Aversions	Traps			

Troll

Damage	5-14*	Natural Armor	17
Alignment	Evil		
Strength	156-175	Hit Points	156-175
Dexterity	36-45	Stamina	36-45
Intelligence	36-50	Mana	0
Parrying	35-45	Resist. Spells	35-50
Tactics	1-20+50	Wrestling	20-70
Food	Meat 15 (3)		
Shelter	Forests (P)	Mountains (P)	
Desires	Gold (C)		
Resources	10 Meat		
Aversions	Traps	Civilization	

*Trolls can carry weapons; damage varies by weapon.

Water Elemental

Damage	4-12	Natural Armor	19
Alignment	Evil		
Strength	116-135	Hit Points	116-135
Dexterity	6-155	Stamina	6-155
Intelligence	61-75	Mana	61-75
Magery	60-75	Parrying	55-65
Resist. Spells	60-75	Tactics	80-100
Wrestling	70-90		
Spell Circle	3-7		
Food	None		
Shelter	Water		
Desires	Water (C)		
Resources	8 Magic		
Aversions	Traps		

Wisp

Damage	25-35	Natural Armor	30		
Spell Circle	8				
Strength	195-215	Hit Points	195-215		
Dexterity	195-215	Stamina	96-115		
Intelligence	195-215	Mana	195-215		
Magery	100	Parrying	100		
Resist. Spells	100	Tactics	100		
Wrestling	100				
Food	None				
Shelter	Swamps (P)	Jungle (P)	Forests (P)		
Desires	None				
Resources	8 Lights				
Aversions	Traps	Civilization			

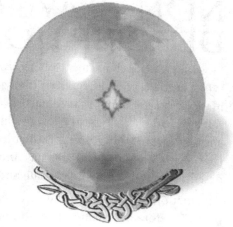

Zombie

Damage	2-8	Natural Armor	5
Alignment	Evil		
Strength	36-50	Hit Points	16-30
Dexterity	10-30	Stamina	10-30
Intelligence	16-20	Mana	16-20
Parrying	10-30	Resist. Spells	15-20
Tactics	35-50	Wrestling	35-50
Food	None		
Shelter	Dungeons (P)	Eerie locations (P)	
Desires	Gold (C)		
Resources	Eeriness		
Aversions	Traps		

NON-PLAYER CHARACTER DESCRIPTIONS

Most non-player characters (NPCs) are based on the Typical statistics given below. When an NPC type differs from the typical statistics, however, the changed information appears under that character's entry. For example, an Alchemist has the same statistics as a Typical NPC, but also desires gold and magical items. For another example, an Animal Trainer has a better *Tactics* skill than most NPCs (between 45 and 68) and also has *Animal Taming* (between 55 and 78). All descriptions apply equally to male and female characters.

Explanations of what each stat means are given on p. 137, before the creature descriptions. There are two statistics that apply only to NPCs:

Sells/Buys lists include all of the items the NPC will buy and sell by default. In a combined list, a (B) after an entry indicates the NPC only buys the item, and (S) indicates he or she only sells it.

Keywords list the words that an NPC of this profession will respond to, in addition to the general and town-specific keywords he or she recognizes. See **Keywords**, p. 125.

Typical NPC

Fencing	15-38	Mace Fighting	15-38
Parrying	15-38	Resisting Spells	15-38
Swordsmanship	15-38	Tactics	15-38
Wrestling	15-38		
Food	Any common food		
Shelter	House (P)		
Desires	Gold (S)	Notoriety (C)	
Resources	8 Meat		
Aversions	Traps	Eerie items and places	

Shopkeeper Keywords

In addition to all of the keywords listed for each character, all characters who run a shop will respond to these keywords:

Keywords	buy	sell	supplies
I <any> sale	sale	can <any> you <any> sell	
thou <any> purchase		what <any> you <any>	
you <any> buy		you <any> purchase	

Guild of Arcane Arts

Alchemist

Strength	36-50	Hit Points	36-50
Dexterity	36-50	Stamina	36-50
Intelligence	51-65	Mana	51-65
Alchemy	55-78	Parrying	25-48
Resisting Spells	25-48	Tactics	25-48
Taste Identif.	55-78		
Desires	Magic (C)		

Sells/Buys	Flasks (empty) (S)		Potions
Reagents	Mortars and pestles		

Keywords	agility	alchem \<any\>	alchemist
alchemy	black pearl	black potion	blind
bloodmoss	blue potion	explode	explosion
garlic	ginseng	green potion	heal
mage	magic	mandrake	mortar
nightshade	orange potion	pestle	poison
potion	purple potion	reagents	red potion
refresh	secret	skill	sleep
spider silk	strength	sulphurous ash	vial
white potion	yellow potion		

Mage (Shopkeeper)

Strength	61-75	Hit Points	61-75
Dexterity	71-85	Stamina	71-85
Intelligence	86-100	Mana	86-100
Inscription	50-65	Magery	86-100
Parrying	45-68	Resisting Spells	55-78
Tactics	35-58		
Spell Circle	3-7		
Desires	Reagents (S)		

Sells	Marker talismans	Potions	Reagents
Scrolls*	Scrolls (blank)	Spell books	Various arcane
items			

*Each shopkeeper mage sells only those scrolls he or she is capable of creating. For example, a First Circle mage sells only scrolls inscribed with First Circle spells, while a Fifth Circle mage sells scrolls inscribed with spells from the First through Fifth Circles.

Keywords	abbey	abilities	ability
arcane	art	cast	casting
component	craft	Des Mani	empath
ether	guild	In Lor	In Mani
In Mani Ylem	In Por Ylem	ingredients	reagent
Rel Wis	relvinian	scroll	skill
spell	spell books	spellbooks	spells
talent	Uus Jux	where \<any\> monks	
Wis Uus	words of power		

Mage (Non-Shopkeeper)

For Hire	Daily Wage 60		
Strength	61-75	Hit Points	61-75
Dexterity	71-85	Stamina	71-85
Intelligence	86-100	Mana	86-100
Inscription	50-65	Magery	86-100
Parrying	55-78	Resisting Spells	65-88
Tactics	55-78		
Spell Circle	7-8		
Desires	Magic (C)	Reagents (S)	

Keywords (see Mage (Shopkeeper) keywords)

Mage (Evil)

Alignment	Evil		
Strength	71-85	Hit Points	71-85
Dexterity	81-95	Stamina	81-95
Intelligence	96-110	Mana	96-110
Evaluating Intel.	55-78	Inscription	76-90
Magery	86-100	Parrying	65-88
Resisting Spells	75-98	Tactics	65-88
Wrestling	20-60		
Spell Circle	3-5		
Desires	Magic (C)	Reagents (S)	

Keywords (see Mage (Shopkeeper) keywords)

Guildmaster

Strength	91-105	Hit Points	91-105
Dexterity	101-115	Stamina	101-115
Intelligence	116-130	Mana	116-130
Evaluating Intel.	55-78	Fencing	75-98
Inscription	76-90	Mace Fighting	75-98
Magery	86-100	Parrying	75-98
Resisting Spells	75-98	Swordsmanship	75-98
Tactics	75-98	Wrestling	75-98
Spell Circle	8		
Desires	Gold (S)	Magic (C)	Reagents (S)
	Bone (S)	Daemon bone (S)	Dirt (S)
	Dragon blood (S)	Ink (S)	Silk (S)
	Serpent scales (S)	Volcanic ash (S)	

Additional Keywords		guild	join
master			

163

Soc. of Cooks & Chefs

(Not currently accepting new members)

Cook

Strength	41-55	*Hit Points*	41-55
Dexterity	56-70	*Stamina*	56-70
Intelligence	56-70	*Mana*	56-70
Cooking	55-78	*Parrying*	35-58
Resisting Spells	35-58	*Tactics*	35-58
Taste Identif.	35-58		

Sells Birds (cooked) Bread (loaves) Cakes
Cheese Chicken legs (cooked) Flour (sacks)
Honey Muffins Mutton (cooked) Pies (baked)
Pigs (roasted) Stews Tomato soup Vegetables

Buys Apples Bananas Birds (raw)
Bread (loaves) Cabbage (heads) Cantaloupe Carrots
Cheese Corn Eggs Fish
Fish (steaks) Flour (sacks) Gourds Grapes
Honey Kindling Lemons Lettuce (heads)
Limes Melons Milk (pitchers) Onions
Peaches Pears Pumpkins Ribs (raw)
Squash Turnips Watermelons

Keywords bacon beef bread
cake chicken consumption cook
craft fish flour food
ham ingredient meal meals
meat oven pastry pork
roast skill sweets vegetables
what <any> you <any> cook

Bardic Collegium

Bard

For Hire	Daily Wage 20		
Strength	16-30	*Hit Points*	16-30
Dexterity	26-40	*Stamina*	26-40
Intelligence	26-40	*Mana*	26-40
Enticement	55-78	*Musicianship*	55-78
Peacemaking	55-78	*Provocation*	55-78

Keywords abbey artifact bard
conservatory cool empath hint
info interesting magic minstrel
music news play relvinian
rumor rumour song tale
to do troubad (e.g., troubadour)
where <any> monks

Guildmaster

Strength	86-100	*Hit Points*	86-100
Dexterity	71-85	*Stamina*	71-85
Intelligence	61-75	*Mana*	61-75
Enticement	55-78	*Musicianship*	55-78
Parrying	65-88	*Peacemaking*	55-78
Provocation	55-78	*Resisting Spells*	65-88
Tactics	65-88		

Additional Keywords guild join
master

Society of Clothiers

Weaver

Desires	Cloth (C)	Cotton (C)	Wool (C)

Sells/Buys Yarn (balls) Cloth (bolts) Cloth (folded)
Cotton (raw) (B) Dye bowls Dye tubs Wool (raw) (B)

Keywords cloth cotton dye
loom weave wool yarn

Guildmaster

Strength	71-85	*Hit Points*	71-85
Dexterity	86-100	*Stamina*	86-100
Intelligence	86-100	*Mana*	86-100
Parrying	65-88	*Resisting Spells*	65-88
Tactics	55-78	*Tailoring*	65-88

Additional Keywords guild join
master

Tailor

Strength	36-50	*Hit Points*	36-50
Dexterity	46-60	*Stamina*	46-60
Intelligence	41-55	*Mana*	41-55
Parrying	25-48	*Resisting Spells*	25-48
Tactics	25-48	*Tailoring*	55-78
Desires	Cloth (C)		

Sells/Buys Aprons Bandannas Cloaks
Cloth (bolts) Cloth (folded) Cotton (raw) Doublets
Dresses Dye bowls Dye tubs Flax (retted)
Hats and caps Jester caps Jester suits Kilts
Leather caps Pants Robes Scissors
Sewing kits Shirts Skirts Thread
Tunics Wool (raw)

Keywords apron cape cloth
clothes clothier clothing coat
dress garment kilt pant
robe sew shawl shirt
skill skirt tailor thread
vest

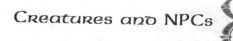

Order of Engineers

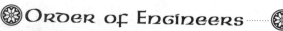

Tinker

Strength	41-55	Hit Points	41-55
Dexterity	66-80	Stamina	66-80
Intelligence	61-75	Mana	61-75
Lockpicking	45-68	Parrying	35-58
Resisting Spells	35-58	Tactics	35-58
Tinkering	45-68		

Sells/Buys

parts	Axles and gears	Butcher knives	Clocks and clock
Drums	Copper keys	Dovetails	Draw knives
Hammers	Froes	Gears	Gold keys
Iron keys	Hinges	Inshaves	Iron ingots
Logs (B)	Key rings	Kindling (B)	Lockpicks
Magic keys (B)	Lumber	Lutes	Lyres
Planes	Metal ingots (B)	Nails (S)	Pickaxes
Scorps	Rusty keys	Saws	Scissors
Shovels	Sewing kits	Sextants	Sextant parts
Sticks	Sledge hammers	Smith hammers	Springs
Tongs	Tambourines	Tinker's tools	Tinker's toolkit

Keywords

clock	device	gear
lumber	machine	part	sextant
skill	spring	sticks	tinker
trade	wood	

Guildmaster

Strength	71-85	Hit Points	71-85
Dexterity	86-100	Stamina	86-100
Intelligence	86-100	Mana	86-100
Lockpicking	65-88	Parrying	65-88
Resisting Spells	55-78	Tactics	65-88
Tinkering	65-88		

Additional Keywords   guild   join

master

Guild of Healers

Healer (Shopkeeper)

Strength	71-85	Hit Points	71-85
Dexterity	81-95	Stamina	81-95
Intelligence	86-100	Mana	86-100
Anatomy	55-78	Forensic Eval.	35-58
Healing	55-78	Parrying	65-88
Resisting Spells	65-88	Spirit Speak	55-78
Tactics	65-88		
Desires	Garlic (S)	Ginseng (S)	Cloth (S)
Aversions	Traps		

Sells/Buys

Bandages	Cloth (folded) (B)	Garlic
Ginseng	Healing potions	Refreshing potions	Spider's silk (B)

Keywords

anatomy	bandage	buy
cure	first aid	heal	healing
healing scrolls	help	hurt	injured
items	knowledge	master	poison
potion	potions	raise dead	resurrect
resurrection	skill	

Healer (Non-Shopkeeper)

Strength	71-85	Hit Points	71-85
Dexterity	81-95	Stamina	81-95
Intelligence	86-100	Mana	86-100
Anatomy	55-78	Camping	35-58
Fishing	35-58	Forensic Eval.	35-58
Healing	55-78	Parrying	65-88
Resisting Spells	65-88	Spirit Speak	55-78
Tactics	65-88		

Keywords (see Healer (Shopkeeper))

Guildmaster

Strength	81-95	Hit Points	81-95
Dexterity	96-110	Stamina	96-110
Intelligence	96-110	Mana	96-110
Anatomy	65-88	Forensic Eval.	45-68
Healing	65-88	Parrying	65-88
Resisting Spells	65-88	Spirit Speak	65-88
Tactics	65-88		

Additional Keywords   guild   join

master

Maritime Guild

Fisherman

Strength	61-75	Hit Points	61-75	
Dexterity	61-75	Stamina	61-75	
Intelligence	41-55	Mana	41-55	
Fishing	45-68	Parrying	35-58	
Resisting Spells	35-58	Tactics	35-58	
Desires	Water (C)			
Sells	Fish	Fish (steaks)	Fishing poles	
Buys	Fish (big and small)			
Keywords	catch	fish <any>	fisher	
fisherman	fishermen	food	nets	
river	sea	skill		

Mapmaker

Strength	21-35	Hit Points	21-35
Dexterity	36-50	Stamina	36-50
Intelligence	36-50	Mana	36-50
Cartography	65-88		
Sells/Buys	Scrolls (blank) (B)		Maps
Maps (blank)			
Keywords	blank	chart <any> course	
empty	make maps	plot <any> course	
sextant	skill	vellum	

Shipwright

Strength	66-80	Hit Points	66-80
Dexterity	71-85	Stamina	71-85
Intelligence	61-75	Mana	61-75
Parrying	45-68	Resisting Spells	45-68
Tactics	45-68		
Desires	Wood (C)		
Sells/Buys	Sextants (S)	Ship deeds	
Keywords	boat	sail	sextant
ship	vessel		

Guildmaster

Strength	81-95	Hit Points	81-95
Dexterity	86-100	Stamina	86-100
Intelligence	81-95	Mana	81-95
Fishing	65-88	Parrying	55-78
Resisting Spells	65-88	Tactics	65-88
Additional Keywords		guild	join
master			

Sailor

For Hire	Daily Wage 50		
Strength	66-80	Hit Points	66-80
Dexterity	66-80	Stamina	66-80
Intelligence	41-55	Mana	41-55
Parrying	45-68	Resisting Spells	45-68
Tactics	45-68		
Desires	Ships (C)	Water (C)	Sailors (C)
Keywords	pirate	sail	sailor
ship			

Merchants' Assoc.

Innkeeper

Strength	66-80	Hit Points	66-80
Dexterity	66-80	Stamina	66-80
Intelligence	61-75	Mana	61-75
Parrying	45-68	Resisting Spells	45-68
Tactics	45-68		
Sells/Buys	Ale (Bottles)	Ale (Pitchers)	Apples
Backpacks	Bananas	Birds (cooked)(S)	Bread (loaves)
Candles	Cheeses	Chicken legs	Cider (jugs)
Cider (pitchers)	Glass pitchers(B)	Grapes	Liquor (bottles)
Liquor (pitchers)	Milk (pitchers)	Mutton (cooked)	Peaches
Pears	Pies (baked)	Ribs (cooked)(S)	Ribs (raw) (B)
Stews	Tomato soup	Torches	Vegetables
Water (pitchers)	Wine (bottles)	Wine (pitchers)	
Keywords	abbey	aleq	artifact
barmaid	bed	beer	breakfast
cool	dinner	empath	food
for the night	hint	info	inn
interesting	lunch	magic	news
relvinian	rent	room	rumor
rumour	sleep	stay the night	tavern
to do	waitress	wench	
where <any> monks			

Merchants' Association (cont.)

Provisioner

Strength	66-80	Hit Points	66-80
Dexterity	61-75	Stamina	61-75
Intelligence	66-80	Mana	66-80
Parrying	45-68	Resisting Spells	45-68
Tactics	45-68		

Sells/Buys Ale (bottles) (S) Apples (S) Armour (most)
Axes (broken) (B) Axles and gears (B)
Backpacks Bags Bandanas Bedrolls (S)
Belt pouches Birds(cooked)(S) Books (various) Boxes (wood)(S)
Bread (loaves) (S) Candles Chicken legs(S)
Cider (jugs) (S) Clocks and clock parts (B) Diamonds (B)
Dovetails (B) Flasks (empty) (S) Froes (B)
Garlic (S) Gears (B) Gemstones (B) Ginseng (S)
Gold ingots (B) Hammerpicks (B) Hammers (B)
Hats and caps (most) Helmets (most) Hinges (B)
House deeds (small) (B) Inshaves (B) Iron ingots (B)
Jointing planes (B) Key rings (B) Kindling
Knives (most) Lanterns Leather clothing (B)
Lockpicks Logs (B) Lumber (B)
Meat cleavers(B) Metal ingots (B) Moulding planes (B)
Oil (flasks) Pears (S) Pickaxes (B) Pitchforks (B)
Saws (B) Scissors (B) Scorps (B) Sewing kits (B)
Sextants and sextant parts (B) Shepherd's crooks (B)
Shields (most) Ship deeds (small) Shovels (B)
Silver ingots (B) Sledge hammers (B)
Smithy hammers (B) Smoothing planes (B)
Springs (B) Staves (B) Sticks (B) Tongs (B)
Torches Weapons (most) Wine (bottles) (S)

Keywords ale apple arrow
bag beer bird bolt
bread candle chicken cider
drink equip food fruit
lantern liquor meat mutton
pack pear pouch provision
ration supply torch wine

Jeweler

Strength	36-50	Hit Points	36-50
Dexterity	51-65	Stamina	51-65
Intelligence	41-55	Mana	41-55
Item Identif.	55-78	Parrying	25-48
Resisting Spells	25-48	Tactics	25-48
Desires	Gold (C)		

Sells Beads Bracelets Earrings
Necklaces Rings
Buys Gemstones Gold ingots Silver ingots
Keywords amber amethyst appraise
bead bracelet citrine diamond
emerald estimate gem gold
jewel necklace quality ring
rubies ruby sapphire silver
skill tourmaline value

Tavernkeeper

Strength	61-75	Hit Points	61-75
Dexterity	66-80	Stamina	66-80
Intelligence	51-65	Mana	51-65
Parrying	45-68	Resisting Spells	45-68
Tactics	45-68		

Sells/Buys Ale (bottles) Ale (pitchers) Cheese
Cider (jugs) Cider (pitchers) Birds (cooked) Bread (loaves)
Chickens Glass pitchers Liquor (bottles) Liquor (pitchers)
Milk (pitchers) Mutton (cooked) Pies (baked) Stews
Tomato soup Vegetables Water (pitchers) Wine (bottles)
Wine (pitchers)

Keywords abbey ale artifact
barmaid beer breakfast cool
dinner empath food hint
info interesting lunch magic
news relvinian rumor rumour
tavern to do waitress wench
where <any> monks

Guildmaster

Strength	71-85	Hit Points	71-85
Dexterity	86-100	Stamina	86-100
Intelligence	86-100	Mana	86-100
Item Identif.	55-78	Parrying	27-50
Resisting Spells	27-50	Tactics	27-50

Additional Keywords guild join
master

League of Rangers

Ranger

Strength	71-85	Hit Points	71-85
Dexterity	76-90	Stamina	76-90
Intelligence	61-75	Mana	61-75
Animal Lore	55-78	Archery	55-78
Camping	55-78	Fencing	35-58
Herding	45-68	Hiding	45-68
Mace Fighting	35-58	Parrying	65-88
Resisting Spells	65-88	Swordsmanship	35-58
Tactics	65-88	Tracking	45-68
Wrestling	35-58		

Keywords alligator, animal, bear, bird, cat, chicken, corpser, cow, daemon, deer, dog, dolphin, dragon, eagle, elemental, ettin, fish, fowl, gargoyle, goat, gorilla, hide, horse, hunt, llama, meat, monster, mountain cat, pelt, pig, rabbit, ranger, seal, sheep, skill, spirituality, track, wolf

Guildmaster

Strength	91-105	Hit Points	91-105
Dexterity	96-110	Stamina	96-110
Intelligence	81-95	Mana	81-95
Animal Lore	65-88	Archery	75-98
Camping	65-88	Herding	55-78
Hiding	65-88	Parrying	75-98
Resisting Spells	75-98	Tactics	75-98
Tracking	65-88		
Shelter	Forest (P)	House (P)	

Additional Keywords guild, join, master

Bowyer

Strength	66-80	Hit Points	66-80
Dexterity	71-85	Stamina	71-85
Intelligence	61-75	Mana	61-75
Archery	65-88	Bowcraft/Flet.	65-88
Fencing	25-48	Mace Fighting	25-48
Parrying	45-68	Resisting Spells	45-68
Swordsmanship	25-48	Tactics	45-68
Wrestling	25-48		
Desires	Wood (C)	Feathers (C)	

Sells/Buys Arrow shafts (S), Arrows, Bolts, Bows, Crossbows, Feathers, Lumber (B)

Keywords archery, arrow, bolt, bow, cross, feather, fletching, shaft, stick

Animal Trainer

Strength	66-80	Hit Points	66-80
Dexterity	66-80	Stamina	66-80
Intelligence	71-85	Mana	71-85
Animal Lore	45-68	Animal Taming	55-78
Parrying	45-68	Resisting Spells	45-68
Tactics	45-68	Veterinary	35-58

Sells tamed: Black bears, Brown bears, Cats, Dogs, Eagles, Horses, Panthers, Rabbits, Rats, Ravens, Timber wolves

Buys Apples, Birds (raw), Carcasses, Carrots, Grain bundles, Lettuce heads, Ribs (raw)

Keywords animal, cat, dog, horse, mount, saddle, steed, train, trainer, whip

Mining Cooperative

Miner

Strength	66-80	Hit Points	66-80
Dexterity	51-65	Stamina	51-65
Intelligence	41-55	Mana	41-55
Mining	35-58	Parrying	35-58
Resisting Spells	35-58	Tactics	35-58
Desires	Stone (C)		

Keywords dig, hole, mine, ore, shaft

Guildmaster

Strength	86-100	Hit Points	86-100
Dexterity	61-75	Stamina	61-75
Intelligence	71-85	Mana	71-85
Item Identif.	65-88	Mining	65-88
Parrying	65-88	Resisting Spells	65-88
Tactics	65-88		

Additional Keywords guild, join, master

Society of Smiths

(Not currently accepting new members)

Armourer

Strength	86-100	Hit Points	86-100
Dexterity	76-90	Stamina	76-90
Intelligence	61-75	Mana	61-75
Arms Lore	65-88	Blacksmithy	55-78
Fencing	45-68	Mace Fighting	45-68
Parrying	55-78	Resisting Spells	55-78
Swordsmanship	45-68	Tactics	55-78
Wrestling	45-68		
Desires	Metal (C)		

Sells — Shields — Ring (if ring specialty)

Chainmail (if chainmail specialty)

Leather and studded leather (if leather specialty)

Plate (if plate or leather specialty) — Helmets (if plate specialty)

All armourers **buy** all armour, shields and helmets, plus:

Lumber — Metal ingots

Keywords — armor — skill — smith

Blacksmith

Strength	86-100	Hit Points	86-100
Dexterity	66-80	Stamina	66-80
Intelligence	61-75	Mana	61-75
Arms Lore	45-68	Blacksmithy	65-88
Fencing	45-68	Mace Fighting	45-68
Parrying	55-78	Resisting Spells	55-78
Swordsmanship	45-68	Tactics	55-78
Wrestling	45-68		
Desires	Metal (S)		

Sells/Buys — Armour (all) — Iron ingots — Kindling (B)

Metal ingots (B) — Tongs — Weapons (all)

Keywords

armor	axe	bardiche
blacksmith	bow	buckler	chain
club	crossbow	cutlass	forge
fork	gauntlet	gorget	halberd
heater	helm	kitana	knife
kryss	mace	maul	meat cleaver
padded	plate	ring	scimitar
shield	smith	spear	staff
steel	sword	war hammer	weapon

Weaponsmith

In a unique arrangement, weaponsmiths have been allowed membership in both the Society of Smiths and the Warriors' Guild. Since the Smiths are not currently accepting new members, new weaponsmiths can only join the Warriors' Guild, and typical Weaponsmith stats are found on p. 171.

Society of Thieves

Beggar

For Hire	Daily Wage 10		
Attitude	50		
Strength	26-40	Hit Points	26-40
Dexterity	21-35	Stamina	21-35
Intelligence	16-30	Mana	16-30
Begging	55-78	Snooping	25-48
Stealing	15-38		
Shelter	House (T)		
Desires	Gold (each instance of begging)		

Keywords

artifact	beggar	coin
cool	donate	gold	help
hint	info	interesting	magic
money	news	rumor	

Thief

For Hire	Daily Wage 60		
Strength	61-75	Hit Points	61-75
Dexterity	86-100	Stamina	86-100
Intelligence	71-85	Mana	71-85
Detecting Hidden	35-58	Fencing	55-78
Hiding	45-68	Lockpicking	35-58
Parrying	55-78	Poisoning	35-58
Resisting Spells	55-78	Snooping	45-68
Stealing	45-68	Swordsmanship	35-58
Tactics	55-78	Wrestling	25-48
Shelter	House (T)		
Desires	Jewels (S)		
Aversions	Guards (becomes uneasy)		

Keywords

authorities	copper	fork <any> gold
guard	hide	lock	Lord British
<any> fork	silver	skill	soldiers
trap			

Guildmaster

Strength	91-105	Hit Points	91-105
Dexterity	91-105	Stamina	91-105
Intelligence	91-105	Mana	91-105
Detecting Hidden	55-78	Fencing	75-98
Hiding	65-88	Lockpicking	65-88
Mace Fighting	45-68	Parrying	75-98
Poisoning	65-88	Resisting Spells	65-88
Snooping	65-88	Stealing	65-88
Swordsmanship	55-78	Tactics	75-98
Wrestling	55-78		

Additional Keywords — guild — join

master

Warriors' Guild

Fighter

For Hire	Daily Wage 60		
Strength	86-100	Hit Points	86-100
Dexterity	81-95	Stamina	81-95
Intelligence	61-75	Mana	61-75
Arms Lore	52-75	Fencing	45-68
Mace Fighting	45-68	Parrying	65-88
Resisting Spells	45-68	Swordsmanship	55-78
Tactics	65-88	Wrestling	45-68

Keywords
armor	axe	bardiche
bow	bucket helm	buckler	bullwhip
chain	club	crossbow	cutlass
fight	fork	gauntlet	gorget
halberd	heater	helm	idiot
kill	kitana	kryss	mace
maim	maul	meat cleaver	moron
norse helm	open faced helm	padded	plate
provisions	ring	scimitar	shield
skill	spear	staff	stupid
sword	thou <any> idiot moron		trouble
weapon	you <any> idiot thou <any>		
you <any> moron			

Warrior

For Hire	Daily Wage 70		
Strength	86-100	Hit Points	86-100
Dexterity	76-90	Stamina	76-90
Intelligence	61-75	Mana	61-75
Arms Lore	52-75	Fencing	45-68
Mace Fighting	45-68	Parrying	65-88
Resisting Spells	45-68	Swordsmanship	55-78
Tactics	65-88	Wrestling	45-68

Keywords (see Fighter keywords)

Mercenary

For Hire	Daily Wage 80		
Strength	86-100	Hit Points	86-100
Dexterity	71-85	Stamina	71-85
Intelligence	71-85	Mana	71-85
Arms Lore	52-75	Fencing	45-68
Mace Fighting	45-68	Parrying	65-88
Resisting Spells	45-68	Swordsmanship	55-78
Tactics	65-88	Wrestling	45-68

Keywords (see Fighter keywords)

Paladin

For Hire	Daily Wage 80		
Strength	96-110	Hit Points	96-110
Dexterity	96-110	Stamina	96-110
Intelligence	81-95	Mana	81-95
Arms Lore	52-75	Fencing	45-68
Mace Fighting	45-68	Parrying	75-98
Resisting Spells	75-98	Swordsmanship	65-88
Tactics	75-98	Wrestling	55-78

Keywords
armor	axe	bardiche
bow	bucket helm	buckler	bullwhip
chain	club	crossbow	cutlass
fork	gauntlet	gorget	halberd
heater	helm	honor	kitana
kryss	mace	maul	meat cleaver
norse helm	open faced helm	padded	paladin
plate	provisions	ring	scimitar
shield	skill	spear	staff
sword	weapon		

Weapons Trainer

Strength	96-110	Hit Points	96-110
Dexterity	91-105	Stamina	91-105
Intelligence	71-85	Mana	71-85
Fencing	67-90	Mace Fighting	67-90
Parrying	75-98	Resisting Spells	65-88
Swordsmanship	67-90	Tactics	75-98
Wrestling	67-90		

Keywords
abilities	ability	axe
bow	dagger	defend	fight
hammer	mace	sword	weapon

Guildmaster

Strength	96-110	Hit Points	96-110
Dexterity	91-105	Stamina	91-105
Intelligence	81-95	Mana	81-95
Arms Lore	55-78	Fencing	55-78
Mace Fighting	65-88	Parrying	75-98
Resisting Spells	65-88	Swordsmanship	65-88
Tactics	75-98	Wrestling	55-78

Additional Keywords
	guild	join
master		

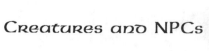

Warriors' Guild (cont.)

Weaponsmith

Strength	86-100	Hit Points	86-100
Dexterity	86-100	Stamina	86-100
Intelligence	81-95	Mana	81-95
Arms Lore	45-68	Blacksmithy	65-88
Fencing	45-68	Mace Fighting	45-68
Parrying	55-78	Resisting Spells	55-78
Swordsmanship	45-68	Tactics	55-78
Wrestling	45-68		
Desires	Wood (C)	Metal (C)	

Bladed Weaponsmith Sells/Buys

Axes (broken)	Bardiches	Battle axes	Bows
Broadswords	Butcher knives	Crossbows	Cutlasses
Daggers	Halberds	Hatchets	Double axes
Hammerpicks	Heavy crossbows (B)		
Iron ingots (B)	Kitanas	Kryss knives	Lrg. Battle Axes
Longswords	Lumber (B)	Meat cleavers	Pickaxes
Pitchforks	Scimitars	Skinning knives	
Two-handed axes	Viking swords	War axes	

Blunt Weaponsmith Sells/Buys

Black staffs	Clubs	Iron ingots (B)	Lumber (B)
Maces	Mauls	Metal ingots (B)	Quarterstaves
Shepherd crooks	Short spears	Smith hammers	Spears
Staffs (gnarled)	War hammers		
War maces			

Keywords	axe	bardiche	bow
bullwhip	club	crossbow	cutlass
dagger	forge	fork	halberd
hammer	kitana	knife	kryss
mace	maul	meat cleaver	scimitar
smith	spear	staff	sweat
sword	weapon	what <any> do	

Other Characters

Actor

Strength	21-35	Hit Points	21-35
Dexterity	26-40	Stamina	26-40
Intelligence	26-40	Mana	26-40

Keywords	actor	actore	art
clothe	costume	Noble	perform
priss	real	sissy	stage
theater	theatre	wuss	

Architect

Strength	21-35	Hit Points	21-35
Dexterity	36-50	Stamina	36-50
Intelligence	36-50	Mana	36-50
Sells/Buys	House deeds		

Keywords	architect	build	building
domicile	home	house	lot
material			

Artist

Strength	16-30	Hit Points	16-30
Dexterity	31-45	Stamina	31-45
Intelligence	16-30	Mana	16-30
Anatomy	25-48		

Keywords	art	canvas	draw
paint	picture	portrait	

Baker

Strength	34-48	Hit Points	34-48
Dexterity	33-47	Stamina	33-47
Intelligence	26-40	Mana	26-40
Cooking	55-78		
Desires	Flour (C)		

Sells/Buys	Bread (loaves)	Cakes	Cookies (B)
Cookies (pan) (S)	Eggs (B)	Flour (sacks)	Honey (B)
Kindling (B)	Milk (pitchers) (B)		Muffins
Pies (baked)	Pizzas		

Keywords	bake	baker	bread
cake	dough	egg	flour
honey	loaf	loaves	milk
muffin	pastry	pie	

Banker

Strength	71-85	Hit Points	71-85
Dexterity	66-80	Stamina	66-80
Intelligence	66-80	Mana	66-80
Parrying	45-68	Resisting Spells	45-68
Tactics	45-68		

Keywords account bank coin
copper currency deposit gold
hold up money rob silver
steal transaction

Beekeeper

Strength	21-35	Hit Points	21-35
Dexterity	36-50	Stamina	36-50
Intelligence	36-50	Mana	36-50
Desires	Gold (S)	Beehives (C)	Honey (C)

Sells/Buys Honey
Keywords apiarist bee bees
flower honey

Brigand

For Hire Daily Wage 60

Strength	66-80	Hit Points	66-80
Dexterity	81-95	Stamina	81-95
Intelligence	61-75	Mana	61-75
Camping	45-68	Fencing	45-68
Hiding	45-68	Lockpicking	35-58
Mace Fighting	25-48	Parrying	55-78
Poisoning	35-58	Resisting Spells	55-78
Snooping	35-58	Stealing	45-68
Swordsmanship	35-58	Tactics	55-78
Wrestling	35-58		

Keywords bandit brigand crime
rob steal thief villain

Butcher

Strength	76-90	Hit Points	76-90
Dexterity	71-85	Stamina	71-85
Intelligence	61-75	Mana	61-75
Parrying	55-78	Resisting Spells	55-78
Tactics	55-78		
Desires	Gold (S)	Meat (C)	

Sells/Buys Bacon (S) Birds (raw) Chicken (legs)
Hams Knives Mutton (legs) Ribs (raw)
Sausages
Keywords beef butcher buy
cut fresh ham meat
poultry

Carpenter

Strength	71-85	Hit Points	71-85
Dexterity	66-80	Stamina	66-80
Intelligence	51-65	Mana	51-65
Carpentry	55-78	Parrying	45-68
Resisting Spells	45-68	Tactics	45-68
Desires	Wood (C)		

Sells/Buys Armoires (B) Benches (B) Chairs (B)
Boxes(wood) (B) Chests (B) Crates (B) Dovetails
Draw knives Drums Froes Hammers
Inshaves Logs (B) Lumber Lutes
Lyres Nails (S) Planes Saws
Scorps Shelves (B) Sticks Stools (B)
Tables (B) Tambourines
Keywords carpent chisel hammer
joining lumber nail plane
saw skill tool wood
woodcarving

Cobbler

Strength	36-50	Hit Points	36-50
Dexterity	36-50	Stamina	36-50
Intelligence	26-40	Mana	26-40
Desires	Leather (C)		

Sells/Buys Boots Hides (Cut, Llama, Pile) (B)
Sandals Shoes
Keywords boot cobbler hide
leather sandal shoe

Farmer

Strength	10	Hit Points	6
Dexterity	10	Stamina	30
Intelligence	10	Mana	6
Fencing	10	Mace Fighting	10
Parrying	30	Resisting Spells	30
Swordsmanship	10	Tactics	10
Wrestling	10		

Sells Apples Cabbage Cantaloupes
Carrots Corns Fresh eggs Gourds
Grain (bundles) Grapes Lemons Lettuce
Limes Melons Milk (pitchers) Onions
Peaches Pears Pumpkins Squash
Turnips Watermelons
Buys Grain (bundles) Kindling Flour (sacks)
Keywords crops farm hoe
plow plowshare rodents tools
vermin

Fur Trader

Strength	66-80	Hit Points	66-80
Dexterity	51-65	Stamina	51-65
Intelligence	41-55	Mana	41-55
Animal Lore	65-88	Camping	55-78
Parrying	45-68	Resisting Spells	55-78
Tactics	55-78		
Desires	Fur (C)		

Sells	Hides (pile)		
Buys	Birds (cooked)	Bread (loaves)	Cakes
Cheeses	Chicken legs	Cookies	Hides (pile)
Muffins	Mutton (cooked)	Pies (baked)	Ribs (cooked)
Stews	Tomato soup	Vegetables	

Keywords	animal	bird	bread
cake	camp	carrots	cheese
chicken	corn	creature	critter
fleece	food	hungry	lettuce
muffin	mutton	peas	pelt
pie	potatoes	ribs	skill
skin	soup	stew	wool

Gambler

For Hire	Daily Wage 40		
Strength	31-45	Hit Points	31-45
Dexterity	51-65	Stamina	51-65
Intelligence	56-70	Mana	56-70
Evaluating Intel.	45-68	Item Identif.	35-58
Parrying	25-48	Resisting Spells	25-48
Snooping	55-78	Stealing	35-58
Tactics	25-48		
Desires	Gambling (C)		

Keywords	appraise	evaluate	peek
cheat	gamble	game	skill

Glassblower

Strength	51-65	Hit Points	51-65
Dexterity	61-75	Stamina	61-75
Intelligence	51-65	Mana	51-65
Parrying	35-58	Resisting Spells	35-58
Tactics	35-58		

Sells/Buys	Flasks (empty) (S)		Jars (empty)
Glass pitchers	Vials (empty)		

Keywords	containers	glass	jar
objets d'art	vessels	vial	

Guard

Alignment	Good		
Strength	151-165	Hit Points	151-165
Dexterity	151-165	Stamina	151-165
Intelligence	151-165	Mana	151-165
Detecting Hidden	90-100	Fencing	90-100
Forensic Eval.	90-100	Mace Fighting	90-100
Parrying	90-100	Resisting Spells	90-100
Swordsmanship	90-100	Tactics	90-100
Wrestling	90-100		
Shelter	Guardposts (P)		
Desires	None		
Aversions	Anyone with negative notoriety (shows aggression)		

Standard guard:	plate armor, halberd
Blackthorn guard:	plate armor, red over-armor, double battle axe, chaos shield
Lord British guard:	plate armor, blue over-armor, Viking sword, order shield

Keywords	armor	armour	arrow
axe	bolt	bow	club
crossbow	dagger	guard	mace
pike	quarrel	shield	soldier
spear	sword	weapon	

Gypsy

Strength	41-55	Hit Points	41-55
Dexterity	51-65	Stamina	51-65
Intelligence	61-75	Mana	61-75
Begging	45-68	Camping	45-68
Hiding	45-68	Item Identif.	45-68
Lockpicking	45-68	Parrying	35-58
Resisting Spells	35-58	Snooping	45-68
Stealing	45-68	Tactics	35-58
Shelter	House (T)		
Desires	Stone (C)		

Keywords	appraise	camp	freeman
gypsie	gypsy	hide	lock
skill	steal	thief	thiev

Herbalist

Strength	21-35	Hit Points	21-35	
Dexterity	36-50	Stamina	36-50	
Intelligence	36-50	Mana	36-50	
Alchemy	35-58	Cooking	35-58	
Taste Identif.	35-58			
Desires	Herb (C)			

Sells/Buys   Blood moss   Flasks (S)   Garlic
Ginseng   Mandrake root   Mortars and pestles
Nightshade

Keywords   alchem   flower   herb
onion   poison   skill   taste

Jailor

Strength	96-110	Hit Points	96-110
Dexterity	96-110	Stamina	96-110
Intelligence	71-85	Mana	71-85
Parrying	75-98	Resisting Spells	75-98
Tactics	75-98		
Aversions	Traps		

Keywords   guard   jail   keeper
prison   prisoner   turnkey

Judge

Strength	66-80	Hit Points	66-80
Dexterity	61-75	Stamina	61-75
Intelligence	76-90	Mana	76-90
Evaluating Intel.	65-88	Forensic Eval.	45-68
Parrying	55-78	Resisting Spells	55-78
Tactics	55-78		

Keywords   court   judge

Magincia Council Member

Strength	41-55	Hit Points	41-55
Dexterity	41-55	Stamina	41-55
Intelligence	41-55	Mana	41-55
Parrying	25-48	Resisting Spells	25-48
Tactics	25-48		

Keyword   parliament

Magincia Servant

For Hire	Daily Wage 20		
Strength	16-30	Hit Points	16-30
Dexterity	21-35	Stamina	21-35
Intelligence	26-40	Mana	26-40

Keywords   labor   servant

Mayor

Strength	36-50	Hit Points	36-50
Dexterity	36-50	Stamina	36-50
Intelligence	51-65	Mana	51-65
Parrying	25-48	Resisting Spells	25-48
Tactics	25-48		

Keyword   mayor

Miller

Strength	41-55	Hit Points	41-55
Dexterity	36-50	Stamina	36-50
Intelligence	26-40	Mana	26-40

Sells/Buys   Grain (bundles)   Flour (sacks)

Keywords   flour   grain   mill
miller   oat   wheat

Minter

Strength	71-85	Hit Points	71-85
Dexterity	66-80	Stamina	66-80
Intelligence	66-80	Mana	66-80
Parrying	45-68	Resisting Spells	45-68
Tactics	45-68		

Keywords   coin   copper   currency
die   gold   mint   minter
money   plates   press   silver

Monk

Strength	21-35	Hit Points	21-35
Dexterity	36-50	Stamina	36-50
Intelligence	41-55	Mana	41-55
Evaluating Intel.	55-78		

Keywords   abbey   empath   knowledge
monk   relvinian   scholar   wisdom
wine

Noble

Strength	31-45	Hit Points	31-45
Dexterity	41-55	Stamina	41-55
Intelligence	51-65	Mana	51-65
Parrying	25-48	Resisting Spells	25-48
Tactics	25-48		
Aversions	Traps	Eerie items and places	
		Carnivores (3+ units / bite)	

Keywords   are you well   art thou well   blue-blood
diamond   gold   how are you   how art thee
how art thou   important   money   nobility
noble   wealth   wealthy blue blood
what is thy   what is your   what <any> do

Ocllo Cashual

Strength	61-75	Hit Points	61-75	
Dexterity	71-85	Stamina	71-85	
Intelligence	86-100	Mana	86-100	
Alchemy	55-78	Inscription	50-65	
Magery	86-100	Parrying	55-78	
Resisting Spells	65-88	Tactics	55-78	
Taste Identif.	55-78			
Spell Circle	7-8			
Desires	Magic (C)	Reagents (S)	Bone (S)	
	Daemon Bone(S)	Dirt (S)		
	Dragon Blood (S)	Serpent Scales(S)	Ink (S)	
	Silk (S)	Volcanic Ash (S)		
Sells	Marker talismans	Potions	Reagents	
Scrolls*	Scrolls (blank)	Spell books	Arcane items	

* Each shopkeeper cashual sells only those scrolls he or she is capable of creating. For example, a First Circle cashual sells only scrolls inscribed with First Circle spells, while a Fifth Circle cashual sells scrolls inscribed with spells from the First through Fifth Circles.

Keywords	book	cashual	mage
magic	potion	reagent	scroll
skill	spell		

Ocllo Priestess/Priest

Strength	41-55	Hit Points	41-55
Dexterity	51-65	Stamina	51-65
Intelligence	61-75	Mana	61-75
Parrying	35-58	Resisting Spells	35-58
Tactics	35-58		
Keywords	arpana	god	huansuytin
priest			

Ocllo Runner

Strength	26-40	Hit Points	26-40
Dexterity	31-45	Stamina	31-45
Intelligence	16-30	Mana	16-30
Keywords	cashual	message	runner

Peasant

For Hire	Daily Wage 10		
Strength	26-40	Hit Points	26-40
Dexterity	21-35	Stamina	21-35
Intelligence	16-30	Mana	16-30
Aversions	Traps	Eerie items and places	
Carnivores (3+ units / bite)			
Keyword	labor		

Pirate

For Hire	Daily Wage 70		
Strength	86-100	Hit Points	86-100
Dexterity	86-100	Stamina	86-100
Intelligence	71-85	Mana	71-85
Fencing	25-48	Mace Fighting	25-48
Parrying	65-88	Resisting Spells	65-88
Swordsmanship	55-78	Tactics	65-88
Wrestling	45-68		
Desires	Pirates (C)	Jewels (C)	
Keywords	captain <any> ?	matey	pirate
sail	sailor	scum	ship

Prisoner

Strength	11-25	Hit Points	11-25
Dexterity	11-25	Stamina	11-25
Intelligence	31-45	Mana	31-45
Shelter	Jail (P)		
Keywords	bail	escape	jail
prison	prisoner		

Rancher

Strength	36-50	Hit Points	36-50
Dexterity	34-48	Stamina	34-48
Intelligence	28-42	Mana	28-42
Animal Lore	55-78	Animal Taming	35-58
Herding	35-58	Veterinary	55-78
Sells	Horses (tame)		
Keywords	cattle	cow	horse
mount	ranch	steed	

Scribe

Strength	16-30	Hit Points	16-30
Dexterity	26-40	Stamina	26-40
Intelligence	31-45	Mana	31-45
Evaluating Intel.	45-68		

Sells/Buys	Books (large, small; blank, published)		
Ink	Pen	Scrolls (blank)	

Keywords	ink	knowledge	oppressor
relvinian	scholar	scribe	scroll
wisdom			

Sculptor

Strength	16-30	Hit Points	16-30
Dexterity	26-40	Stamina	26-40
Intelligence	21-35	Mana	21-35
Anatomy	25-48		

Keywords	carve	sculpt	statue

Shepherd(ess)

Strength	51-65	Hit Points	51-65
Dexterity	41-55	Stamina	41-55
Intelligence	31-45	Mana	31-45
Camping	55-78	Herding	55-78
Parrying	25-48	Resisting Spells	25-48
Tactics	25-48		
Desires	Sheep (S)		

Sells	Shepherd's crooks	Wool (raw)	

Buys	Birds (cooked)	Bread (loaves)	Cakes
Cheese	Chicken legs	Cookies	Hay
Muffins	Mutton (cooked)	Pies (baked)	Ribs (cooked)
Stews	Tomato soup	Vegetables (bowls)	

Keywords	sheep	shepherd	

Tanner

Strength	51-65	Hit Points	51-65
Dexterity	61-75	Stamina	61-75
Intelligence	41-55	Mana	41-55
Parrying	35-58	Resisting Spells	35-58
Tactics	35-58		
Desires	Leather (C)	Hide (C)	

Sells/Buys	Leather and studded leather armour		
Belts	Backpacks	Cut hides	Llama hides (B)
Pile hides (B)	Skinning knife		

Keywords	backpack	fur	gloves
hide	pouch		

Vegetable Seller

Strength	51-65	Hit Points	51-65
Dexterity	41-55	Stamina	41-55
Intelligence	31-45	Mana	31-45
Animal Lore	35-58	Herding	35-58
Parrying	25-48	Resisting Spells	25-48
Tactics	25-48	Veterinary	35-58

Sells/Buys	Apples	Cabbages (heads)	Cantaloupes
Carrots	Corn	Eggs	Gourds
Grain (bundles)	Grapes	Lemons	Lettuces
(heads)	Limes	Melons	Milk (pitchers)
Onions	Peaches	Pears	Pumpkins
Squash	Turnips	Watermelons	

Keywords	crops	farm	hoe
plow	plowshare	rodents	tools
vermin			

Veterinarian

Strength	56-70	Hit Points	56-70
Dexterity	56-70	Stamina	56-70
Intelligence	56-70	Mana	56-70
Animal Lore	55-78	Parrying	35-58
Resisting Spells	35-58	Tactics	35-58
Veterinary	55-78		

Sells	Bandages	Cats (tame)	Dogs (tame)
Horses (tame)			

Buys	Apples	Bandages	Birds (raw)
Carcasses	Carrots	Cloth (folded)	Grain (bundles)
Lettuce (heads)	Ribs (raw)		

Keywords	bear	bird	buy
cat	cure	dog	dragon
gorilla	heal	healing scrolls	help
horse	hurt	injured	llama
mount	mule	pet	poison
potion	potions	raise <any> dead	resurrect
resurrect	resurrection	steed	toxin
venom	vet		

Waitress/Waiter

Strength	36-50	Hit Points	36-50
Dexterity	36-50	Stamina	36-50
Intelligence	21-35	Mana	21-35

Sells	Ale (bottles)	Ale (pitchers)	Birds (cooked)
Bread (loaves)	Cheese	Cider (jugs)	Cider (pitchers)
Chickens	Glass pitchers	Liquor (bottles)	Liquor (pitchers)
Milk (pitchers)	Mutton (cooked)	Pies (baked)	Stews
Tomato soup	Vegetables	Water (pitchers)	Wine (bottles)
Wine (pitchers)			

Keywords	ale	cider	drink
food	server	service	waiter
waitperson	wine		

Town Cryer

MEDITATIONS ON THE LIFE OF A HEALER

By Eagle Spirit of Yew

The life of a healer can be thankless to the bitter extreme. 'Twas long a goal of mine to become an adept in the arts of healing. I struggled profusely and labored many long hours to master the brewing of healing potions, the casting of healing spells and the bandaging of wounds. My goal was to one day become capable of the greatest feat known to a healer — the resurrection of my fellow travellers.

Many sheep did I shear and many bolts of cloth did I weave to create bandages, which I applied to the wounded with care. I wandered for days among the humid swamps, braving all sorts of foul creatures to procure the ingredients for potions. With my work, I hoped to send travellers on their way with some measure of comfort should they fall victim to misfortune.

Aye, I never charged for my services. My conscience could not require something of others for what I could bestow as a gift — the precious holds of life and health. Nevertheless, donations from kind strangers kept me fed and clothed and helped to buy the supplies I needed as a healer.

One dark night, at the north gate to Trinsic, I heard a voice cry out in pain. As I walked north on the path, I spied a man near death, wearing the robes of recent tragedy. His belongings were strewn about him, and as I neared and attempted to help, I was set upon by two bandits who quickly reduced my world to darkness.

Without my belongings, I could not heal. I could not even shear a sheep for wool to make cloth, nor did I have the means to cut the cloth into bandages. My mortar and pestle were lost, as were my spellbook and reagents, and what little gold I had.

Yet I did not falter. There was little I could do but start afresh, and it cost me another life of gathering in the swamps. But, soon again, I was set upon uawares by a fearsome alligator. Were it not for a passing healer, I would not have been revived.

Slowly, painfully, I built up my profession again. I was unable to procure another spellbook or mortar and pestle, as my funds were limited. So I followed my life's work simply, healing only with bandages, and moved to the great fork where the roads to Minoc and Vesper and Britain meet.

'Twas here that I stood ready to aid weary travellers, and many I did heal. But I was to learn yet again of the sacrifices a healer must make. A traveller in gold and blue did pass, by the name of Vernex. Seeing that he was hurt, I offered to heal him. He accepted, and in return handed me a gleaming sword.

Though I am not by any means a fighter, I thought perhaps I could sell it for supplies, or another mortar and pestle. But as fate had shown me twice before, this was not to be. I saw him leave, and circle around in a nearby stand of willow trees. I watched him sneak into my backpack — a common occurrence in these times of lawlessness and chaos.

What came next caught me completely off guard. Though he wore plate, and I only a robe, he took great pleasure in shooting me with a crossbow from a distance. Thus, again, I fell. I watched as he plundered my corpse, and with dismay I saw that the only thing he left was the one thing I did not desire — the sword.

In my present days, I grow weary of the poison in the land. There was once a time when I thought I could heal some of the wounds and staunch a few tears. But after having fallen to the hands of those I struggled to save, I feel a dark and loathsome presence seeking to twist my mind toward anger and hatred, seeking to undo all for which I have struggled.

As I once more return to this mortal coil, I wonder how many more deaths I must endure. But I know that the lives I save will outnumber my deaths, and so I must persevere.

INFLUX BRINGS ECONOMIC CONSEQUENCES

By Fatman

Towns of Britannia are abuzz with talk of the many newcomers that have appeared in recent days. While many merchants at first have welcomed the newcomers as a chance to expand their clientele and turn greater profits, others are now worried about the long-term impact that such a mass immigration could have on the economy.

Blacksmiths as the whole are upbeat on the situation. Master Smith Gregor Ivanov of Trinsic summed it up as follows, "More adventurers mean more armour and swords! Methinks 'tis time to acquire a new apprentice ..."

On the other hand, weavers and tailors are expressing worries over growing competition. "I've 'eard tell that many of these adventurers are somewhat skilled in the arts of tailoring" stated Tailor Margeret Mandell. "Mark my words, they'll soon be setting up shop just outside my own — and then who will buy my clothes?"

Overall, there exists a strong concern that newcomers knowledgable in crafts and trades may put honest, well-established Britannian merchants out of work. The earnest work of adventurers may also result in a glut of foodstuffs, according to Butcher Reynold Eamon.

"All day long, I see warriors returing from the wilds with great hunks of deer and rabbit meat. Do they not realize that Britannia doesn't have that many mouths to feed? I'm having to salt and store most of what they sell to me now, and I barely have space for my sausage. It's a waste, I tell thee."

Farmer Blair of Britain agrees, but in a different sense. "Aye, I wish these adventurers would go back to killin' dragons and ettins and such. Tailors and carpenters! Why, in my day, ye'd be laughed out of the city if ye showed up with a sewin' kit and green trousers!"

Britain's royal economist, Sir Lovalet, has publicly made light of the situation, avowing that an increased populace can do no harm and would inject many thousands of gold pieces into the economy.

RELVINIAN THOUGHT RESPONSIBLE FOR MAZE

The Guild of Arcane Arts has focused a considerable amount of attention on the mysterious maze that appeared south of Britain two days ago, and they are finding more and more evidence pointing to Relvinian as the one responsible for its creation. "Relvinian is the only one who is both capable of the power needed to make this thing and whose whereabouts are currently unknown," said Turnius, guildmaster for the Guild. "And as it sprang up within a week of the disaster in Castle Britannia, I suspect that he's sequestered himself in the middle of it and doesn't want to come out."

The maze appeared three days ago, replacing valuable farmland and hunting habitat with what appears to be bits and pieces taken from all parts of Britannia. Creatures from all over the land seem attracted to the maze and wander about aimlessly inside it, according to sources who have briefly entered the place. "There were all kinds of monsters, and a bunch of brigands seem to have taken to it pretty quickly too. I guess they're counting on being safe from the law."

Relvinian was the mage responsible for the daemon attack inside Castle Britannia, and is, therefore, ultimately to blame for the fourteen deaths that occurred that night. Virgil Hassen, the lone survivor of the kitchen staff, who was crippled and seriously burned in the attack, said, ""An army needs to storm that maze and hang that mage on a short rope from a tall tree." When asked if he thought Relvinian had planned the attack inside the castle, Virgil replied, "I don't know. Sure. And don't say that name in my presence again."

An official scouting party is being formed by Lord British to try and map the maze, and to find out if Relvinian is, literally, at the center of it.

CLASSIFIEDS

NICE QUIET NEIGHBORHOOD, large three-room house in the middle of a usually quiet town. First reasonable offer accepted. Contact Adam in Minoc.

SINGLE MAST FRIGATE, good repair, only one year old. Supply your own crew. Owner wants a new career. Will trade for a bakery. Pastry ovens a plus. Contact One-Eye Fitzhugh in Trinsic.

Combat

Come hear the tale of Byrne of Yew
The stories he told, the Daemons he slew.
For valiant was he, and swiftest of swords,
But hardly, oh hardly, so quick with his words —
Recounts of his Exploits drug on through the night
As he hotly described each blow of each fight.

Now hear the sad cry of his Lady Irene,
Who quickly grew tired of the marvels he'd seen,
And left without warning while he was away,
To seek a new life by Britannia Bay.

But soon she would learn it was fighting she knew
('Twas all she had heard of from ol' Byrne of Yew),
So using her knowledge of weapons and gore,
She began training Fighters and Thugs by the score.

And she took most delight in dashing the Pride
Of brilliant young Warriors who eagerly tried
To craft stirring tales of their Fencing Renown,
When all they had fought was a doll stuffed with loam.

Her remedy? A trial — where all could see
A loudmouth defeated by silent Lady
For in but a moment, with a flick of her Kryss,
She'd slit ope' their trousers and blow them a kiss.

— Dag Errel

COMBAT SYSTEM

Although *Ultima Online* lets you pursue many peaceful career opportunities, combat can be an integral part of your gaming experience. Rule #1, however, is that fighting is not allowed inside towns. If any NPC sees or hears you fighting in the city, guards will inevitably show up to spoil your day. They're very tough, and few combatants can escape the consequences if caught fighting by a guard.

Physical and Magical Combat

Physical combat occurs anytime a player fights another player, an NPC or a monster. Blows are delivered through punches or weapon strikes. Armor or other protections (if available) absorb part of the damage. Fighting continues until one participant gives up or dies.

Magical combat works in essentially the same way. Not all spells are useful in combat, but many are — *Fireball, Meteor Swarm, Reactive Armor, Magic Arrow* and *Summon Elemental*, to mention a few. Other spells attack your opponent indirectly, such as *Clumsy* and *Mana Drain*. Both temporarily reduce your opponent's vital statistics, and thus, the ability to attack you.

How Combat Works

To initiate combat, your character must be in WAR mode. (This activates automatically if you're attacked.) If you have a weapon in hand, you fight with that weapon. If not (for instance, if your weapon is in your backpack), your *Wrestling* skill is automatically triggered. You can also cast attack spells if you have the reagents and the necessary spell inscribed in your spellbook. (For creatures, the attack skill is usually hand-to-hand *Wrestling* with tooth and claw.)

When you swing at a defender (another player, NPC or monster), the game follows this sequence:

1. Check for **weapon type/speed**
2. Check for **hit or miss**
3. Determine **base damage** (hit)
4. **Modify** damage
5. Check for **magical defenses**
6. Check for **shield and** *Parrying* **skill**
7. Determine **hit location**
8. Check for **armor**
9. **Apply** damage

Each step is explained in detail on the following pages.

1 — Check for Weapon Type/Speed

First, attack speeds are figured for each fighter. Attack speeds for the active weapons are based on each weapon's assigned speed (see weapons descriptions, beginning on p. 187) and each fighter's Dexterity.

$$\text{Attack Speed} = \frac{10{,}000}{(\text{Dexterity} + 100) \ \text{x Weapon Speed}}$$

You don't necessarily trade swings with your opponent — you simply strike as quickly as you can. For novice fighters with slow weapons, the time between swings can be as long as 5 seconds. Experienced players with higher-speed weapons can strive for up to two attacks per second. The table below lists sample strike speeds — seconds of delay between strikes.

Sample Strike Speeds

Examples	Weapon Speed	Attacker's Dexterity				
		5	25	50	75	100
Halberd	20	4.8	4.0	3.3	2.8	2.5
Battle Axe	40	2.4	2.0	1.7	1.4	1.3
Club	60	1.6	1.3	1.1	1.0	0.8
Skinning Knife	80	1.2	1.0	0.8	0.7	0.6

2 — Check for Hit or Miss

Whoever starts the fight gets to attack first. The chance of hitting is based on the attacker's ability is with the wielded weapon — reflected in specific weapon skills, such as *Fencing*, *Mace Fighting* and *Swordsmanship*. Success is also determined by the defender's ability and the attacker's *Tactics* skill with his or her weapon (See Tactics, p. 93.)

$$\text{Hit Chance} = \frac{(\text{Attacker's Weapon Ability} + 50)}{(\text{Defender's Weapon Ability} + 50) \ \text{x } 2}$$

Here are some examples of percentages. Note that regardless of the attacker's weapon ability, or the defender's lack of it, there's still a chance to hit.

		Defender's Ability				
Attacker's Ability		5	25	50	75	100
5		50	37	28	22	18
25		68	50	38	30	25
50		91	67	50	40	33
75		114	83	63	50	42
100		136	100	75	60	50

(% Chance to Hit)

A successful strike helps you learn and improves your combat-based skills. If you miss, your skills don't improve, but your target's defensive battle skills do.

If you're much more skilled than your opponent, you probably can't really improve your attack skills during the fight. Conversely, if you're evenly matched with your opponent, or slightly less skilled, you'll gain the most improvement.

3 — Determine Base Damage (Hit)

Once a hit is successful, the base damage is randomly determined from the weapon's range of damage. A war axe, for example, inflicts anywhere from 4 to 36 points of damage. See **Weapon, Clothing and Armor Descriptions**, p. 186

4 — Modify Damage

After base damage is determined, it is then modified.

Strength adds from 1 to 20% additional weapon damage, depending on your current strength.

$$\frac{\text{Strength}}{5} = \text{\% Bonus Damage}$$

5 — Check for Magical Defenses

Magical items or spells always have first chance at reducing or increasing damage. *Reactive Armor* can reflect damage from physical attacks. This means that if you're wearing bone armor with a *Reactive Armor* charge, the *Reactive Armor* reflects that damage back at the attacker.

If a magical weapon is being used for an attack, one charge is subtracted now, and damage is delivered similarly to a physical attack.

6 — Check for Shield and Parrying Skill

If the defender uses a shield, the chance of blocking a blow is half of the defender's *Parrying* skill. For example, if your *Parrying* skill is 76, there's a 38% chance of catching an attack on your shield. (*Parrying* only affects your skill with your shield. If you aren't using one, *Parrying* won't help.)

If your shield misses the blow, the shield isn't damaged, and all damage passes directly to your armor (and possibly your body).

If the blow is deflected, the shield absorbs damage. This is figured by subtracting the shield's armor from the attack damage. A Buckler shield has an armor rating of 7. This means that if a 25-point attack hits the shield, the shield takes absorbs 7 points of damage and the remaining 18 points pass through to your body.

If a shield is hit and absorbs damage, it will probably lose one hit point to wear and tear.

7 — Determine Hit Location

Any damage that gets past the shield attacks a specific part of the body. If armor protects that location, the armor absorbs at least part of the damage. If the defender is wearing only clothing, the clothing absorbs a minimal amount of the damage. Any other damage that gets through attacks the character directly.

Hits cannot be targeted to a specific location — where a successful hit strikes is randomly determined:

Location	% Chance	Protective Armor
Torso	44%	Chest/breast plate*
Arms	14%	Arm plates
Head	14%	Helmet
Legs/Feet	14%	Leg plates
Neck	7%	Gorget
Hands	7%	Gloves

* A chain mail tunic covers both the torso and arms.

Note: Dresses, capes, cloaks and shirts cover the torso; pants and skirts cover the legs and feet.

8 — Check for Armor

Once a location is determined, the game checks for protective covering there. Although you can wear multiple pieces of armor (or armor and clothing) on the same location, only the item with the highest armor value is checked when you're hit. Stacking pieces of armor has no additional effect.

Each piece of armor has an armor value. Additionally, each piece of armor is capable of absorbing a range of damage per hit. The damage that can be absorbed is a random amount falling between half and all of the armor's armor value. Excess damage (if there is any) strikes the defender's body, subtracting that many hit points.

For instance, bone armor arm plates have an armor rating of 30. This means they can absorb from 15 to 30 points of damage each time they're hit. If damage is no greater than 15, the arm plates absorb all the damage without harming the arm beneath the plate. If damage is greater than 30, at least part of the blow injures the defender.

If damage is between 15 and 30, the arm plate absorbs at least 15 points, and possibly as much as 30 points. A 25-point blow will be fully absorbed about a third of the time. Otherwise, the excess damage is inflicted on the defender.

Creatures have natural "armor" (fur, hide or whatever). It absorbs damage like man-made armor, but never wears out.

9 — Apply Damage

To character. Whatever damage is not deflected by shields, armor or clothing affects the body directly. This damage is subtracted from the character's hit points. Magic effects and the effects of poisoned weapons are also applied at this time.

To equipment. Each shield and piece of armor also has hit points — each time you're hit, this subtracts from the shield's and/or armor's condition. You might lose a point or two every time something strikes your armor. (The exact amount is random.)

On the attacker's side, one point of damage may be applied to the attacking weapon to reflect normal wear and tear. Weapons and armor can be repaired by an armourer or weaponsmith, or you can learn how to repair them yourself. However, they wear out over time, and eventually repairs don't help.

If you unsuccessfully try to repair an object, you'll further damage it.

WEAPONS, ARMOR AND CLOTHING

As with every other aspect of *Ultima Online*, these descriptions are subject to change. In addition, there might be items with extreme attributes that go beyond the values listed here (either extremely good *or* extremely bad).

Ranges of numbers. If the value listed is a range (for example, 15-38), that stat will vary from creature to creature (or NPC to NPC) between the two numbers.

Damage (weapons). How much damage the weapon can inflict with each blow.

HP. How much damage the item can sustain before becoming completely useless.

Spd (weapons). The speed with which the weapon can be wielded. (Lower numbers are better.)

Skill Req. (weapons). What skill is used with the weapon.

Str. The minimum Strength a character must have to use or wear this item.

Two-Handed? (weapons). Whether two hands must be used to wield the weapon. (If so, a shield cannot be used in conjunction with the weapon.)

AR (armor and clothing). The armor defense of the item.

Weapons

Practice Weapons

If any new character is supplied with a weapon (because of a skill selected) that weapon will always be a starting variant of the usual weapon. Its stats differ from the usual weapons as follows: **Damage** is 2-8 and **Strength** required is 10.

Axes

Weapon	Damage	HP	Spd	Skill	Req. Str.	Two-Hands?
Executioner's Axe	4-28	31-90	50	Swordsmanship	35	Yes
Axe	4-28	31-80	40	Swordsmanship	25	Yes
Large Battle Axe	4-36	31-110	20	Swordsmanship	45	Yes
Double Axe	7-31	31-110	35	Swordsmanship	35	Yes
Hatchet	5-23	31-80	55	Swordsmanship	15	
Pickaxe	4-32	31-60	40	Fencing	25	
Two-Handed Axe	4-32	31-70	30	Swordsmanship	40	Yes
War Axe	8-33	31-80	35	Mace Fighting	35	Yes

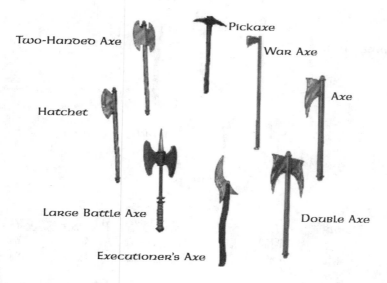

Two-Handed Axe · Pickaxe · War Axe · Hatchet · Axe · Large Battle Axe · Executioner's Axe · Double Axe

Knives and Daggers

Weapon	Damage	HP	Spd	Skill	Req. Str.	Two-Hands?
Butcher Knife	2-8	31-40	80	Swordsmanship	5	
Cleaver	3-12	31-50	70	Swordsmanship	10	
Dagger	3-12	31-40	55	Fencing	1	
Kryss	6-18	31-90	50	Fencing	10	
Skinning Knife	2-8	31-40	80	Swordsmanship	5	

Kryss · Cleaver · Butcher's Knife · Skinning Knife · Dagger

Maces and Hammers

Weapon	Damage	HP	Spd	Skill	Req. Str.	Two-Hands?
Club	3-12	31-40	60	Mace Fighting	10	
Hammer Pick	9-33	31-70	30	Mace Fighting	35	Yes
Mace	4-16	31-70	55	Mace Fighting	20	
Maul	9-21	31-70	40	Mace Fighting	20	
Smithy Hammer	4-16	31-60	60	Mace Fighting	30	
War Hammer	4-36	31-110	20	Mace Fighting	40	Yes
War Mace	6-34	31-110	30	Mace Fighting	30	

Maul War Hammer

Hammer Pick Club

War Mace Mace Smithy Hammer

Pole Arms

Weapon	Damage	HP	Spd	Skill	Req. Str.	Two-Hands?
Bardiche	7-35	31-100	30	Swordsmanship	40	Yes
Halberd	4-48	31-80	20	Swordsmanship	45	Yes

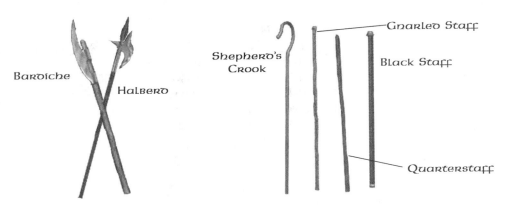

Gnarled Staff

Shepherd's Crook

Black Staff

Bardiche Halberd

Quarterstaff

Staves

Weapon	Damage	HP	Spd	Skill	Req. Str.	Two-Hands?
Black Staff	7-23	31-70	35	Mace Fighting	35	Yes
Gnarled Staff	9-21	31-50	40	Mace Fighting	20	Yes
Quarterstaff	6-18	31-60	50	Mace Fighting	30	
Shepherd's Crook	3-12	31-50	70	Mace Fighting	10	Yes

Swords

Weapon	Damage	HP	Spd	Skill	Req. Str.	Two-Hands?
Broad Sword	5-25	31-100	35	Swordsmanship	25	
Cutlass	6-18	31-70	45	Swordsmanship	10	
Katana	4-20	31-90	40	Swordsmanship	10	
Long Sword	4-28	31-110	35	Swordsmanship	25	
Scimitar	6-22	31-90	45	Swordsmanship	10	
Viking Sword	4-32	31-100	35	Swordsmanship	40	

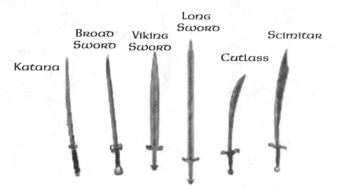

Spears and Forks

Weapon	Damage	HP	Spd	Skill	Req. Str.	Two-Hands?
Pitchfork	5-20	31-60	50	Fencing	15	Yes
Short Spear	7-19	31-70	55	Fencing	15	
Spear	7-27	31-80	30	Fencing	30	
War Fork	4-28	31-110	35	Fencing	35	

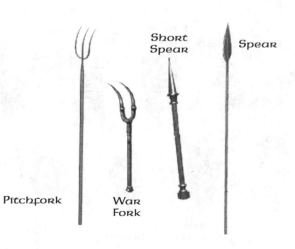

Bows and Crossbows

Weapon	Damage	HP	Spd	Skill	Req. Str.	Two-Hands?
Bow	9-24	31-60	20	Archery	20	Yes
Crossbow	6-26	31-80	20	Archery	30	Yes
Heavy Crossbow	6-34	31-100	20	Archery	40	Yes

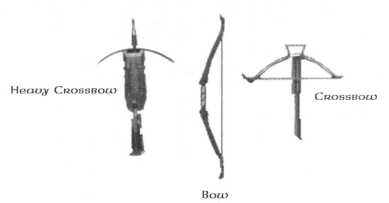

Heavy Crossbow   Crossbow

Bow

Shields

Shield	AR	HP	Req. Str.
Buckler	7	41-51	15
Chaos Shield	32	101-115	0
Heater Shield	23	31-37	30
Metal Shield	11	51-65	15
Kite Shield (wooden)	16	46-58	30
Order Shield	30	101-115	0
Round Bronze Shield	10	26-30	20
Kite Shield (metal)	12	101-115	20
Wooden Shield	8	21-23	5

Kite Shield
(metal)   Heater

Chaos Shield

Metal Shield

Buckler

Kite
Shield
(wooden)

Wooden
Shield

Order
Shield

Round
Bronze
Shield

ARMOR

(Many pieces of armor specifically conform to a male or female body. This distinction doesn't affect any of the stats listed below, so those pieces are not split into two listings.)

Bone

Armor	AR	HP	Req. Str.
Armor (Breast Plate)	30	26-30	40
Arm Plates	30	26-30	40
Gauntlets	30	26-30	40
Helm	30	26-30	40
Leg Plates	30	26-30	40

Chainmail

Armor	AR	HP	Req. Str.
Coif	23	36-44	20
Leggings	23	46-58	20
Tunic*	23	46-58	20

*A chainmail tunic protects the arms as well as the torso.

Leather

Armor	AR	HP	Req. Str.
Gloves	13	31-37	10
Gorget	13	101-115	10
Leggings	13	31-37	10
Sleeves	13	31-37	10
Tunic	13	31-37	15
Cap	13	31-37	15

Plate

Armor	AR	HP	Req. Str.
Sleeves	30	51-65	40
Breast	30	51-65	60
Gauntlets	30	51-65	30
Gorget	30	51-65	30
Helm	20	46-58	40
Leggings	30	51-65	60

Ringmail

Armor	AR	HP	Req. Str.
Gauntlets	20	41-51	20
Leggings	20	41-51	20
Sleeves	20	41-51	20
Tunic	20	41-51	20

Studded Leather

Armor	AR	HP	Req. Str.
Armor	15	101-115	20
Gloves	16	36-44	25
Gorget	16	36-44	25
Leggings	16	36-44	35
Sleeves	16	36-44	25
Tunic	16	36-44	35

Additional Helmets

Armor	AR	HP	Req. Str.
Bascinet	18	101-115	10
Closed Helm	22	101-115	20
Helmet	15	51-65	0
Nose Helm	22	101-115	0
Orc Helm	20	31-70	0

Bascinet

Closed Helm

Orc Helm

Helmet

 Nose Helm

Clothing

Clothing	AR	HP
Apron (Full)	4	21-30
Apron (Half)	4	21-25
Bandana	1	21-23
Belt	1	11-40
Cloak	5	11-40
Doublet	3	11-40
Dress	5	21-30
Hats*	3	21-23
Jester's Suit	7	11-40
Kilt	3	21-24
Knee Boots (Black)	7	21-29
Mask (Bear)	6	21-23
Mask (Deer)	6	21-23
Mask (Tribal)	5	21-23
Pants (Fancy)	4	11-40
Pants (Short)	3	11-40
Robe	7	11-40
Sash	1	11-40
Shirt (Fancy)	4	21-23
Shirt (Poor) (no arms)	3	21-23
Shoes (also sandals)	3	21-25
Skirt	4	21-24
Skullcap	1	51-60
Thigh Boots	6	21-33
Tunic (has arms)	3	11-40

*bonnet, cap, feathered hat, floppy hat, jester hat, jester's cap, straw hat, tall straw hat, tricorne hat, wide-brim hat, wizard's hat

The 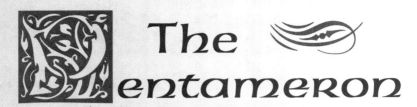 Pentameron

of Andrew P. Morris

 ood reader, what you have before you is not original material. Rather, it is five tales of mirth and moral performed by the greatest storytellers of the land in honor of Lord British's thirty-sixth birthday, and then recorded by this humble scribe (with but slight stylistic embellishment, I assure you). It is done so in the interest of posterity for our king's future enjoyment and, mayhaps more importantly, for the amusement of any unfortunate enough to miss our liege's exciting celebration. Each story contains not only elements of danger and excitement, but also perhaps a bit of insight into the dealings and difficulties faced daily within our very society. Read on, good lords and ladies, both young and old, and see what lessons may be learned to help you succeed in the roles of life that you play.

The Tale of the Guild Master

he flames from the logs crackled and frisked about the inside of the fireplace as the woman stood before the mantle, seemingly concentrating on the very stones of the wall. Though no longer wearing her hauberk and coif, her left hand resting on the hilt of her sword gave away her profession. Seated at the small table by the door were two men, also warriors.

"Guild Master?" asked the first.

She turned to regard them, her pursed lips an obvious sign that she still focused more on her thoughts than on her audience.

"Guild Master, we need an answer," urged the other male. "The Knights of the Ankh have shown us great dishonor. Do we issue challenge or not?"

Both fighters looked anxiously at each other, yet another minute passed before the woman responded.

"I have spent years fighting wars for other people," she began. "My first post was with a caravan, where little more than food and a sleeping pallet was my pay to fend off brigands. I've since battled headlesses, ogres and drakes. I've even faced the undead skeletons of warriors I had slain the very day before."

"Aye, Guild Master."

"And yet never have I known such an outrage as what you say the Knights have done. Our guilds were formed for the very same purpose, to help spread Lord British's ideals throughout Britannia. But now they speak blasphemy towards the very king himself! Why, to challenge them would be like challenging siblings. Yet such words cannot go unpunished." With her final statement, the Guild Master leaned on the table, looking her lieutenants in the eyes. "We are warriors all, and warriors we shall die, one day or another. Send notice to all our members — tomorrow we, the Protectors of Virtue, demonstrate our loyalty to the realm, and put an end to the Knights of the Ankh."

"Aye, Guild Master."

It did not take long for the news to spread to the other guild members, and by noon fighting had already started. The skirmishes in the streets were small, for neither side wished to draw attention from the guards, but in the surrounding countryside, the ringing of steel on steel was a common sound. But even after a month had passed, the conflict had not ended.

"The listing of the dead, Guild Master," the lieutenant said, handing her the scroll as she paced within her office.

She took the parchment, unrolled the skin, and began to read the names of the deceased. As the lieutenant turned to leave, she stopped him at the door.

"Wait, warrior. These dozen names at the end ... I know them not. They are members of our guild?"

"Guild Master?" The fighter peered at the list. "Nay, milady, they are not."

Her questioning look told him to continue.

"Conscripts, Guild Master."

"I do not understand. The Protectors of Virtue do not take 'conscripts.'"

"Our members battle with heart and soul, Guild Master. It takes much to keep morale high between battles ..."

"I know about the effects of warfare, lieutenant," she said between clenched teeth. "What does this have to do with forced membership?"

"Well, Guild Master, when some of the others are on hunt, they are oft times inclined to stop any who cross their path, and," he paused in anticipation of her wrath, "those who do not declare loyalty to the Protectors are put to the blade."

"What?" she asked with alarming coldness.

"They are given a choice ... to join the guild as friend, or be slaughtered as foe."

"By the Virtues, what have I done?" the Guild Master exclaimed as she sank to her chair. She swallowed hard and then spoke plainly.

"This will stop, Lieutenant. The challenge was made by our

guild, and our guild alone. We chose to band together to further our cause, not to bully peasants. It is our fight, and if we cannot face it alone, we do not deserve to win. When I gave command to confront the Knights of the Ankh, my intent was to defend the welfare of the people of Britannia, not threaten it. You will control your warriors, Lieutenant, and if you cannot, you will answer to me."

"Aye, Guild Master."

As the lieutenant moved for the second time to leave, a knock came from the door.

"Enter," said the Guild Master.

The door opened and in walked half a dozen royal guards. The captain stepped forward to speak.

"Guild Master of the Protectors of Virtue, you have brought bloodshed into the town of Trinsic, and as leader of your guild you are hereby charged by order of the King with multiple counts of slaughter. You are to come with us." Turning to the lieutenant, he added, "you are now charged with the leadership of this guild. It is not a role to be taken lightly. I suggest you consider the larger ramifications of any actions you or your guild may take in the future, for as your Guild Master has just learned, it is easier to inspire and enforce ideals within one man, than in many."

This story focuses on the hazards sometimes hidden to those inexperienced with the responsibilities of leadership like the Guild Master. It demonstrates the need to imagine the consequences resulting from one's actions, and of realizing how widespread they might be. This is an excellent example of the decisions Lord British must make on a daily basis, but applies equally well to any leader of nearly any sized group.

The Tale of the Merchant

o War."

Basilio held his wine glass high, waiting for the man across the table to raise his drink in return salute.

"To War," replied the other, and both drank.

"Tell me, Basilio," he asked, setting his glass on the polished oak desk, "what is it about this guild war that pleases you so?"

A wry smile crossed the merchant's face, but he paused to check the sleeve ties of his robe before responding, seemingly to let the question sit momentarily before sharing his wisdom.

"What pleases me so? Why, I will tell you, my friend. Gold. Gold is what makes this petty war so welcome to me."

"You speak of profit, obviously, but from where? How?"

"Why, from the very guilds themselves. Ah, I see by your puzzled look I must explain." Basilio reached for the carafe of wine. "The Protectors of Virtue have challenged The Knights of the Ankh, yes? And so they battle. And those who battle need arms and armour, yes? So they come to me. It is a simple matter of demand."

"But you are not the only merchant to sell weapons and armour to one of the guilds. Why do you seem to profit so much more than the others?"

"Ah, and there you have it, my friend. I do not sell to 'one' of the guilds — I sell to both. I have found a few scavengers who are willing to collect what the dead lose in these battles. They bring the arms to me, I pay them a modest price, and then sell them again to either guild at a profit. Of course, since I rarely have to make new wares, I can sell more in less time, so I can afford to charge a little less than everyone else. Thus, I get more business. Same cost outlay for me, double the customers, half the time ... it adds up. See," Basilio shrugged, palms held upward, "who is hurt but my competitors?"

"Ingenious," admitted the companion. "To war, then!"

"To war —" again Basilio raised his glass, but stopped his words mid-sentence. "What is that noise coming from outside?"

His friend opened the shuttered windows to the din below.

"Apparently, the fighting is over. I can see warriors with markings from both guilds shaking hands and banging shields. I would say your bit of profiteering has come to an end."

Basilio's brow furrowed for a moment, then with a sigh he took a drink.

"'Tis little matter. There will always be conflict. If not in our city, than with the orcs in the hills, or trolls in the mountains, or the brigands on the plains. My profits will drop to normal, but I have driven enough others out of business that I can keep up with the demand at little cost to myself. As long as the guilds continue to purchase from me, I am set."

"Then perhaps you should take a look outside this window, Basilio. I see the fighters trading weapons with each other, and there seems to be recognition on their faces, as if they are reclaiming the arms of brothers lost."

Basilio's eyes grew wide.

"Indeed, the Guild Masters themselves are inspecting the pommels of their swords. I think they are comparing the blacksmiths' markings, Basilio."

Basilio rose to his feet with a look of panic, his hands pulling his gown around him protectively.

"And now they point and come this direction. Basilio, I think they come to speak with you. Basilio?"

But Basilio was gone.

This interesting tale illustrates the error of practicing indifference and exploitation, especially at the misfortune of others. In a world sometimes as harsh and violent as ours, there is little long-term benefit gained from taking advantage of one's fellow men and women, and will ultimately, in fact, lead to one's ruin. Lord British was particular pleased with this anecdote for its example of the fallacy of greed.

The Tale of the Bard

nother round, Caleb?"

"My thanks, Dennal. Singing is thirsty work." The bard reached for the tankard.

"Not much of a crowd this eve, I'm afraid. Traffic to the city is light now that rumors of the liche have reached Jhelom. How flows the gold?"

"Well, let me phrase it thus — is the cot in the pantry taken?"

"Now, Caleb, you know better than that," replied the tavernkeeper, running a rag along the oaken bar top, "as long as you are singing here, you have a bed."

"Again, my thanks, Dennal. As usual."

"But ..." Dennal picked at a splinter along the edge of the bar.

"Aye, friend?"

"Well, I could use a bit of help in a matter other than coin."

"Speak plainly, friend."

"We've had a bit of trouble here lately. Trouble with the guilds."

Caleb's brow rose in surprise, but then slowly his lips curled into a grin.

"Trouble here, at the Quail? So the miller's been pressing you for his share of your efforts, eh? A little spittle in the flour if you don't send more gold his direction. Perhaps followed by a thrashing with the rolling pin?" he added with a wink.

"Nay, Caleb." The absence of a smile on the tavernkeeper's face meant he considered the situation quite serious. "I'm not speaking of the service guilds. I mean the mercenary guilds."

"The mercenary guilds, as in all of them?"

"No, no. Just two. The Knights of the Ankh and the Protectors of Virtue."

"But I thought Lord British's men put that feud to an end."

"Aye, in the city. But here they are less concerned about interference from the guards. Both sides have begun to frequent the Quail much more often this past week, and last night a fistfight nearly started over a spilled drink."

"And how is it that I can help you?" asked Caleb, already guessing the answer.

"With that silver tongue of yours, lad. I've seen you keep an angry mother from taking the lash to her noisy children, and I'll never forget the time you calmed Adrianna when she found Wilton with the scullery maid." For the first time since the topic had moved to the guilds, Dennal smiled. "We thought he was fodder certain as goblins have fleas!"

"Well, I make no promise, but I will do what I can."

"Well and good, Caleb. I can ask no more."

The bard finished his ale and returned to his stool in the corner, where he began to sing a love song. As the time for the evening meal drew nearer, the Quail became a bit more crowded, and Caleb's purse became a bit fuller. Still, Caleb was concerned, for the majority of the patrons were not local farmers, but mercenaries from the city. No doubt something was planned for the evening. Judging by the look on Dennal's face, he was thinking the very same thing.

As expected, the insults started flying by the third round of drinks. In response, Caleb began to play softer, more soothing pieces, hoping to pacify the crowd. It seemed to work, at least for a little while. But as more of the regulars departed, and more members of the opposing guild factions filled the establishment, the effects of his calming music began to wane.

Sensing the increasing tension, Caleb called out, "How about a jig?" As the bard began to play, one of the patrons grabbed a serving wench and swung into step. Soon, those who had had enough to drink were dancing, and those who hadn't were drinking more.

But the ruse didn't last long, for when drunks dance, dancers collide. And when hot-tempered warriors collide, trouble follows. Just as the first mug was raised to be brought down on another's head, Caleb stuck two fingers in his mouth and whistled. All turned their eyes toward him.

"I see we have a bit of a conflict here, my lords and ladies."

"No trouble, troubadour, just some cleaning that needs doing," someone in the back called out, to the cheers of some and the growls of others.

"Ah, so it is cleaning you wish. Excellent! Though I must confess, never before have I seen such fine sword arms on maids before ..."

A mercenary's eyes flashed in anger and he started to push toward the stool, but a comrade chuckled and slapped him on the back. The minstrel continued.

"Surely cleanliness is a worthy endeavor, but hardly lucrative."

"This is not about gold, bard."

"I beg your pardon, good lady," said Caleb. "I did not realize this fight is about love."

"Nay, this is not about love, either."

"Oh, then, 'tis about truth."

"Nay, 'tis not about truth," came the reply, following some muttering from the crowd.

"Not about love, not about truth? Well, then it must be about courage!"

Upon those words, several shouts filled the room, but Caleb did not falter.

"But it could not be about courage, for the fight is between men, not man and beast. And there is certainly nothing more heroic than slaying some loathsome beast!"

A little more shouting, and a little more muttering, but all were still listening.

"So, no one is fighting over a love, in search of the truth, or with great courage. Thus, you must be fighting for money, else why risk your lives when nothing of value is at stake. Right?"

Much less shouting, and much more muttering.

"I ask again, are not those the most important reasons to wage war?"

This time the response verged on agreement.

"So without the tremendous benefits earned from fighting over one of those four reasons, is there anything gained by fighting for any other reason?"

"Your words are just words," said one mercenary, stepping forward from the others. "They do nothing to change the dishonor cast upon us by the foul Knights!"

"Nor do they give us less reason to crush the Protectors," declared another fighter, pulling the leg off a nearby chair.

"True," admitted Caleb. "My speech has done nothing to mitigate your desire for revenge, nor to make you think this fight is not worth your efforts. However, my speech has done one very important thing."

"And what's that?" shouted yet another mercenary, ready for the brawl.

"Why, it has delayed you long enough to give Dennal's young son time to return with the guards," Caleb replied with a smirk. "And I suggest you cooperate with them fully."

That said, the bard lifted his lute and began to play a pleasant ballad about truth, love, courage and gold.

This light-hearted story reveals the value of wit and charm above anger and violence. It shows how simple it can be to ignore reason when ingrained hatred fills one's soul, and yet how reason can be used avoid a dangerous situation. I seem to remember Lord British once telling of a companion of his being in a similar situation, and of using rhetoric and wordplay to confuse a hostile audience.

The Tale of the Mage

o, you wish for me, Morkidan the Great, to journey with you to the liche's tower, whereupon I will cast a powerful spell of death and destroy the foul creature, at which point in time you will fall about yourselves claiming the glory. Do I understand you correctly?"

"Aye."

"Yes."

"Exactly, milord."

The small band of adventurers standing before the skilled wizard spoke first, and then confirmed with each other before nodding their agreement.

"Very well, then," continued the mage. "You realize, of course, that this requires a considerable amount of gold, yes?"

"Aye."

"Yes."

"Of course, milord."

"Fine, then. I agree to your terms," said Morkidan. "First I will need a few days to ensure I have the proper reagents for my magics, and then we may be off. I will send word to you at your inn when I am ready. Go now, for we are done."

With that, the band departed, and Morkidan bid his servants to set about locating the requisite components for his spell, as well as preparing a really comfortable sleeping roll. Most of what the powerful spellcaster needed was procured immediately, save one rather significant item.

"What do you mean we have no sulphurous ash?" he bellowed at the apprentice before him.

"Begging your pardon, Master, but we used the last ounce creating the illusionary gold that went toward paying your debt to the brothel —"

"Never you mind that, fool! We have to find some, and find it soon."

"Again begging the Master's pardon, Master, but perhaps some scrapings from from the Brazier of Enchanting? 'Tis an inferior amount, but certainly one so skilled as you are, Master, could draw full power from within it."

"Hmmm ...," mused the mage, "perhaps indeed. All right, then, scrape the remnant from the Brazier and put it in my pouch. Once that is done, send a page to inform that band of misfits at the Wayfarer's Inn that we will be leaving in the morrow."

At dawn the next morning, Morkidan set off with the adventurers toward the countryside, where the liche was said to be terrorizing the locals with his undead minions.

Along the way they encountered many villagers and farmers, all of whom were quite pleased to see that something was being done to rid the land of the liche scourge. Three days passed before the horror's lair was spied by their scout. They camped briefly to sharpen their blades and tighten their armour straps, while Morkidan mixed the ash with the other reagents required for his spell of death.

Then they were ready. The warriors rushed the gates of the tower, while the scouts skirted the edges to flank any guardians. Morkidan stood bravely behind several large stones. But the liche was just as ready.

As the portal to its home swung wide to release skeletal defenders, the liche drew an intricate pattern in the air with its hands, summoning bolts of lightning from the sky to rain upon the bold adventurers. Morkidan took that moment to begin the gesturing that would create his powerful Death Vortex. He flailed his arms wildly and called out the words of power.

"Vas Corp Hur!"

Then Morkidan reached into the bag of reagents and scattered the mixed components into the air. Soon ... nothing happened.

Morkidan stared with amazement at that which he had not wrought.

"Vas Corp Hur!" he yelled again, following it with the appropriate gestures.

Again, nothing happened. No swirling mist, no black cloud, not even a hint of gray steam.

"Bedeviled brazier ash!" Morkidan shouted at his apprentice, who was still at his master's house in Britain, pleasantly enjoying some imported venison.

"What?" called out the others, struggling to keep the mass of bony death at bay.

"Er, nothing," came Morkidan's not quite so reassuring reply. With another wave and different words of power, he disappeared from behind the rocks and reappeared in his laboratory, exactly upon the Mark to which his Recall spell was linked.

To this day, Morkidan politely warns any who journey to the countryside to beware of the liche in the tower, and should anyone come across any sulphurous ash, he gladly pays double the normal cost in gold.

This humorous story imparts a lesson involving the importance of preparation, and of trust. As many a baker will tell you, there is no substitute for ingredients when preparing a birthday cake, but even the most conceited tells the birthday boy when honey replaces glazed sugar, for who knows what fear of bears the boy may have.

The Tale of the Burglar

Thylena carefully slipped the knife blade between the two shutters and gently lifted the latch. Precariously perched on the thin ledge of the second-floor window, she again questioned the wisdom of stealing into the home of a wizard, pleading to unknown forces that no magical ward secured the entrance. Fate granted her wish and the shutters opened easily and quietly. Odd, thought Thylena, rumor has it that this Morkidan is quite protective of his house.

Gently lowering herself to the floor, Thylena's soft-soled boots made little sound as they touched the stone below. Leaving the shutters open, she paused a moment to let her eyes become accustomed to the small amount of light coming through the window from the starlit night. She was in a hallway. She knew better than to trust the map sold to her by one of the old mage's apprentices, yet she had no other information on which to base her decisions. Somewhere left of the main corridor was where, according to what she had memorized, the laboratory was located, and where the Brazier was supposedly kept.

Thylena walked slowly across the tiles, her eyes darting back and forth along the walls in search of trap-triggers she knew she would not be able to perceive. But it was too risky to light a candle. She reached the end of the hall and found a pair of doors. She pushed on the handle of the right door, but it did not open, obviously locked. She got the same result from the left door. She would need light after all. With a soft sigh, she removed her gloves and pulled a candle and the set of lock picks from her belt. With a stick of flint which she ran along the tile, she lit the candle. The hallway was surprisingly austere for a man who was said to be so wealthy. She let enough wax drip on the floor to ensure the candle would stand upright and then set upon the task of picking the lock. It, too, opened quite easily ... disturbingly easily. She decided to open the door before blowing out the candle.

Before her was a library, filled with floor-to-ceiling bookshelves. She pried the candle loose — no need to worry that she was leaving wax behind, for once the Brazier was gone, that alone would be evidence that the house had been violated — and entered the room, closing the door behind her. Now where would that hidden latch be? The secret door to a wizard's laboratory was always located in the library, and the stories she had heard indicated that Morkidan's home would be no exception.

First she looked along the bookshelves for the unique book that was set just so, but noticed nothing there. Next were the sconces. No, this library had only candelabras. Ah, the desk. With supple gloves again on her hand, she ran her fingers along the center drawer. Finding nothing suspicious, she pried open the drawer with her blade. Aside from some vellum and dry quills, it was empty. Scanning the top of the desk, she came across a small well of ink (from an octopus, no doubt). Why was it also not in the drawer? She took one of the quills and dipped it in the ink well, pressing deeply. There it was, that familiar click of a door unlatching and coming open. When will these wizards ever learn?

She pulled on the shelf that had moved ever so slightly inwards and was faced with a long, steep staircase. Thylena moved the candle to her left hand, drew her sword, and then cautiously began to descend the stairs. It definitely led past the first floor and below the street outside, perhaps even more than one story below ground, and ended at a large, iron door. Tilting her head so the candle wouldn't burn her honey-colored tresses when she put it in her mouth, she pushed on the door handle. The door gave way easily, but the sound from the top of the stairs indicated that the library door was shutting just as this one was opening.

With the candle back in her hand, Thylena stepped into the chamber. Beyond a doubt, this was the laboratory. Tables and stools were strewn about like so much arcane litter, each covered with beakers, vials, flasks and mortars. On the cobblestone floor in the center of the room was a thaumaturgical circle, drawn in dark red chalk, or something else of that color ... And within the circle was a golden, gem-encrusted brazier, the Brazier of Enchanting. Arkleron had offered a prince's ransom for the cursed thing, and now Thylena was near enough to spit inside it.

Of course, there was one problem. Like any paranoid wizard, Morkidan had bothered to protect his precious artifact. Filling the space between the door and the inner laboratory were several magical fields of energy. Thylena had encountered enough of these in the past to know what would happen were she to try to pass through one. She didn't particularly care for the smell of charred flesh, least of all her own.

Fortunately, she had encountered enough of these fields in the past also to know to be prepared to get around them. There's no way through them, so they can be overcome only by someone who can dispel them. And, since wizards tended to have some sort of unspoken agreement about directly stealing each other's prized possessions, most felt fairly secure leaving the fields in place as a deterrent for the few thieves cunning enough to reach them, but who couldn't cast their way through them. But, few burglars had spent as many years as Thylena had breaking into other people's homes, and having a particular dislike for wizards, she had learned long ago how to read a Dispel Field scroll. So, it was a simple matter for her to sheathe her sword, pull the scroll from her backpack, read aloud the necessary incantation, and make one segment of the field disappear.

With a smile that bordered on arrogance, Thylena walked boldly forward, grasped the Brazier in her hand, and stuffed it into a silk sack. The smile was still there when she turned to head for the exit. And it was still there when she pulled on the handle of the mighty iron door. Only when the door was open wide enough for her see the golem guardian standing at the bottom of the stairs to greet her did the smile fade.

With a quiet moan the golem lifted its great fist to come crashing down on Thylena's head. In a flash, she leapt backwards out of harm's way, simultaneously drawing her sword. The creature lumbered toward her, again preparing for a mighty swing. Realizing her sword would be all but useless against the hard skin of her opponent, Thylena needed an alternative quickly.

Down came the maul-like fist with tremendous force, catching Thylena's blade beneath it as she narrowly dodged the blow. The sword snapped in twain as the stony hand connected with the stony floor. Having never seen a golem before, she did not expect the extent of the guardian's reach.

That's it, the long arms! While the golem was moving into position for another strike, Thylena backed up almost against one of the remaining fields of energy. She knew this would require precision timing or she would be pounded squarely into a cobblestone-shaped mound of flesh. She waited as the massive hand reached its zenith, and then just as it began to fall, she rolled into the empty space where the dispelled field once sparked with energy. Again, the fist crashed into the floor, but this time it also broke the barrier of the magical field.

Thylena heard a thunderous crash, and just barely managed to duck as chunks of rock flew past her head. The huge behemoth, now missing most of one arm and part of the other, began to crumble before her eyes.

Realizing her opponent had surely made enough noise to rouse the entire neighborhood, let alone the wizard into whose home she had broken, Thylena wasted no time. She rushed to the stairs, carefully pulled shut the door, and bounded up the steps in time to slip through the upper door that had been opened by the closing of the one below. She dashed through the library and into the hallway, past the servants who were brave enough to investigate (Thylena learned later than Morkidan was off on some expedition, which explained why she did not have to face him that evening), and through the window. The drop to the ground below was painful, but her rolling landing minimized the broken bones. And like a bolt, she was off into the night.

Unfortunately for Thylena, wealthy Arkleron had miscalculated the amount of mandrake root to use in his latest experiment, and a wizard who has hurled himself in pieces throughout the city can hardly pay for expensive magical artifacts. And the Brazier of Enchantments, though quite powerful indeed, is a hard item to get rid of without attracting undue attention. So now, having been abandoned somewhere on the wharves of Britain, it sits in the study of Lord British's wizardly advisor, Nystul, perhaps one of the few mages powerful enough to make Morkidan think twice about taking it back. Of course, there are rumors that Morkidan knows someone who might be able to get it back for him ....

At first glance, it seems this story, one of cunning and guile, is designed to do nothing more than amuse. It is difficult to detect a moral or a lesson to be learned. But closer inspection reveals the hidden message. The careful words within demonstrate the danger of overconfidence, of hubris, itself, and is visible in more than one character. It is a clever story, for in it the parable is disguised beneath the very story itself. Lord British was particularly attentive to this tale, for our king recognizes that she learns best who does not realize she is being taught. And, by the by, for the record, Nystul denies knowledge of the whereabouts of any kind of enchanted coal-burning container.

And so have passed the five tales of life and learning, humor and harmony. Perhaps you have heard these stories before, or at least recognize elements within. Be that so, it is a testament to their relevance, not a mark against their originality. Consider carefully all that you have read for it will help mitigate the struggle of daily life in Lord British's realm of Virtue.

Magic

MAXIL

Magic is power. It is the strength of raging storms distilled to a few potent drops. It is the might of a lightning bolt, folded into a graven wand no thicker than a finger. It is the raw energy drawn from the cosmos and coerced to follow the whims of fragile mortals.

But magic is not omnipotence. Know that the cost of necessary and vital reagents prevents the acquistion of fortune. Long hours of study ruin health and doom companionable friendships. Those few of you (and you will number few) who survive both your lessons and your first combat experiences will know the demands of commercial inventory and the fine points of legal contracts no less than the intricacies of reagents and incantations. You will grow to be paranoid and garrulous, sarcastic and bitter, dyspeptic and chronically exhausted. You will be betrayed unto death, and none shall mourn you.

But you won't believe me, and even if you did you wouldn't care. So study diligently and remember before all this one basic precept:

    ➛ Always enunciate carefully, no matter what is about to bite your head off.

Inspirational Speech of Xathron, Elder Mage,
to the entering candidates of the Academy

THE SECRETS OF MAGIC

Skill

In *Ultima Online*, your magical abilities are measured in terms of *Magery* skill, a numerical scale that measures your magical proficiency. You can select this skill when you create a character. Your skill can rise as high as 100, once you've spent time in practice.

When you've acquired a little bit of magery skill and attempt to work magic, the program uses your magery skill to compute your chances of success. If your skill is 40, then you have a 40 percent chance of success; if it's 80, then you have an 80 percent chance. A successful spell subtracts mana points and depletes your current stock of reagents.

For more information on Magery skill, see p. 81.

Improving Magery Skill

Observation is the slowest way to improve your spellcasting abilities, but it also requires the least effort. If you're in the market for new spells, however, visit all of the local magic shops. While you're there, inquire about any local mages' guilds. Just as in the real world, any reliable contacts you make can put you ahead.

Bandits and adventurers can make good sources for new spells as well — most of them don't have any use for scrolls and are more than happy to sell them.

One last note — if you watch or approach NPC mages who cross your path, be extremely kind to them. They've earned their skills the hard way, and if you insult or trick them, they can be extremely vengeful.

♀   If you want to increase your magery skill, cast spells. Start with lower-circle, non-harmful spells (like *Heal*) on yourself or friends. The more you successfully cast them, the more your skill improves. Later, casting more powerful, higher-circle spells will increase your magery skills even faster.

♀   You'll need the *Inscription* skill to create a scroll of a spell that you know.

♀   If you have a spell inscribed on a scroll you can cast it without reagents.

♀   If you plan to pursue a career in magic, you might select these skills and values when you create your character:

Magery	35 (or about half your available points)
Resist Spells	20 (or about a third of your available points)
Alchemy	10 (or about a sixth of your available points)

(See **Developing Your Character**, p. 20, for an alternative approach.)

Circles of Magic

Spells are currently grouped into eight circles containing eight spells apiece. Each circle marks an increase in the power of spells that can be cast and the amount of mana that they require. At first, you will only have the ability to cast spells of the First Circle. Each time you cast a spell, the game checks your current circle and your *Magery* skill. To advance from one circle to another, you must learn at least four of the spells in your current circle. To move from the First Circle to the Second, you must learn four First Circle spells and achieve a *Magery* skill of 50 or greater.

Nothing within the game will tell when you've advanced — no magical information scrolls appear, no kind citizen will inform you of your new powers. (No one said the ancient arts were user friendly.) You must keep track of the spells you have cast and your *Magery* skill yourself, or simply acquire a few spells of the next circle and attempt to cast them from time to time.

☥ By the way, you'll know a spell was successful if you see the effect happen, or see sparkles appear around the affected item or person. If the spell fails, your character will utter something like "Oh drat, it didn't work!"

Circles

Spells	1st	2nd	3rd	4th	5th	6th	7th	8th
	Reactive Armor	Agility	Bless	Archcure	Blade Spirits	Dispel	Chain Lightning	Earthquake
	Clumsy	Cunning	Fireball	Archprotect	Dispel	Energy Bolt	Energy Field	Energy Vortex
	Create Food	Cure	Magic Lock	Curse	Incognito	Explosion	Flamestrike	Resurrection
	Feeblemind	Harm	Poison	Fire Field	Magic Reflection	Invisibility	Gate Travel	Summon Air Elemental
	Heal	Magic Trap	Telekinesis	Greater Heal	Mind Blast	Mark	Mana Vampire	Summon Daemon
	Magic Arrow	Remove Trap	Teleport	Lightning	Paralyze	Mass Curse	Mass Dispel	Summon Earth Elemental
	Night Sight	Protection	Unlock	Mana Drain	Poison Field	Paralyze Field	Meteor Swarm	Summon Fire Elemental
	Weaken	Strength	Wall of Stone	Recall	Summon Creature	Reveal	Polymorph	Summon Water Elemental

How to Acquire and Cast Spells

Scrolls. Once you've found (or bought or stolen) a spell scroll, you can do one of two things with it — you can place the spell into your spellbook or cast the spell directly from the scroll.

Placing the spell in your spellbook — you will only be able to place a spell in your spellbook if you have already reached that spell circle (i.e., you must be a Sixth-Circle mage to put a Sixth Circle spell in your book). Once the spell is in your spellbook, you can cast it anytime, as long as you have the required reagents and mana.

Casting the spell from the scroll — Anyone can cast any spell directly from a spell scroll, regardless of his or her skill, Circle, mana, or the reagents in his or her possession. But there's a catch — you can only use the scroll once.

With any luck, you will be able to find some scrolls, and you can also purchase them from other players or from NPCs. Most spell scrolls you find (versus purchasing them) will be First or Second Circle spells. Occasionally, you'll find a real jewel (like an Eighth Circle spell), but not often. Figure that, of the scrolls you find while adventuring, less than one in a hundred will contain an Eighth Circle spell.

If you have cultivated the *Inscribe* skill, you will be able to copy spells from your own spellbook on to scrolls, which you can then give or sell to others.

Spellbook. To have continued access to a spell, place it in your spellbook (drag the scroll icon over your book — you will be able to do this only if you've advanced to the required circle of magic. Having a spell in your book doesn't guarantee that you'll be able to cast it — you'll need to have the necessary mana and reagents. You can buy blank spellbooks from other players or alchemy shops, and you may occasionally get lucky and find one that already contains spells. You can carry multiple spellbooks in your backpack.

Potions. Some spells can be condensed into magical potions. Potions are created by alchemists, and are sold at alchemy shops. (Human players can sell the potions they own anywhere.) You do not have to have any *Magery* skill to use a potion. They almost always work, but can be used only once.

Double-left-click on a potion to use it. Potions are color-coded, so you know their general effects, but some potions can have varying intensities. You may want to use the *Taste Identification* skill on it — or find someone who can. This skill will identify the potion without releasing its magical effect. See **Potions**, p. 244.

Magic Items. Several kinds of enchanted items — swords, statues, wands and rings among them — exist in the land of Britannia. These items cast spells when used, or possess certain magical qualities such as increased durability.
See **Magic Items**, p. 242.

Magic Resource Bank

While not necessary to play the game, a good understanding of the value of mana and how it is distributed in the real world can give an increased appreciation for the powerful occupation of magery.

Like all other resources in the natural world, mana is in limited supply in Britannia. Each region has a *resource bank* with a specific amount of base mana resources. As those resources are apportioned to scrolls and magical items, the amount of resources in the mana bank drops.

The passage of mana resources from the bank into the world of mortals is only temporary, however. After a spell scroll is cast, a potion is drunk, someone dies, or the last magical charge on an item is used, the associated mana is transferred back into the resource pool where it originated.

The amount of mana needed to support spells, sustain magical abilities or power charges varies by item. For example, a First Circle spell is worth about 5 mana resources in bank terms, while an Eighth Circle spell draws 800.

Reagents

To the ignorant and untrained eye, reagents can appear to be nothing more than plants or other natural substances. Yet for the knowing they provide a vital link connecting the physical world and the nebulous fields of ethereal energy. Of course, there are about this world other, similar items, purported to be reagents by some and occasionally found in shop displays. These are curiosities to most, but a few may well hold hidden powers.

If you're practicing alchemy or magic, you need to become intimately familiar with reagents. Alchemists extract the essence of reagents to form potions with magical properties. Mages, on the other hand, combine several different reagents in casting different spells. Before you can successfully cast a spell from your spellbook, you must have the necessary reagents present in your backpack. The only exception to this comes once you've practiced magic long enough to master higher-circle skills — then, you will be able to use almost any reagent to cast lower-circle spells.

While creating a potion might require more than one unit of a particular reagent, casting a spell (or creating a scroll) always requires just one unit of each reagent that is listed in the spell description.

Acquiring and learning spells can be somewhat daunting, but obtaining reagents is a relatively straightforward task. You can find them in the wild, or purchase them in the cities at a price anywhere from 2 to 5 gold pieces. Some reagents are more plentiful in certain areas, but you should be able to find anything you need within an hour's walking distance, especially if you search underground.

Black Pearl

Black pearls are rare, and are often referred to as the reagent of movement. When finely ground into a powder, black pearls can invoke spells that teleport or propel the caster to another location.

Main effect   Teleportation/propulsion

Needed for

Fireball (3)	Mind Blast (5)	Energy Field (7)
Magic Lock (3)	Poison Field (5)	Gate Travel (7)
Lightning (4)	Energy Bolt (6)	Mana Vampire (7)
Mana Drain (4)	Explosion (6)	Mass Dispel (7)
Recall (4)	Mark (6)	Energy Vortex (8)
Blade Spirits (5)	Paralyze Field (6)	Resurrection (8)
Dispel Field (5)	Chain Lightning (7)	

Blood Moss

Blood moss takes its name from its reddish color. Those familiar with mycology theorize that blood moss is a magical offshoot of the Hyalopycris blepharistoma fungi.

Prevalent in wetter surroundings (such as marshes or swamps), this type of fungi is a base reagent for spells involving locomotion or animation.

Main effect   Locomotion/animation

Needed for

Clumsy (1)	Incognito (5)	Polymorph (7)
Agility (2)	Summon Creature (5)	Earthquake (8)
Remove Trap (2)	Invisibility (6)	Energy Vortex (8)
Telekinesis (3)	Mark (6)	Summon Air Elemental (8))
Teleport (3)	Reveal (6)	Summon Daemon (8)
Unlock (3)	Chain Lightning (7)	Summon Earth Elemental (8)
Wall of Stone (3)	Mana Vampire (7)	Summon Fire Elemental (8)
Recall (4)	Meteor Swarm (7)	Summon Water Elemental (8)

Garlic

The ground paste of a ripe bulb of garlic has a reputation for warding off evil. This effect accurately describes its use a reagent as well. Modern magicians use garlic in spells that protect the caster (or a specified target) or dispel danger.

Garlic is the most plentiful reagent — you can find and pick it in all areas of Britannia.

Main effect   Protection/dispel danger or evil

Needed for

Create Food (1)	Bless (3)	Incognito (5)
Reactive Armor (1)	Magic Lock (3)	Magic Reflection (5)
Heal (1)	Wall of Stone (3)	Paralyze (5)
Magic Arrow (1)	Archcure (4)	Dispel (6)
Weaken (1)	Archprotection (4)	Mass Curse (6)
Cure (2)	Curse (4)	Mana Vampire (7)
Harm (2)	Fire Field (4)	Mass Dispel (7)
Magic Trap (2)	Greater Heal 4)	Meteor Swarm (7)
Protection (2)	Dispel Field (5)	Resurrection (8)

Ginseng

Ginseng is hailed as the reagent of health, as its syrup bestows both healing and restoration. Common Britannia folk use it as a home remedy for fatigue and sickness, but true magicians appreciate ginseng for its magical qualities and always keep a healthy portion on hand.

Main effect   Healing/enhancement

Needed for

Create Food (1)	Magic Trap (2)	Paralyze Field (6)
Feeblemind (1)	Protection (2)	Earthquake (8)
Heal (1)	Archcure (4)	Resurrection (8)
Cure (2)	Archprotection (4)	
Harm (2)	Greater Heal (4)	

Mandrake Root

Mandrake root is harder to find than other reagents, although it is probably the most commonly used of the eight base reagents. Like blood moss, it thrives in dark, dank areas where most dare not venture. Those that do search out this precious root are rewarded by being able to cast spells invoking strength and energy.

Main effect   Strength/power/energy

Needed for

Create Food (1)	Recall (4)	Gate Travel (7)
Agility (2)	Blade Spirits (5)	Mana Vampire (7)
Cunning (2)	Magic Reflection (5)	Mass Dispel (7)
Strength (2)	Mind Blast (5)	Meteor Swarm (7)
Bless (3)	Paralyze (5)	Polymorph (7)
Telekinesis (3)	Summon Creature (5)	Earthquake (8)
Teleport (3)	Dispel (6)	Energy Vortex (8)
Archcure (4)	Explosion (6)	Summon Air Elemental (8)
Archprotection (4)	Mark (6)	Summon Daemon (8)
Greater Heal (4)	Mass Curse (6)	Summon Earth Elemental (8)
Lightning (4)	Chain Lightning (7)	Summon Fire Elemental (8)
Mana Drain (4)	Energy Field (7)	Summon Water Elemental (8)

Nightshade

The nightshade plant is as deadly as its long-standing reputation. Its touch can poison a human; in a magical spell, it invokes powers of death, damage and illusion.

Most mages would rather pay a steep price for nightshade than search for it in swamps. Because its flowers bloom only at night, it must be picked in the late evening hours — coinciding with the feeding habits of many dangerous swamp inhabitants.

Main effect   Harm/damage/illusion

Needed for

Clumsy (1)	Magic Trap (2)	Mind Blast (5)
Feeblemind (1)	Strength (2)	Poison Field (5)
Heal (1)	Poison (3)	Energy Bolt (6)
Magic Arrow (1)	Curse (4)	Invisibility (6)
Weaken (1)	Blade Spirits (5)	Mass Curse (6)
Cunning (2)	Incognito (5)	Energy Vortex (8)

Spider's Silk

Spider's silk is an inexpensive reagent, as it is quite plentiful and light on one's back, even in large quantities. However, it is so fine that massive amounts of fibers are consumed by a single spell. True to its origin as webbing, this reagent calls forth summoning and binding spells.

Main effect   Summoning/binding
Needed for

Night Sight (1)	Paralyze (5)	Polymorph (7)
Reactive Armor (1)	Poison Field (5)	Summon Air Elemental (8)
Fire Field (4)	Summon Creature (5)	Summon Daemon (8)
Greater Heal (4)	Paralyze Field (6)	Summon Earth Elemental (8)
Mana Drain (4)	Energy Field (7)	Summon Fire Elemental (8)
Dispel Field (5)	Flamestrike (7)	Summon Water Elemental (8)
Magic Reflection (5)	Mana Vampire (7)	

Sulphurous Ash

Foul-smelling but powerful, sulphurous ash is a dusty volcanic residue. It is found mainly in Britannia's mountainous regions and is a common element of any spell releasing fire, light or explosive energy.

Main effect   Explosions/light
Needed for

Night Sight (1)	Fire Field (4)	Energy Field (7)
Reactive Armor (1)	Lightning (4)	Flamestrike (7)
Remove Trap (2)	Dispel Field (5)	Gate Travel (7)
Protection (2)	Mind Blast (5)	Mana Vampire (7)
Fireball (3)	Dispel (6)	Mass Dispel (7)
Magic Lock (3)	Explosion (6)	Meteor Swarm (7)
Unlock (3)	Mass Curse (6)	Earthquake (8)
Archprotection (4)	Reveal (6)	Summon Daemon (8)
Curse (4)	Chain Lightning (7)	Summon Fire Elemental (8)

False Reagents

Adventurers in Britannia may notice that NPC mages take a marked interest in certain "reagent-like" substances, including Dragon Blood, Daemon Bone, Serpent Scales and Volcanic Ash. (And those who are familiar with the world of Pagan — visited in *Ultima VIII* — may know that these substances do, in fact, function as reagents in that barbaric land.) It should therefore be noted that, while NPCs may have use for these substances in conjunction with certain theoretical inquiries, they are of no use whatsoever at this time to player mages, except as commodities to be sold or traded to those who desire him. To speak plainly, there are *no* "secret spells" in *Ultima Online* at this time, and these "occult objects" should not be construed as evidence of some kind of secret power to be unearthed.

Runic Lexicon

Every mage worth his or her spellbook knows that to cast any spell, you must know the magical words of power. These aren't any ordinary words — uttering them can cause the reagents you're carrying to combine and spew out a spell.

Syllable	Letter	Meaning	Syllable	Letter	Meaning
An	ᚨ	Negate or Dispel	Nox	ᚴ	Magic
Bet	ᛒ	Small	Ort	ᛉ	Poison
Corp	ᚴ	Death	Por	ᚴ	Move or Movement
Des	ᛙ	Lower or Down	Quas	ᛈ	Illusion
Ex	ᛗ	Freedom	Rel	ᚱ	Change
Flam	ᚹ	Flame	Sanct	ᚻ	Protect or Protection
Grav	ᚷ	Field	Tym	↑	Time
Hur	ᚦ	Wind	Uus	ᚾ	Raise or Up
In	ᛁ	Make, Create or Cause	Vas	ᚥ	Great
Jux	ᚿ	Danger, Trap or Harm	Wis	ᛝ	Know or Knowledge
Kal	ᚴ	Summon or Invoke	Xen	ᛚ	Creature
Lor	ᚱ	Light	Ylem	ᛘ	Matter
Mani	ᛗ	Life or Healing	Zu	ᛉ	Sleep

Lexicon

Spell Names

Acquiring spells is an art in and of itself (see **How to Acquire and Cast Spells**, p. 217). Once you've collected a few, however, be ready to study what you have, and what's to come. Magery is an occupation unlike any other, and it behooves one to be intimately familiar with all spells — not just those personally known.

The first lesson in spellcasting is that each spell has several names — *common*, *lexicon* (spoken) and *runic* (written). While most spells are referred to in common terms, you should be able to recognize all spells by their aural and visual representations.

1st Circle

Common	Lexicon	Runic
Reactive Armor	Rel An	
Clumsy	Uus Jux	
Create Food	In Mani Ylem	
Feeblemind	Rel Wis	
Heal	In Mani	
Magic Arrow	In Por Ylem	
Night Sight	In Lor	
Weaken	Des Mani	

2nd Circle

Common	Lexicon	Runic
Agility	Ex Uus	
Cunning	Uus Wis	
Cure	An Nox	
Harm	An Mani	
Magic Trap	In Jux	
Remove Trap	An Jux	
Protection	Uus Sanct	
Strength	Uus Mani	

3rd Circle

Common	Lexicon	Runic
Bless	Rel Sanct	
Fireball	Vas Flam	
Magic Lock	An Por	
Poison	In Nox	
Telekinesis	Ort Por Ylem	
Teleport	Rel Por	
Unlock	Ex Por	
Wall of Stone	In Sanct Ylem	

4th Circle

Common	Lexicon	Runic
Archcure	Vas An Nox	
Archprotection	Vas Uus Sanct	
Curse	Des Sanct	
Fire Field	In Flam Grav	
Greater Heal	In Vas Mani	
Lightning	Por Ort Grav	
Mana Drain	Ort Rel	
Recall	Kal Ort Por	

5th Circle

Common	Lexicon	Runic
Blade Spirits	In Jux Hur Ylem	
Dispel Field	An Grav	
Incognito	Kal In Ex	
Magic Reflection	In Jux Sanct	
Mind Blast	Por Corp Wis	
Paralyze	An Ex Por	
Poison Field	In Nox Grav	
Summon Creature	Kal Xen	

6th Circle

Common	Lexicon	Runic
Dispel	An Ort	
Energy Bolt	Corp Por	
Explosion	Vas Ort Flam	
Invisibility	An Lor Xen	
Mark	Kal Por Ylem	
Mass Curse	Vas Des Sanct	
Paralyze Field	In Ex Grav	
Reveal	Wis Quas	

7th Circle

Common	Lexicon	Runic
Chain Lightning	Vas Ort Grav	
Energy Field	In Sanct Grav	
Flamestrike	Kal Vas Flam	
Gate Travel	Vas Rel Por	
Mana Vampire	Ort Sanct	
Mass Dispel	Vas An Ort	
Meteor Swarm	Kal Des Flam Ylem	
Polymorph	Vas Ylem Rel	

8th Circle

Common	Lexicon	Runic
Earthquake	In Vas Por	
Energy Vortex	Vas Corp Por	
Resurrection	An Corp	
Smn. Air Elmtl.	Kal Xen Hur	
Smn. Daemon	Kal Xen Corp	
Smn. Earth Elmtl.	Kal Xen Ylem	
Smn. Fire Elmtl.	Kal Xen Flam	
Smn. Water Elmtl.	Kal Xen An Flam	

SPELL DESCRIPTIONS

This section is meant to be used as a mage's reference, and lists the following aspects of each spell, by circle:

Reagents. What natural reagents must be present and combined to cast the spell. Reagents are consumed during the casting of a spell, whether it is successful or not. See p. 218-222 for information on each of the eight reagents.

Effect. What the spell does when it is cast. Some spells affect only the caster, others the target, and others an entire area.

Damage. How much damage the spell applies to the target object or person. This number is subtracted from the object or person's Health. Not all spells inflict damage.

Mana Cost. How much mana the spell consumes. This number is subtracted from your total reserve of mana.

Duration. How long the spell's effects last.

1st Spell Circle

Reactive Armor
RA

Reagents	Garlic, Sulphurous Ash, Spider's Silk
Effect	Reflects partial damage back at attacker Does not work with ranged or magical attacks
Damage	Reflects each blow's damage, up to 10 points. (Damage over 10 points evaporates.)
Mana Cost	2
Duration	1 second x (caster's skill/2)

Clumsy
NA

Reagents	Bloodmoss, Nightshade
Effect	Reduces target's Dexterity by (caster's skill/10)
Damage	-NA-
Mana Cost	2
Duration	6 seconds x (caster's skill/5)

Create Food
IMA

Reagents	Garlic, Ginseng, Mandrake Root
Effect	Creates 1 of 10 food items: grapes, ham, cheese, muffins, fish, ribs, chicken, sausage, apple or peach
Damage	-NA-
Mana Cost	2
Duration	Permanent (until consumed ...)

1st Spell Circle

Feeblemind
ᚱᚻ

Reagents	Ginseng, Nightshade
Effect	Reduces target's Intelligence by (caster's skill/10)
Damage	-NA-
Mana Cost	2
Duration	6 seconds x (caster's skill/5)

Heal
ᛁᛗ

Reagents	Garlic, Ginseng, Nightshade
Effect	Restores Health: (caster's skill/10), plus 1 to 6 more
Damage	-NA-
Mana Cost	2
Duration	Single use

Magic Arrow
ᛁᚲᚻ

Reagents	Garlic, Nightshade
Effect	Casts flaming fireball at target
Damage	Reduces target's Health by (2 to 5) x (caster's skill/10)
Mana Cost	2
Duration	Single use

Night Sight
ᛁᚱ

Reagents	Spider's Silk, Sulphurous Ash
Effect	Sharpens night vision
Damage	-NA-
Mana Cost	2
Duration	1 minute x (caster's skill/10)

Weaken
ᛪᛈ

Reagents	Garlic, Nightshade
Effect	Reduces target's Strength by (caster's skill/10)
	High skill or stamina on recipient reduces effect
Damage	-NA-
Mana Cost	2
Duration	6 seconds x (caster's skill/5)

2nd Spell Circle

Agility
MΛ

Reagents	Blood Moss, Mandrake Root
Effect	Increases target's Dexterity by (caster's skill/10)
Damage	-NA-
Mana Cost	4
Duration	6 seconds x (caster's skill/5)

Cunning
ΛN

Reagents	Nightshade, Mandrake Root
Effect	Increases target's Intelligence by (caster's skill/10)
Damage	-NA-
Mana Cost	4
Duration	6 seconds x (caster's skill/5)

Cure
ᚿ

Reagents	Garlic, Ginseng
Effect	Counteracts poison
Damage	-NA-
Mana Cost	4
Duration	Single use

Harm
NN

Reagents	Garlic, Ginseng
Effect	Forms circle of harm around target (anyone within circle takes damage)
	Directly opposes Heal (An Mani, First Circle)
Damage	Reduce's target's Health by (caster's skill/10), plus 1 to 12 more
Mana Cost	4
Duration	Single use

2nd Spell Circle

Magic Trap |❶

Reagents	Garlic, Ginseng, Nightshade
Effect	Places explosive trap on a useable objects (activates when object is used)
Damage	Reduces Health by 10
Mana Cost	4
Duration	Single use

Remove Trap |❶

Reagents	Blood Moss, Sulphurous Ash
Effect	Deactivates magical trap on a single object
Damage	-NA-
Mana Cost	4
Duration	Single use

Protection |❶

Reagents	Garlic, Ginseng, Sulphurous Ash
Effect	Increases target's armor rating by (caster's skill/10)
Damage	-NA-
Mana Cost	4
Duration	6 seconds x (caster's skill/5)

Strength |❶

Reagents	Mandrake Root, Nightshade
Effect	Increases target's Strength by (caster's skill/10)
Damage	-NA-
Mana Cost	4
Duration	6 seconds x (caster's skill/5)

Bless
ᚱᚻ

Reagents	Garlic, Mandrake Root
Effect	Increases target's Health/Dexterity/Strength/Intelligence by (caster's skill/10)
Damage	-NA-
Mana Cost	6
Duration	6 seconds x (caster's skill/5)

Fireball
ᚾᛈ

Reagents	Black Pearl, Sulphurous Ash
Effect	Launches powerful fireball at target
Damage	Reduces target's Health by (1 to 6) x (caster's skill/10)
Mana Cost	6
Duration	Single use

Magic Lock
ᚠᚴ

Reagents	Black Pearl, Garlic, Sulphurous Ash
Effect	Places magical lock on a chest
Damage	-NA-
Mana Cost	6
Duration	Single use

Poison
ᚻ

Reagents	Nightshade
Effect	Poisons target
	Can be countered by Cure (An Nox, Second Circle)
Damage	Gradually reduces target's Health over several minutes, but will not kill
Mana Cost	6
Duration	Single use

3rd Spell Circle

Telekinesis

ᚠᚲᚻ

Reagents	Blood Moss, Mandrake Root
Effect	Use or move a single object that is beyond reach
Damage	-NA-
Mana Cost	6
Duration	Single use

Teleport

ᚱᚲ

Reagents	Blood Moss, Mandrake Root
Effect	Transports caster to target location (within same screen) Higher-circle mages have more destinations
Damage	-NA-
Mana Cost	6
Duration	Single use

Unlock

ᛗᚲ

Reagents	Blood Moss, Sulphurous Ash
Effect	Picks and opens magical locks
Damage	-NA-
Mana Cost	6
Duration	Single use

Wall of Stone

ᛁᚻᚻ

Reagents	Blood Moss, Garlic
Effect	Erects temporary stone wall on open ground
Damage	-NA-
Mana Cost	6
Duration	10 seconds

4th Spell Circle

Archcure
ΛΡΨ

Reagents	Garlic, Ginseng, Mandrake Root
Effect	Counteracts poisoning for all targets within two or three paces
Damage	-NA-
Mana Cost	10
Duration	Single use

Arch-protection
ΛΛ4

Reagents	Garlic, Ginseng, Mandrake Root, Sulphurous Ash
Effect	Increases target's ability to withstand harm
	Protects all targets within two or three paces
Damage	-NA-
Mana Cost	10
Duration	Single use

Curse
ΜΨ4

Reagents	Garlic, Nightshade, Sulphurous Ash
Effect	Reduces target's Health/Skill/Dexterity/Intelligence by (caster's skill/10)
Damage	-NA-
Mana Cost	10
Duration	Single use

Fire Field
ΙΨΧ

Reagents	Garlic, Spider's Silk, Sulphurous Ash
Effect	Erects a 3' x 9' flaming area on open ground
Damage	Reduces Health of anyone touching field by 10 per touch
Mana Cost	10
Duration	20 seconds

4th Spell Circle

Greater Heal
ΙΛΜ

Reagents	Garlic, Ginseng, Mandrake Root, Spider's Silk
Effect	Improves target's Health by (4) x (caster's skill/10)
Damage	-NA-
Mana Cost	10
Duration	Single use

Lightning
ΚΜΧ

Reagents	Black Pearl, Mandrake Root, Sulphurous Ash
Effect	Launches small lightning strike on target
Damage	Reduces target's Health by (2 to 7) x (caster's skill/10)
Mana Cost	10
Duration	Single use

Mana Drain
ΜΡ

Reagents	Black Pearl, Mandrake Root, Spider's Silk
Effect	Drains all mana from target (although mana will regenerate normally)
	Defend against this with Magic Reflection (In Jux, Fifth Circle)
Damage	-NA-
Mana Cost	10 (but target's mana transfers to caster)
Duration	Single use

Recall
ΚΜΚ

Reagents	Black Pearl, Blood Moss, Mandrake Root
Effect	Tranports user to object's original marked location
	Must be used on object marked with Mark spell (Kal Por Ylem, Sixth Circle)
Damage	-NA-
Mana Cost	10
Duration	Single use

5th Spell Circle

Blade Spirits
ᛁᚩᛈᛗ

Reagents	Black Pearl, Mandrake Root, Nightshade
Effect	Creates spinning column of blades that detects and chases moving targets within a one-yard radius
Damage	15 points
Mana Cost	16
Duration	120 seconds

Dispel Field
ᚠᚷ

Reagents	Black Pearl, Garlic, Spider's Silk, Sulphurous Ash
Effect	Creates a gap in field (e.g., Poison Field) spells through which you can walk. Dispel field is created perpendicularly to caster and is 15' x 3'
Damage	-NA-
Mana Cost	16
Duration	120 seconds

Incognito
ᚻᛁᛗ

Reagents	Blood Moss, Garlic, Nightshade
Effect	Sets target's notoriety to "neutral"
Damage	-NA-
Mana Cost	16
Duration	6 seconds x (caster's skill/5)

Magic Reflection
ᛁᚠᚻ

Reagents	Garlic, Mandrake Root, Spider's Silk
Effect	Reflects spell back at person who cast it. Can also harm caster
Damage	Varies by spell type
Mana Cost	16
Duration	Single use

5th Spell Circle

Mind Blast
KAN

Reagents	Black Pearl, Mandrake Root, Nightshade, Sulphurous Ash
Effect	Compares the Intelligence of the caster and target, then further reduces the lower Intelligence by the difference between the two.
Damage	See Effect
Mana Cost	16
Duration	Single use

Paralyze
AMK

Reagents	Garlic, Mandrake Root, Spider's Silk
Effect	Temporarily paralyzes target
Damage	-NA-
Mana Cost	16
Duration	1 second x (caster's skill/2)

Poison Field
HX

Reagents	Black Pearl, Nightshade, Spider's Silk
Effect	Creates 3' x 9' wall of poison on open ground
Damage	same as poison
Mana Cost	16
Duration	20 seconds

Summon Creature
h入

Reagents	Blood Moss, Mandrake Root, Spider's Silk
Effect	Summons a slave creature for combat support
Damage	-NA-
Mana Cost	16
Duration	Caster's skill, in seconds

6th Spell Circle

Dispel
ᛘᛜ

Reagents	Garlic, Mandrake Root, Sulphurous Ash
Effect	Permanently destroys undead targets; powerful mages can occasionally dispel elementals and daemons
Damage	-NA-
Mana Cost	26
Duration	Caster's skill, in seconds

Energy Bolt
ᛣᚴ

Reagents	Black Pearl, Nightshade
Effect	Fires bolt of energy at target
Damage	Reduces target's Health by (caster's skill)
Mana Cost	26
Duration	Single use

Explosion
ᛚᛜᛦ

Reagents	Black Pearl, Mandrake Root, Sulphurous Ash
Effect	Causes explosion at target location
Damage	Reduces Health of target by 1 to 8 per (caster's skill/20)
Mana Cost	26
Duration	Single use

Invisibility
ᚠᛏᛣ

Reagents	Blood Moss, Nightshade
Effect	Makes target temporarily invisible
Damage	-NA-
Mana Cost	26
Duration	6 seconds x (caster's skill/5)

6th Spell Circle

Mark
ᚠᚴᛗ

Reagents	Black Pearl, Blood Moss, Mandrake Root
Effect	Makes an object a teleport marker
	Using *Recall* (Kal Ort Por, Fourth Circle) on a Marked object teleports caster to original location where object was Marked
Damage	-NA-
Mana Cost	26
Duration	Single use

Mass Curse
ᚪᛉᛄ

Reagents	Garlic, Mandrake Root, Nightshade, Sulphurous Ash
Effect	Curses all creatures within a pace or two
	Delivers increased effect of Curse (Des Sanct, Fourth Circle), although some creatures can resist
Damage	-NA-
Mana Cost	26
Duration	6 seconds x (caster's skill/5)

Paralyze Field
ᛁᛗᛉ

Reagents	Black Pearl, Ginseng, Spider's Silk
Effect	Creates 3′ x 9′ wall of paralysis on open ground
	Some creatures can resist paralysis
Damage	-NA-
Mana Cost	26
Duration	20 seconds

Reveal
ᚾᚥ

Reagents	Blood Moss, Sulphurous Ash
Effect	Unveils all invisible objects, creatures and/or players in within 2 or 3 paces
Damage	-NA-
Mana Cost	26
Duration	Single use

7th Spell Circle

Chain Lightning
ΛℲX

Reagents	Black Pearl, Blood Moss, Mandrake Root, Sulphurous Ash
Effect	Casts lightning bolt within a pace or two of focal point
Damage	Reduces Health of all affected by (2 to 7) x (caster's skill/10)
Mana Cost	52
Duration	Single use

Energy Field
IℲX

Reagents	Black Pearl, Mandrake Root, Spider's Silk, Sulphurous Ash
Effect	Creates 3' x 9' wall of electricity on open ground
	Some creatures take only 50% damage
Damage	25
Mana Cost	52
Duration	20 seconds

Flame-strike
ℲΛԿ

Reagents	Spider's Silk, Sulphurous Ash
Effect	Casts down a pillar of flames onto target
Damage	Reduces target's Health by (caster's skill/2), plus 4 to 32 more
Mana Cost	52
Duration	Single use

Gate Travel
ΛRK

Reagents	Black Pearl, Mandrake Root, Sulphurous Ash
Effect	Teleports caster to location where item was Marked (Kal Por Ylem, Sixth Circle)
	Others can teleport as well for the duration of the spell
	Must be cast on Marked object
Damage	-NA-
Mana Cost	52
Duration	10 seconds

7th Spell Circle

Mana Vampire

Reagents	Black Pearl, Blood Moss, Garlic, Mandrake Root, Spider's Silk, Sulphurous Ash
Effect	Transfers mana from target to caster
	Target's mana restores normally
	Some creatures/players/NPCs can resist
Damage	-NA-
Mana Cost	52 (but target's mana transfers to caster)
Duration	Single use

Mass Dispel

Reagents	Black Pearl, Garlic, Mandrake Root, Sulphurous Ash
Effect	Destroys all undead within 2 or 3 paces of target
Damage	-NA-
Mana Cost	52
Duration	Single use

Meteor Swarm

Reagents	Blood Moss, Garlic, Mandrake Root, Sulphurous Ash
Effect	Casts flaming meteor storm
	Harms anyone within a pace or two of focal point
Damage	Reduces Health by (1 to 6) x (caster's skill/10)
Mana Cost	52
Duration	Single use

Polymorph

Reagents	Blood Moss, Mandrake Root, Spider's Silk
Effect	Transforms target into random creature type
	Some creatures can resist polymorphing
Damage	-NA-
Mana Cost	52
Duration	6 seconds x (caster's skill/5)

8th Spell Circle

Earth-quake
ΙΛΚ

Reagents	Blood Moss, Ginseng, Mandrake Root, Sulphurous Ash
Effect	Creates tremor that makes nearby mobile creatures stumble and fall
	Does not affect caster
Damage	-NA-
Mana Cost	52
Duration	10 seconds

Energy Vortex
ΛϞΚ

Reagents	Black Pearl, Blood Moss, Mandrake Root, Nightshade
Effect	Creates moving vortex of energy that attacks targets moving within its half-yard sensor radius
Damage	Harm (ϞϞ, 2nd Circle) Reduces target's Health by (caster's skill/10), plus 1 to 12 more
	Poison (Ϟ, 3rd Circle) Same as Poison spell
	Curse (Ϟϟ, 4th Circle) Reduces target's Intelligence by (caster's skill/10)
Mana Cost	78
Duration	Single use

Resurrec-tion
ϞΚ

Reagents	Black Pearl, Garlic, Ginseng
Effect	Brings human player ghost back to life
	Does not affect creatures or NPCs
Damage	-NA-
Mana Cost	78
Duration	Single use

Summon Air Elemental
ϞΛΡ

Reagents	Blood Moss, Mandrake Root, Spider's Silk
Effect	Summons air elemental for combat support
Damage	-NA-
Mana Cost	78
Duration	(Caster's skill) in seconds

8th Spell Circle

Summon Daemon

Reagents	Blood Moss, Mandrake Root, Spider's Silk, Sulphurous Ash
Effect	Summons daemon for combat support
Damage	-NA-
Mana Cost	78
Duration	(Caster's skill) in seconds

Summon Earth Elemental

Reagents	Blood Moss, Mandrake Root, Spider's Silk
Effect	Summons earth elemental for combat support
Damage	-NA-
Mana Cost	78
Duration	(Caster's skill) in seconds

Summon Fire Elemental

Reagents	Blood Moss, Mandrake Root, Spider's Silk, Sulphurous Ash
Effect	Summons fire elemental for combat support
Damage	-NA-
Mana Cost	78
Duration	(Caster's skill) in seconds

Summon Water Elemental

Reagents	Blood Moss, Mandrake Root, Spider's Silk
Effect	Summons water elemental for combat support
Damage	-NA-
Mana Cost	78
Duration	(Caster's skill) in seconds

MAGIC ITEMS

Throughout your travels in Britannia, you may encounter magic items — swords, armor, wands and so forth, that have magic spells cast on them. Unlike the spells in your spellbook, you do not need to possess any magic skill to use the items, nor do you need to have the proper reagents or have achieved the proper spell circle for the spell you wish to cast. The magical energy required for the spell is contained in the magical item — you do not need incantation or reagents to summon it.

The following percentages control magic items created entirely at random. Each percentage is the chance that particular type of item will be created:

25%	Magic weapon	6%	Magic clothing
25%	Magic armor	5%	Magic brazier or statue
25%	Scroll	1%	Ring
13%	Magic wand or staff		

But of course, things rarely happen entirely at random. Also, the are different types of magic — an enchanted breastplate that improves the wearer's weapon skills can't be created because weapon magic is only found on weapons, armor magic is only found on armor, and so forth.

The Substantial Sword of Demon's Breath

Sounds pretty sharp, but what can it do? The following tables list the magical qualities that magic items can have, and a description of each quality. For example, the sword mentioned above has 10 more hit points than average, and (while enchanted) casts the *Fireball* spell on whatever it strikes. The percentages listed are the chances that a particular effect will be cast on the weapon. (For example, if a helmet is enchanted, there is a 12% chance it will be a *Durable Helmet*, an 6% chance it will be a *Substantial Helmet* and so forth.)

Magic Armor

Boosts in armor value only apply to the areas covered by the magical armor.

All of these effects are permanent.

37%	Defense	+5 to AR		12%	Durable	+5 armor hit points
19%	Guarding	+10 to AR		6%	Substantial	+10 armor hit points
11%	Hardening	+15 to AR		4%	Massive	+15 armor hit points
6%	Fortification	+20 to AR		2%	Fortified	+20 armor hit points
2%	Invulnerability	+25 to AR		1%	Indestructible	+25 armor hit points

Magic Weapons

All of the effects listed below are permanent.

16%	Ruin	+5 damage		3%	Exceedingly Accurate	+20 to weapon skill
8%	Might	+10 damage		1%	Supremely Accurate	+25 to weapon skill
4%	Force	+15 damage		13%	Durable	+10 hit points
2%	Power	+20 damage		6%	Substantial	+20 hit points
1%	Vanquishing	+25 damage		3%	Massive	+30 hit points
18%	Accurate	+5 to weapon skill		2%	Fortified	+40 hit points
9%	Surpassingly Accurate	+10 to weapon skill		1%	Indestructible	+50 hit points
5%	Eminently Accurate	+15 to weapon skill				

The following effects cause a spell to be cast on anything the weapon hits, in addition to the damage normally delivered. The duration of the effect is the same as the duration for the spell.

1%	Clumsiness	Clumsy spell		1%	Ghoul's Touch	Paralyze spell
1%	Feeblemindedness	Feeblemind spell		.5%	Daemon's Breath	Fireball spell
1%	Burning	Magic Arrow spell		.5%	Evil	Curse spell
1%	Weakness	Weakness spell		.5%	Mage's Bane	Mana Drain spell
1%	Wounding	Harm spell		.2%	Thunder	Lightning spell

Magic Braziers and Statues

17%	Restoration		4%	Summon Creature		1%	Summon Air Elemental
17%	Heal		2%	Greater Heal		1%	Summon Earth Elemental
12%	Cure		2%	Clumsy		1%	Summon Fire Elemental
8%	Agility		2%	Feeblemind		1%	Summon Water Elemental
8%	Cunning		2%	Weaken		.5%	Summon Daemon
8%	Strength		2%	Wounding (Harm)		.5%	Curse
5%	Protection		1%	Mage's Bane (Mana Drain)			
4%	Bless		1%	Ghoul's Touch (Paralyze)			

Magic Wands and Staves

13%	Identification		11%	Weaken		7%	Dragon's Breath (Fireball)
13%	Heal		10%	Magic Arrow		5%	Thunder (Lightning)
11%	Clumsy		8%	Harm		3%	Mage's Bane (Mana Drain)
11%	Feeblemind		7%	Greater Heal			

Magic Clothing

33%	Night Eyes (Night Sight)		8%	Invisibility (Invisible)		4%	Clumsiness (Clumsy)
13%	Protection		5%	Spell Reflection (Magic Reflection)		4%	Weakness (Weaken)
8%	Agility					3%	Blessings (Bless)
8%	Cunning		4%	Feeblemindedness (Feeblemind)		2%	Evil (Curse)
8%	Strength						

Magic Rings

There are only two known kinds of magic rings — a *Teleport* ring and an *Invisibility* ring. There is a 50% chance of either being created when a magic ring is made.

Magic Scrolls

Scrolls might have any known spell inscribed upon them. However, as the Circle increases, the odds grow slimmer that a particular spell will be inscribed on a scroll you find. The odds of a scroll having a spell of a particular Circle are:

39%	First Circle	10%	Fourth Circle	2%	Seventh Circle
24%	Second Circle	6%	Fifth Circle	1%	Eighth Circle
15%	Third Circle	3%	Sixth Circle		

Potions

Each of the eight reagents is the principle ingredient in one or more potions. The potions that can currently be concocted, along with the amount of reagents needed (in units) and the minimum *Alchemy* skill necessary to mix them (see p. 54), include:

Reagent	Color	Potion	Units	Min. Skill	Effect when consumed
Black Pearl	Red	Refresh	1	-	Restores 25% of lost Fatigue
		Total Refreshment	5	50	Removes all Fatigue
Blood Moss	Blue	Agility	1	40	Improves Dexterity by 10 for 30 sec.
		Greater Agility	3	60	Improves Dexterity by 20 for 30 sec.
Garlic	Black	Nightsight	1	-	Lets you see in the dark (lasts until lighting around you gets brighter)
Ginseng	Yellow	Lesser Heal	1	-	Heals 3-10 hit points
		Heal	3	40	Heals 6-20 hit points
		Greater Heal	7	80	Heals 9-30 hit points
Mandrake	White	Strength	2	50	Improves Strength by 10 for 30 sec.
		Greater Strength	5	70	Improves Strength by 20 for 30 sec.
Nightshade	Green	Poison	1	25	Gradually reduces your hit points over several minutes, but doesn't kill
		Greater Poison	3	50	Similar to Poison, but can also reduce your Strength and Dexterity
Spider Silk	Orange	Cure (Sleep)	1	-	Counteracts poison
Sulfurous Ash	Purple	Lesser Explosion	3	30	Explodes, causing 5-10 hit points damage
		Explosion	5	60	Explodes, causing 10-20 hit points damage
		Greater Explosion	10	90	Explodes, causing 20-40 hit points damage

Towns

Kerrick,

I hope that you and your parents are well, and that the weather is clement. I trust your life is beginning to take a strong path, in a worthy direction. One that will give your life meaning. One you will never have to doubt. Or regret. Regret is a bitter thing.

I do not regret my own path. I live by the sword and by violence, but such has ever been my nature. I am a fighter. When I made the choice to fight only for true and just causes, to lend my strength to the weak, I knew that it would be a hard life. I knew I would never grow rich, or live comfortably, or die in peace. I accepted that stricture, and thought it was my best chance to make a difference ... to shed light and scatter shadows. I believed I would be Called to Quest wherever I was most needed.

But now I don't know. As I write this, I am filled with doubt.

I passed through the honest village of Cove today, and it is beset by orcs, and lies in ruins. And I could not stop.

I can feel the call summoning me to some unknown place in the north. I do not know how far I must go. I do not know how long I will be. I cannot even tell if after my quest is complete will I return to Cove, that I might assail its enemies and avenge its losses. I would have spilled out my lifeblood to protect that small hamlet, and yet I heard no call when its hour of need came. I slept soundly through nights when the noble lighthouse stood dark, when the brute creatures overran the walls and pitched torches through windows. I didn't know. I couldn't aid them. And now I have the geas of a quest upon me, and as I rode through Cove, a place I'd come to love as my own home, I could do nothing more than wonder at the fortifications and encampments and grieve. And know that if I had been a mercenary, I could have drawn my sword and fought back the minions of evil that have infested this innocent woodland. But I did nothing, and perhaps nothing will be done. Where there was once a light, will there only be a scabrous place in the dust?

My heart grieves for Cove. And I fear, as I have never feared man nor creature, that my path may not return there.

Gareth

MAPS OF THE TOWNS

The world of Britannia encompasses many regions, some dark and dank, others frigid, or tropical and sunny. Theses maps you see before you have been painstakingly inked by the gentle-handed Fodor Fain, cartographer extraordinaire, whose intricate mappings of Britannia are hailed as collector's items. May they guide you well on your journey.

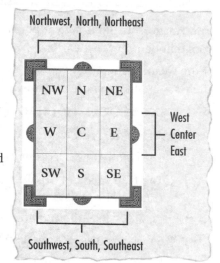

Northwest, North, Northeast

NW	N	NE
W	C	E
SW	S	SE

West
Center
East

Southwest, South, Southeast

(Should you desire to explore the less-traveled dungeons of the land, see Fodor's **Dungeon Maps**, p. 284.)

To interpret these maps, you should become familiar with their icons and terminology.

Map Icons

[NW] **Directions.** All maps are oriented so that North is at the top. In the key for each city, each location has a compass direction — [NW], [SE], etc. These directions correspond to the general areas on the map for that city. (See the above scroll.)

Signposts point in the general direction you need to follow if you're traveling to a neighboring town.

Map Keys

Map Keys are divided into categories. Each has a list of locations marked with an oval icon and a compass direction (see the above scroll). The letter inside each icon describes the category, and the number specifies a location within that category (S1 is the first shop, S2 the second shop, etc.).

A#	Arms & Armour	**H#**	Healing
C#	Civic & Common	**M#**	Magic
E#	Entertainment	**S#**	Shops
F#	Food & Provisions	**T#**	Taverns, Inns & Traveller's Aid
G#	Guilds	**U#**	Unique Locations

Reccurring locations are marked with two letters: (CC) Cemetery, (CG) City Gate, (CP) Guard Post, (CS) Stable, (CW) Warehouse and (GC) Counselors' Guildhall.

5A **5B** **Teleporters** are keyed numerically at their entrance point (a black box marked with a white number followed by "A") and exit points (a white box with the same number, followed by "B"). Some teleporters (marked "2", "3"etc.) allow two-way travel.

⚔ Britain (West) ⚔

The Warriors' Guild is a great place to train. There are six training dummies on the roof, enough for most parties.

If the weapon and armour shops around town are sold out of what you need, there's a little-known shop in the northern part of Lord British's castle.

Key to Both Maps (West and East)

Arms & Armour

(A1) The Lord's Arms (Blacksmith) [W]

(A2) The Hammer and Anvil (Blacksmith) [NW]

(A3) Quality Fletching (Bowyer) [C]

(A4) Strength and Steel (Armourer) [C]

(A5) Heavy Metal Armourer [C]

(A6) Artistic Armour [SE]

Civic & Common

(C1) The First Bank of Britain [SW]

(C2) Barracks [W]

(C3) Britain Public Library [W]

(C4) The First Library of Britain [S]

(C5) Customs [S]

(C6) The Bucking Horse Stables [N]

(CS) Stables [W, SW]

(CW) Warehouse [SW, S, SE]

(CC) Cemetery [NW]

(CP) Guard Post [SW, C (x2)]

(CG) Main Gate [C]

Entertainment

(E1) The King's Men Theater [C]

Food & Provisions

(F1) Good Eats (Bakery) [C]

(F2) Britain's Premier Provisioner and Fish Shoppe [C]

(F3) Profuse Provisions [SE]

(F4) The Cleaver (Butcher's Shop) [S]

Guilds

(GC) Counselors' Guild Hall [N, SE]

(G1) Warriors' Guild [SW]

(G2) The Sorcerer's Delight: Shop, Library and Guild [N]

(G3) Mining Cooperative [NW]

(G4) Merchants' Association [C]

(G5) Order of Engineers [W]

(G6) Artists' Guild [C]

(G7) Guild of Cavalry & Horse [NE]

Healing

(H1) Britannia Animal Care (Veterinary Clinic) [N]

(H2) Good Health Healers [C]

(Keys to Britain continued on page 250.)

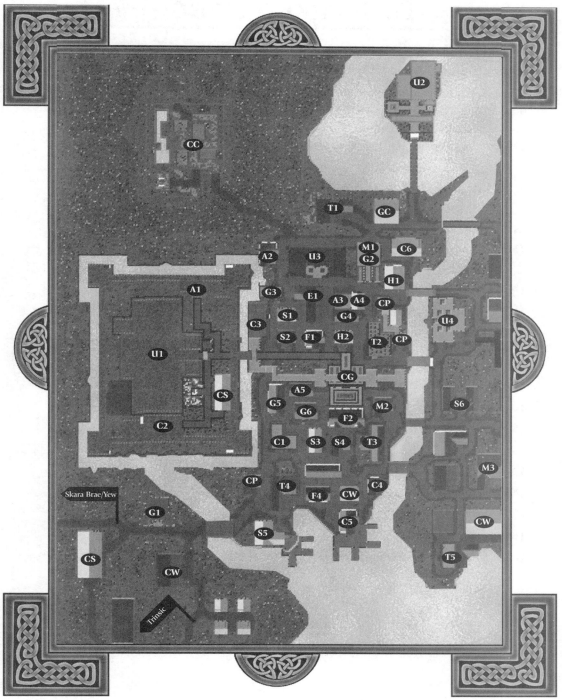

⇒ Britain (East) ⇐

Britain is a land of everything, and a grand place to begin a life of adventure. Fishing is nearby; woods are close to hand; plentiful ore is but a short stroll away.

It may seem fortuitous that there are so many guilds in this, the largest of cities, but since it costs 500 gold pieces to join, and becoming a guildsmember simply buys you discounts on certain goods, it's not the first thing on which a new character needs to spend hard-earned gold.

Key to Both Maps (continued)

Magic

(M1) The Sorcerer's Delight: Shop, Library and Guild [N]

(M2) Ethereal Goods (Magic Shop) [C]

(M3) Sage Advice (Magic Shop) [SE]

(M4) Incantations and Enchantments (Magic Shop) [E]

Shops

(S1) The Saw Horse (Woodworking) [W]

(S2) The Best Hides of Britain (Tanner) [W]

(S3) Premier Gems (Jeweler) [S]

(S4) The Lord's Clothier [S]

(S5) The Oaken Oar (Shipwright) [SW]

(S6) The Right Fit (Tailor) [E]

(S7) A Girl's Best Friend (Jeweler) [E]

Taverns, Inns & Traveller's Aid

(T1) The North Side Inn [N]

(T2) Sweet Dreams (Inn) [C]

(T3) The Blue Boar (Tavern) [S]

(T4) The Cat's Lair (Tavern) [SW]

(T5) The Unicorn's Horn (Tavern) [SE]

(T6) The Wayfarer's Inn [E]

(T7) The Salty Dog (Tavern) [E]

Unique

(U1) Lord British's Castle [W]

(U2) Blackthorn's Castle [N]

(U3) Lord British's Conservatory of Music [N]

(U4) The Chamber of Virtue (Temple) [E]

(U5) Gazebo [NE]

(U6) Lookout Tower [SE]

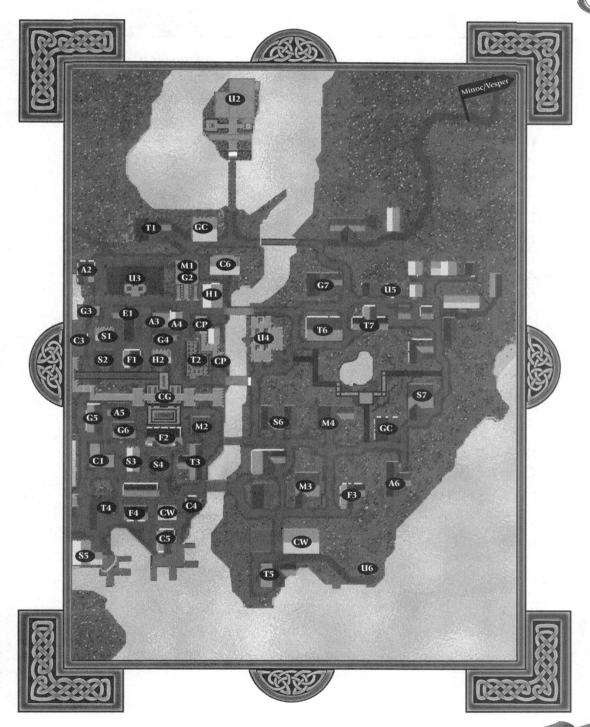

Buccaneer's Den

The lure of Buccaneer's Den is that it is so completely uncharming. It is only for the strong of arm and ruthless of character, since even the town proper is "guard free" and crime goes unpunished save by the retaliation of the local populace.

It is, essentially, a good place to learn the niceties of being a nasty person.

There are very few shops of any longstanding duration, but those people strong enough to make their way there can be very useful comrades at arms … though never make the mistake of trusting them!

This is not a good place for the untried to venture.

Key to the Map

Arms & Armour

(A1) Cutlass Smithing (Blacksmith) [NW]

Civic & Common

(C1) Bath House [NW]

(C2) Docks [E]

Food & Provisions

(F1) Pirate's Provisioner [SE]

Guilds

(G1) Pirate's Den (Society of Thieves) [SW]

Healing

(H1) The Bloody Scab [C]

Shops

(S1) Violente Woodworks [NW]

(S2) Buccaneer's Den Leatherworks (Tanner) [C]

Taverns/Inns & Traveller's Aid

(T1) The Peg Leg Inn [NE]

(T2) The Pirate's Plunder (Tavern) [SW]

Cove

Cove is a small village, once uneventful, now beset by a tribe of orcs. There are few places within the besieged walls that are of any note to the average traveller, and it is, in fact, a fairly dangerous place to visit.

It is, however, a playground for the dauntless. Training can be had just south of the armourer (where there can be found training dummies and archery butts), and the orcs to the south provide a nearly endless supply of fighting opportunities.

Orc fighting is dangerous, of course, but also lucrative. If you live long enough to rifle their pockets, you'll find they carry their fiendish wages in gold.

Key to the Map

Arms & Armour

(A1)   Armourer

Civic & Common

(C1)   Dock
(CG)   City Gate
(CP)   Guard Post

Food & Provisions

(F1)   Provisioner

Healing

(H1)   Healer

Unique

(U1)   Orc Camp

Jhelom

The city of Jhelom is a stable, gentle environment in which to begin a career — in particular a career as a fighter or a blacksmith. There are several forges to provide practice at shaping iron, and ore is not difficult to obtain in the area. A fighter will find that the practice dummies in the guilds are free to be used even by non-members, and the arena provides even more opportunities to hone your skills.

Wood gathering, fishing and snaring animals are possible in the nearby woods.

Key to the Map

Arms & Armour

(A1) First Defense (Blacksmith) [N]

(A2) Second Skin (Armourer) [N]

(A3) Armour [E]

(A4) Blacksmith [C]

(A5) Deadly Intentions (Weapons) [NW]

(A6) Weapons [E]

Civic & Common

(C1) Storage [S]

(C2) Docks [NE, C, S]

(C3) Jhelom Library [C]

(CC) Cemetery [NW]

(CG) City Gate [C]

(CP) Guard Post [C]

(CW) Warehouse [C]

Entertainment

(E1) Performing Arts Theater [S]

Food & Provisions

(F1) Baker's Dozen (Bakery) [NW]

(F2) Provisioner [C]

(F3) Finest Cuts (Butcher) [S]

Guilds

(GC) Counselors' Guild Hall [S]

(G1) Brothers in Arms Warriors' Guild [NW]

(G2) Armourers' Guild [C]

(G3) Farmers Market (Guild) [C]

Healing/Magic

(H1) Healer [C]

(M1) Jhelom Mage [S]

Shops

(S1) Sailor's Keeper (Shipwright) [NE]

(S2) Treasure of Jhelom (Jeweler) [W]

(S3) Adventurer's Needle (Tailor) [W]

(S4) Gadgets and Things (Tinker) [C]

(S5) Woodworker [C]

(S6) Pearl of Jhelom (Jeweler) [S]

(S7) Fine Tailoring [S]

(S8) Ocean's Treasure (Fish Shop) [N]

Taverns/Inns & Traveller's Aid

(T1) The Horse's Head (Tavern) [E]

(T2) The Morning Star Inn [W]

Unique

(U1) Arena [N]

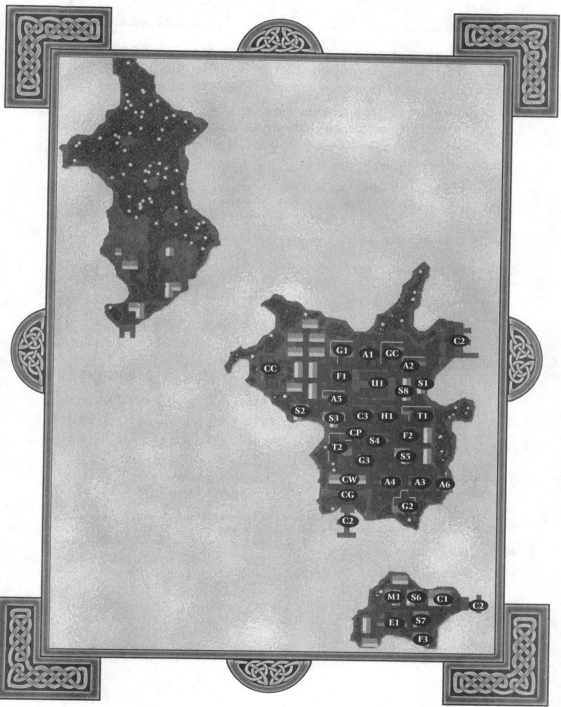

Magincia

One of Magincia's greatest charms is that it is not nearly so crowded as the "entrance" cities. It holds no real attraction for the fighter mentality, but others will find that things get done far more quickly and pleasantly in Magincia.

This is a popular area for mining and other forms of raw material gathering. Shops stand ready to purchase the fundamental materials of their trade, and the area is not so quickly picked over by hordes of new people. Metal is always a popular material on the open market.

A guild is a good place to buy tools, plus joining a guild is the best way of getting your implements and essentials at a reasonable rate.

There is a Moongate to the west, in the forest.

Key to the Map

Civic & Common

(C1)   Temple [NE]

(C2)   Parliament [SE]

(C3)   Docks [SW]

(CW)   Warehouse [E]

Food & Provisions

(F1)   The Baker's Dozen [SE]

Guilds

(GC)   Counselors' Guild Hall [C]

(G1)   Mining Cooperative [W]

(G2)   Fishermen's Guild & Supplies [S]

(G3)   Merchants' Association [S]

Magic

(M1)   Magincia's Magicka [S]

Shops

(S1)   The Tic Toc Shop (Tinker) [E]

(S2)   The Family Jewels (Jeweler) [W]

(S3)   Stitchin' Time (Tailor) [SW]

(S4)   The Furled Sail (Shipwright) [SW]

Taverns/Inns & Traveller's Aid

(T1)   The Stag & Lion Inn [C]

(T2)   Soldier's Sanctuary [S]

(T3)   The Great Horns Tavern [SE]

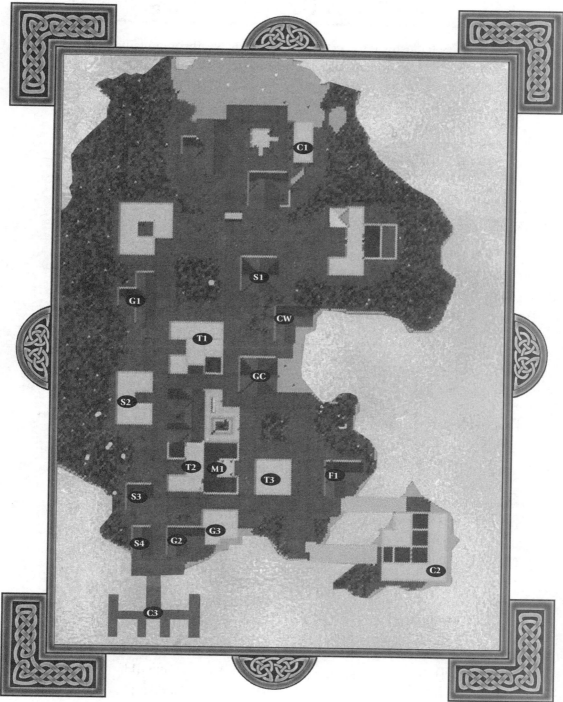

Minoc

Minoc is a hospitable town for a skilled blacksmith. Nearby mountains contain substantial deposits of iron ore, and many Minocians are employed in the mining trade. Blacksmiths can purchase raw ore and convert it to ingots, and then sell the ingots, or convert them to weapons and sell those.

For the more nomadic, Vesper lies only a short distance away through the wilderness. By keeping an eye on surpluses and shortages in each town, one might be able to earn a living trading, while avoiding the dangers of a long land voyage and the expense of a sea voyage.

Key to the Map

Arms & Armour

(A1)	The Forgery (Blacksmith) [S]
(A2)	The Warrior's Battle Gear (Armourer) [S]

Civic & Common

(C1)	Minoc Town Hall [W]
(CS)	Stable [N]

Entertainment

(E1)	The Mystical Lute (Music Hall) [SW]

Food & Provisions

(F1)	The Slaughtered Cow (Butcher) [NW]
(F2)	The Old Miners Supplies (Provisioner) [N]
(F3)	The Survival Shop (Provisioner) [S]

Healing

(H1)	The Healing Hand (Healer) [SE]

Guilds

(GC)	Counselors' Guild Hall [N]
(G1)	The New World Order (Warriors' Guild) [N]
(G2)	The Golden Pick Axe (Mining Cooperative) [N]
(G3)	The Matewan (Miners' Guild) [C]

Shops

(S1)	Gears and Gadgets (Tinker) [N]
(S2)	The Oak Throne (Architect) [C]
(S3)	The Stretched Hide (Tanner) [C]

Taverns/Inns & Traveller's Aid

(T1)	The Barnacle (Tavern) [N]

Unique

(U1)	Statue [C]
(U2)	Cave [E]
(U3)	Mt. Kendall [E]
(U4)	Mining Camp [E]
(U5)	Gypsy Camp [S]

GC
CS
T1
F1
F2
G1
G2
S1
S2
G3
U2
U3
U1
C1
S3
U4
E1
F3
A1
A2
H1
Vesper/Britain
U5

Moonglow

As the seat of knowledge for the realm, Moonglow is naturally attractive to mages. Every book ever written is rumored to appear somewhere within this domain.

Key to the Map

Arms & Armour

(A1) The Mighty Axe (Weapons) [NW]

(A2) Second Defense (Armoury) [C]

Civic & Common

(CC) Cemetery [S]

(C1) Lycaeum [NW]

(C2) Moongate [C]

Food & Provisions

(F1) The Scholar's Goods (Provisioner) [C]

(F2) Fruits and Vegetables (Provisioner) [C]

(F3) Mage's Bread (Bakery) [C]

(F4) The Fatted Calf (Butcher) [C]

Guilds

(GC) Counselors' Guild Hall [C]

(G1) Encyclopedia Magicka (Guild of Mages) [C]

(G2) Moonglow Academy of Arts (Artists' Guild) [C]

(G3) Guild of Arcane Arts [C]

(G4) Merchants' Guild [C]

(G5) Masters of Illusion [E]

(G6) Guild of Sorcerery [SE]

Healing

(H1) Healer [C]

Magic

(M1) Moonglow Reagent Shop [C]

Shops

(S1) Scholar's Cut (Tailor) [C]

(S2) The Mage's Seat (Woodworker) [C]

(S3) Herbal Splendor (Herbalist) [C]

Taverns/Inns & Traveller's Aid

(T1) Moonglow Student Hostel (Inn) [C]

(T2) The Scholar's Inn [C]

Unique

(U1) Telescope [E]

(U2) Zoo [S]

Intracity Teleporters

(1A) Teleporter entrance to 1B [C]

(1B) Teleporter exit from 1A [NW]

(2A) Teleporter entrance to 2B [C]

(2B) Teleporter exit from 2A [NE]

(3A) Teleporter entrance to 3B [C]

(3B) Teleporter exit from 3A [E]

(4A) Teleporter entrance to 4B [NW, NE, E, S]

(4B) Teleporter exit from 4A [C]

(5A) Teleporter entrance to 5B [C]

(5B) Teleporter exit from 5A [S]

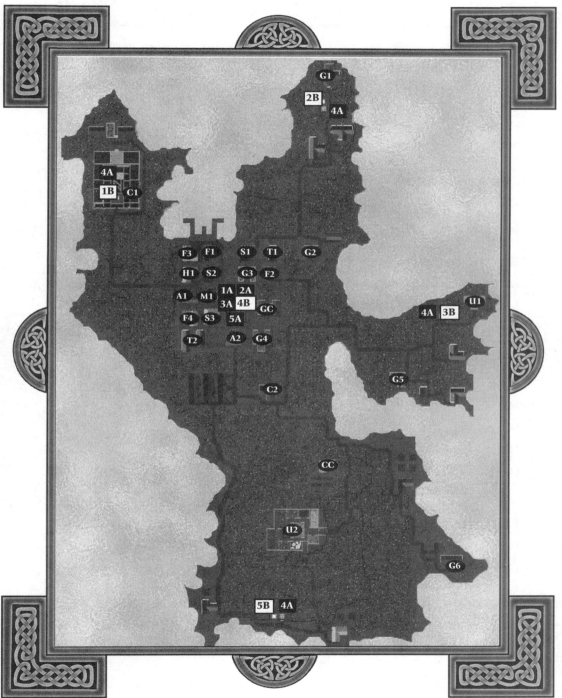

Nujel'm

The greatest attraction of Nujel'm may well be its beauty. The gardens are a delight to explore, and the city proper grew out of a municipal desire to be surrounded by color and nature, rather than a soulless outgrowth of commerce and practicality.

Nujel'm is not the den of iniquity that some people would lead you to believe, but it is a place where the rules are more or less at the whim of the instant. Traditional right and wrong in this city are not so much ignored as adapted to fit the situation.

This sometimes leads to disastrous results in the municipal Chess Field!

Key to the Map

Arms & Armour

(A1)   Weapons (Market Stall) [NW]

(A2)   Blacksmith (Market Stall) [NW]

Civic & Common

(C1)   Customs [C]

(C2)   Dock [SE]

(C3)   Bank [SE]

(C4)   Jail [S]

(CC)   Cemetery [NW]

(CP)   Guard Post
[NW, N (x2), W (x2)]

Entertainment

(E1)   Theater [C]

(E2)   Chess Board [S]

Food & Provisions

(F1)   Butcher (Market Stall) [NW]

Guilds

(GC)   Counselors' Guild Hall [NE]

(G1)   Merchant's Association [S]

Shops

(S1)   Tanner (Market Stall) [NW]

(S2)   Bowyer (Market Stall) [NW]

(S3)   Jeweler [NE]

(S4)   Tailor [E]

Taverns/Inns & Traveller's Aid

(T1)   Mystical Spirits (Tavern) [E]

(T2)   The Silver Bow (Tavern) [C]

(T3)   Restful Slumber (Inn) [S]

Unique

(U1)   Conservatory [N]

(U2)   Palace [C]

(U3)   Garden [SW]

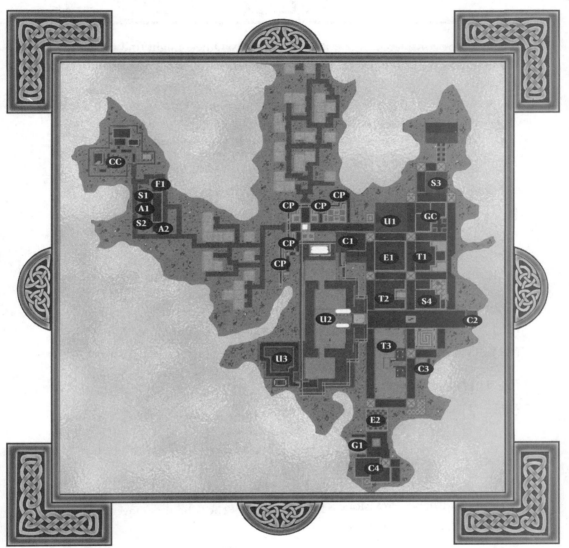

Ocllo

This might be considered the capital city for bards. Others might find it a bit dry, and definitely difficult to get to, as the only entrance to this city is a small inlet to the south.

The Bardic Collegium provides not only good prices to members, but also a wide variety of instruments for practice. Although some have been known to be "borrowed" for a while, it takes a practiced, deft touch to do so and it is generally considered a knavely thing to do.

Key to the Map

Arms & Armour

(A1) Hammer and Steel Smithy [W]

Civic & Common

(C1) Ocllo Public Library [NW]

(C2) Docks [S]

Entertainment

(E1) First Academy of Music (Theater) [N]

Food & Provisions

(F1) Now You're Cookin' (Baker) [W]

(F2) Last Chance Provisioners [W]

(F3) Sweet Meat (Butcher) [S]

Guilds

(GC) Counselors' Guild Hall [N]

(G1) Guild of Sorcery [NW]

(G2) Bardic Collegium [N]

Healing

(H1) Island Sanctuary (Healer) [W]

Shops

(S1) Paint and More (Painter) [NW]

(S2) A Stitch in Time (Tailor) [C]

(S3) Better Leather Tannery [W]

(S4) Anchors Aweigh (Shipwright) [SW]

Taverns/Inns & Traveller's Aid

(T1) The Bountiful Harvest (Inn) [C]

(T2) The Albatross (Tavern) [S]

Unique

(U1) Farm [E (x2), SE (x2)]

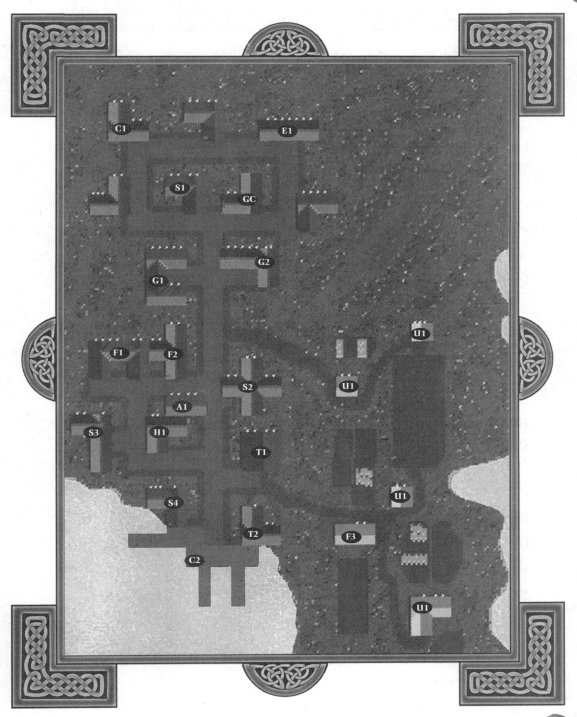

Serpent's Hold

It is impossible to get to Serpent's Hold without a boat or some magical shortcut, so it does not see the traffic that many other cities get.

It is a fine place to be a warrior, however. The Warriors' Guild has a hall there, along with a skilled weaponsmith shop and armoury. Everything that one could need before setting off on an adventure can be found on these two islands ... and for afterwards, there are two talented healers for patching up any wounds.

The stables of Serpent's Hold are a good place to practice any animal-related skills that might need honing.

Key to the Map

Arms & Armour

(A1)   Serpent Arms (Weapons) [C]

(A2)   Blacksmith [C]

Civic & Common

(C1)   Dock [C (x2)]

(C2)   Island Stables [SW]

(C3)   Barracks [NE]

(CS)   Stables [E]

(CP)   Guard Post
[N, NE, W, C, S, SW, SE]

(CG)   City Gate [N]

Food & Provisions

(F1)   Bakery [N]

(F2)   Provisioner [N]

(F3)   Serpent's Hold Meats
(Butcher) [SW]

Guilds

(GC)   Counselors' Guild Hall [N]

(G1)   Warriors' Guild [E]

Healing

(H1)   Healer [N]

(H2)   Healer [C]

Magic

(M1)   Mage Shop [N]

(M2)   Reagent Shop [N]

Shops

(S1)   Bowyer [NE]

(S2)   Silver Serpent Tailors [SW]

(S3)   Tinker [S]

Taverns/Inns & Traveller's Aid

(T1)   The Dog and Lion Pub [C]

(T2)   The Broken Arrow Inn [C]

(T3)   Tavern [C]

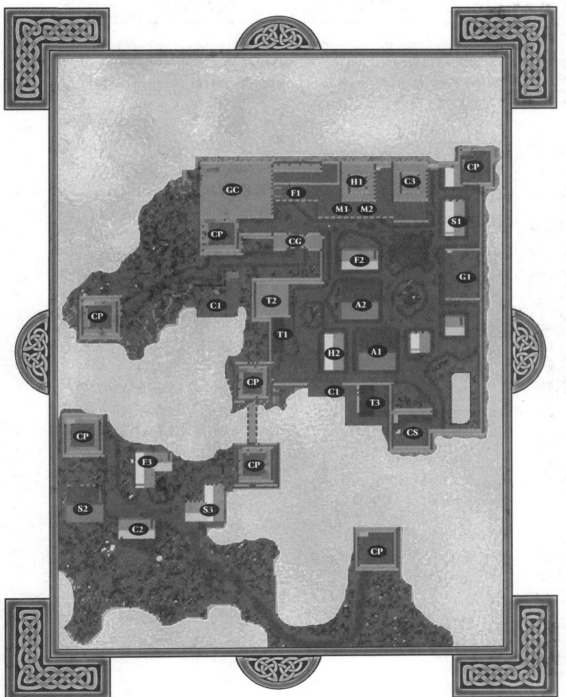

Skara Brae

Rangers congregate at this city in the woods. It's an excellent place to train animals, either in the stables or in the nearby forest. Deer and rabbits won't run away if you don't attack them, and will even make pets. Pets are so prevalent here that supplies specific to their needs are available for sale.

Archery butts are available for practicing at the Rangers' Guild, and are a great way to perfect your style.

Key to the Map

Arms & Armour

(A1) More Than Just Mail (Armourer) [N]

(A2) Gore Galore (Weapons) [NE]

(A3) On Guard Armoury [C]

Civic & Common

(C1) Skara Brae Town Hall [W]

(C2) Docks [S, SE]

(CS) Stable [NW]

Food & Provisions

(F1) Farmer's Market [N]

(F2) Bountiful Meats (Butcher) [C]

(F3) Sundry Supplies (Provisioner) [S]

(F4) The Honey Pot (Beekeeper) [N]

Guilds

(GC) Counselors' Guild Hall [N]

(G1) League of Rangers [NW]

Healing

(H1) Final Aegis (Healer) [C]

Magic

(M1) Mystic Treasure (Reagents) [NE]

(M2) Mage's Menagerie (Magic Shop) [C]

Shops

(S1) Beasts of Burden (Animal Supplies) [NW]

(S2) Builder's Delight (Carpenter) [N]

(S3) Shear Pleasure (Tailor) [E]

(S4) Bloody Bowman (Bowyer) [C]

(S5) Superior Ships (Shipwright) [S]

Taverns/Inns & Traveller's Aid

(T1) The Shattered Skull (Tavern) [W]

(T2) The Falconer's Inn [S]

Trinsic

Almost every shop you need is located near the eastern bridge — this nest of shops also makes it easy for adventurers taking the eastern bridge out of town to sell their newly acquired possessions if they return by the same bridge.

Key to the Map

Arms & Armour

(A1)	Shining Path Armoury [N]
(A2)	Honorable Arms (Weapons) [C]

Civic & Common

(C1)	Barracks [N]
(C2)	Encyclopedia Magicka [NW]
(C3)	Meeting Hall [N]
(C4)	Jail [W]
(C5)	First Trinsic Stablery [C]
(C6)	Bank of Britannia: Trinsic Branch [SW]
(C7)	Docks [SE]
(C8)	Trinsic Stablery [NW]
(CP)	Guard Post [NW (x2), W, SE, E]

Food & Provisions

(F1)	The British Grille (Restaurant) [N]
(F2)	Britannia Provisions [W]
(F3)	Baked Delights (Baker) [C]
(F4)	The Trinsic Cut (Butcher) [SE]

Guilds

(GC)	Counselors' Guild Hall [NW, S]
(G1)	Order of Engineers [NW]
(G2)	Brotherhood of Trinsic (Warriors' Guild) [N]
(G3)	Paladins' Guild [NE]
(G4)	Sons of the Sea (Guild of Fishermen) [SE]

Healing

(H1)	Healer [C]

Shops

(S1)	The Pearl of Trinsic (Jeweler) [C]
(S2)	Adventurer's Clothing (Tailor) [SE]
(S3)	Trinsic Fine Skins (Tanner) [SE]

Taverns/Inns & Traveller's Aid

(T1)	The Traveller's Inn [NW]
(T2)	The Keg and Anchor (Tavern) [C]
(T3)	The Rusty Anchor (Inn) [C]

Unique

(U1)	Training Grounds [NE]
(U2)	Paladins' Hall [NE]
(U3)	Garden [C]

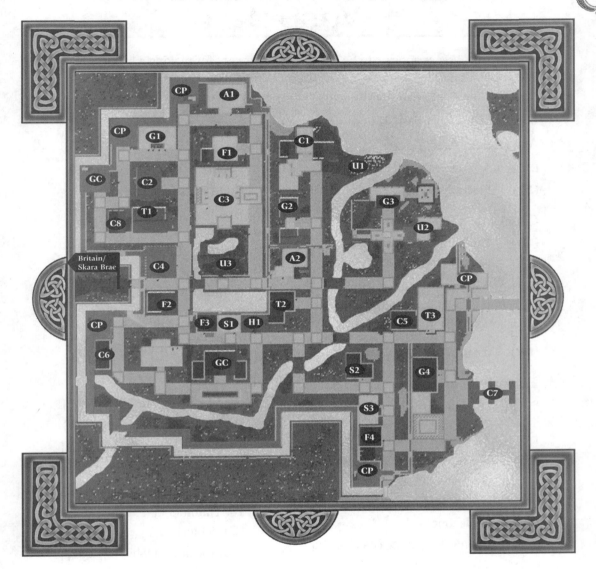

CP
A1
CP
G1
C1
F1
U1
GC
C2
G3
C3
G2
U2
T1
C8
Britain/
Skara Brae
C4
U3
A2
CP
F2
T2
CP
F3 S1 H1
C5 T3
CP
C6
GC
S2
G4
C7
S3
F4
CP

Vesper

As in Trinsic, Vesper appears to be another popular spot for making a bit of gold. The population grows even by the week as hopeful entrepreneurs come to test their mercantile hand in the city's prosperous marketplace.

Key to the Map

Arms & Armour

(A1) Armourer [W]

(A2) Blacksmith [C]

Civic & Common

(C1) The Mint of Vesper [N]

(C2) Docks [E (x2)]

(C3) Vesper Museum [S]

(C4) Vesper Customs [SE]

(CC) Cemetery [W]

(CP) Guard Post [SW]

Entertainment

(E1) The Musicians' Hall [N]

Food & Provisions

(F1) The Adventurer's Supplies (Provisioner) [NE]

(F2) The Twisted Oven (Bakery) [E]

(F3) Provisioner [E]

(F4) The Butcher's Knife (Butcher) [E]

(F5) Fish Shop [E]

(F6) Provisioner [C]

(F7) The Busy Bee (Beekeeper) [N]

Magic

(M1) The Bubbling Brew (Mage) [N]

(M2) Magical Light (Magic Shop) [N]

(M3) The Magician's Friend (Magic Shop) [E]

Guilds

(GC) Counselor's Guild Hall [S]

(G1) Guild of Fishermen [E]

(G2) Society of Thieves [S]

(G3) The Champions of Light (Warriors' Guild) [C]

(G4) The Ore of Vesper (Mining Cooperative) [N]

Healing

(H1) The Herb of Health (Healer) [C]

Shops

(S1) The Spinning Wheel (Tailor) [NE]

(S2) The Colored Canvas (Painter) [N]

(S3) Shimmering Jewel (Jeweler) [N]

(S4) The Ranger Tool (Bowyer) [W]

(S5) The Gadgets Corner (Tinker) [C]

(S6) The Hammer and Nails (Carpenter) [C]

(S7) The Majestic Boat (Shipwright) [E]

(S8) Tanner [S]

Taverns/Inns & Traveller's Aid

(T1) Vesper Youth Hostel (Inn) [SE]

(T2) The Marsh Hall (Tavern) [C]

(T3) The Ironwood Inn [SW]

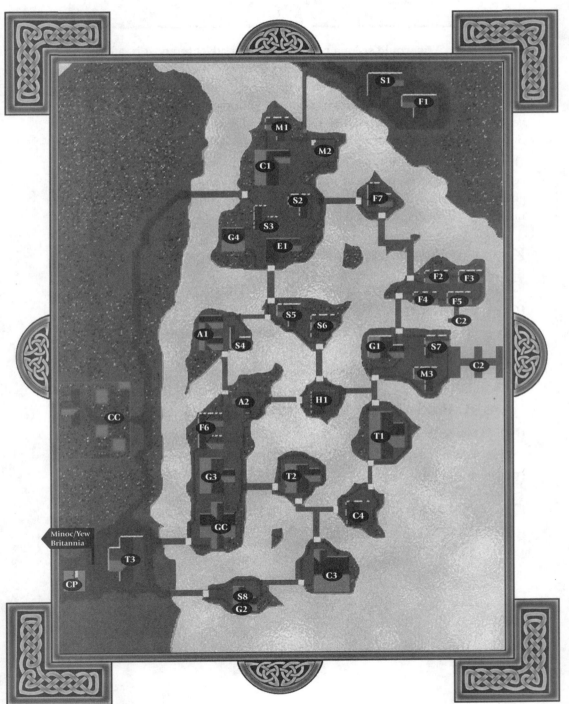

Yew

At first glance, Yew would seem a popular place for adventurers. It is, after all, a village famous for its wine! But perhaps the somber presence of the abbey, or the mellow attitude of the brothers therein, have had a calming effect on the town. While it is a good place to begin one's career, with plenty of wildlife, trees for harvesting and other useful resources nearby, there are no "regular" shops at which to purchase staples for the devil-may-care lifestyle.

That is not to say that it is a waste of time for any passing soldier of fortune. The cemetery nearby is known to be populated by a fair number of undead such as ghosts and skeletons, and these are a fine way to get good practice, improve your notoriety, and perhaps earn a coin or two.

Key to the Map

Civic & Common

(C1)	Prison [NW]
(C2)	Storeroom [NW]
(C3)	Courtroom [NW]
(CC)	Cemetery [SE]

Food & Provisions

(F1)	Market [C]
(F2)	The Jolly Baker [C]
(F3)	Butcher [C]

Guild

(GC)	Counselor's Guild Hall [E]

Healing

(H1)	Healer [C]
(H2)	Deep Forest Healing [SE]

Shops

(S1)	Flour Mill [N]
(S2)	Winery [NE]
(S3)	The Sturdy Bow (Bowyer) [C]
(S4)	Bloody Thumb Woodworking [C]

Unique

(U1)	Empath Abbey [NE]

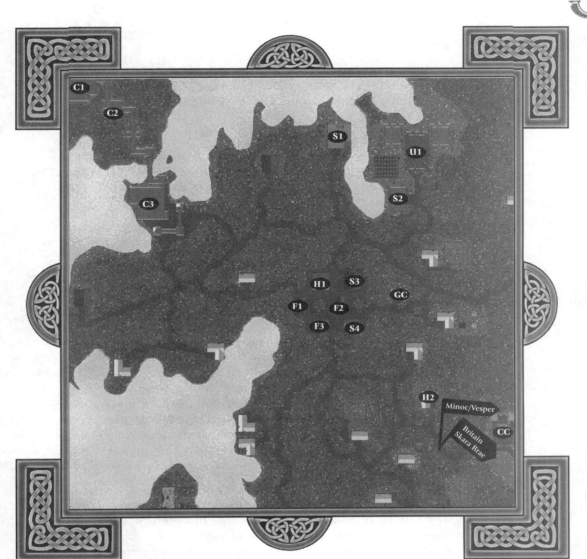

C1
C2
S1
U1
C3
S2
H1
S3
GC
F1
F2
F3
S4
H2
Minoc/Vesper
Britain
Skara Brae
CC

Kerrick,

I have had such an adventure as a bard would take twelve evenings to sing, and I fear that one letter may not be enough to describe it. Let me tell you how it began ....

I was called to a quest for a baby, stolen from its mother in a method most foul and held by a mischievous woman. Although it was no small matter to bring justice to bear, I triumphed and in the end I had the child under my own custody. The next step was to return him to his rightful family. All I knew was that he "belonged to Wind."

Wind, I found, is a legendary city hidden within or near the forest of Samlethe. Everyone from whom I sought advice counseled that it was a fool's errand ... that there was no such city and I was misled. My heart is guided by higher forces, however, and I was determined to go. I bought a basket to hold the infant — with a lid to shield him from the sun — and began the second part of my quest.

Kerrick, you have young brothers. You know I have not. I thought that tending a baby would have been a simple matter, for it weighs less than a mail shirt and sleeps through most of the day. You should have warned me. You should have said: Gareth, do not take an infant across Britannia without a train of pack mules, a wet nurse and a maidservant. You should have mentioned: Gareth, never feed ewe's milk to a baby accustomed to milk from a goat. Or even: Gareth, when you change a boy-child's napkins, lower your visor. I would have been grateful for but a word on what makes an infant wail when it is fed and dry and warm. By the time I reached the Serpent Spine mountains, I was a broken man.

I near wept with relief when I saw greenery of Samlethe's forest. It is a harsh place, filled with monsters and worse creatures, but I was beyond fear and in no mood to dally. Rogue magic has mutated the denizens, and the orcs and humans seem to have banded together into a black brotherhood, but either the wild look on my face or the foul stench from my packs kept them at bay.

On the first evening in the forest I heard the eerie cries of the hungry creatures, but it woke the baby into a fit of screaming, and the nights were peaceful ever after. I will tell you more in my next letter.

Your friend,

Gareth

Kerrick,

At the end of my last letter, I had entered the forest of Samlethe. It seemed as though a path opened up for me to guide me to the fabled city, and that is indeed the case. It is certain that without the aid of the mages of Wind, I would have spent weeks searching for the entrance to that mystical city.

Wind is divided into two parts: flat-faced cliff buildings and platforms that cling tenaciously to the side of the mountains, and the tunnels within the mountain itself. It is almost like two cities, for outside in the cold the people wear furs and drab colors, while within the warm inner city they wear brightly colored flowing robes, slippers and long, unbound hair. That is, at least, what I was told by the guide who came out to greet me.

It seems all the people of Wind are accomplished mages. From what I saw, it is true; they have no technology, but posses a library which is a nigh infinite source for information on the arcane arts. They have magical devices and scrying techniques that let them see anything of interest to them, and use spells of invisibility and similar things to prevent being discovered by those of no interest to them.

Most remained invisible to me, but the family of the infant was welcoming and grateful, and led me to the wonders of their city as an honored and respected guest. I saw their underground farms, where they grow the peculiar glowing fungi which are their main vegetable staples. They showed me the methods that allow them to watch over and care for the mutant races in the Samlethe forest, for which they feel responsible. I even wandered for a time through the magical garden they maintain within the mountain, complete with a magical sun to provide nurturing light and warmth.

Perhaps the most impressive aspect of the people of Wind is their belief in balance. Moderation is their one desire. They say that people cannot be forced to behave ethically, but must instead grow into the desire for and knowledge of right and wrong. This, I believe, is the true reason for their isolationism ... contact with the outer world might upset the balance by bringing in unpredictable elements. They say, instead, it is that they wish to improve the balance of the world, and those who develop the world as a whole must be therefore hidden so that reliance upon them is impossible. They are an undoubtedly powerful people, and I am relieved that they are not an aggressive one.

Your friend,

Gareth

Wind

The location of the city of Wind is secret, but it is not difficult to find — once you have found the Forest of Samlethe. Wind is an underground city, and you will find the sole existing teleporter from the surface to the city inside a cave maze.

Be forewarned, however, that the city of Wind is a city of mages, and that the teleporter to Wind will only allow entry to those who meet two criteria established by the citizens of the town. Entry is granted to any who have a Magery skill equal or greater to 60 and who have cast every spell from every spell circle up to and including the Sixth Circle. The teleporter will deny entry to those who do not meet these requirements, informing them that they are not worthy to enter the city of Wind.

Key to the Map

Civic & Common

(C1)   Bunkhouse [NE]

(C2)   Dining Room [NE]

(C3)   Library [C]

(C4)   Library [C]

Food & Provisions

(F1)   Supplies [W]

(F2)   Kitchen [NE]
(Wind's communal kitchen contains three shops — a butcher's shop, a bakery and a farmer's stall. You can purchase food from all three.)

Healing

(H1)   Healer [C]

Shops

(S1)   Alchemist [NW]

(S2)   Tailor [NW]

(S3)   Alchemist [NE]

Taverns, Inns and Traveller's Aid

(T1)   Inn [NW]

(T2)   Inn [C]

Intracity Teleporters

(1A)   Entrance to/exit from 1B [N]

(1B)   Entrance to/exit from 1A [NW]

(3)   Teleporter to surface [W]

(4)   Teleporter from surface [SW]

Dungeons

My Heroic Adventures: Part XIII, Day 4

I knew my Fate was Glory and Adventure from the day I ~~left~~ strode from the training field to ~~find~~ seek Confront my Destiny. It is not every Warrior who can claim such a complete education in only two weeks.

My Glorious Adventure ~~appeared~~ ~~showed~~ was Made Manifest within hours! I Vanquished a Rogue, Slew ~~an~~ a grewsome Orc and ~~made my own Rabbit Stew~~ dined well upon Nature's Repast.

Much better than school.

The next day I Slayed a Despicable Villain. Righteously.

Evil, however, beckoned me to ~~Right the Wrongs~~ Cleanse a Scourge from our Noble Soil. A villager told me a family of Ettins lived in a cave nearby, and ~~I found it~~ there I went. The air was cold, the walls were ~~damp~~ dank, and the Stench of Depravity Assaulted my Nose. Those are the ~~signs~~ Hallmarks of a Foul Dungeon, so I knew I was in the Right Place.

My first day I Defeated two rats and a Mongbat. The second day I discovered the ~~chewed body~~ ~~Gnawed~~ ~~Corpse~~ Remains of a Thief. There was one Brass-Bound Chest, Filled with treasures, but also surrounded by body parts, so I didn't go near it. I may have been here Overlong. Mayhaps weeks. I keep hearing the sound of footsteps, even when I Stand Silent? I can't find the Ettins and I'm running low on torc

ABANDON ALL HOPE ....

Dungeons are to an adventurer what flour is to a Cook, what a panther is to an Animal Trainer ... or what a metal-bound, locked chest is to a Thief. It is the first real challenge that will prove your mettle. It is the best opportunity for a lucrative day's work. It is the most fun, and also the most dangerous, way to spend a sunny afternoon.

In this section we give you a bird's-eye view of each of the dungeons found in the game. Unique points of interest are individually named, and more common sites are noted with icons.

Campsites are called out with the letter "C." These are not safe places for you to log out, but rather they are camps set up by local monsters. There is a slightly better than average chance of meeting up with a monster at a campsite than you would in other places — and some creatures tend to keep their spending money there!

Traps and other such dangerous locations are marked with exclamation points. You should be able to avoid these dangers if you look closely enough, but wherever you see the Trap Icon, you'll want to be sure you've got your Healing Potions stocked up. There is a variety of traps, just like treasure, and you need to keep your eyes open to see them coming ... and remember where they were for the next time you venture into the area.

Healing areas are marked with an Ankh, and there aren't many of them. Dungeons are dark and evil places, and you should be prepared to look after yourself without having to drag your slaughtered spirit to a shrine for resurrection.

Numbered icons represent areas or lairs where specific monsters tend to congregate. The numbers correspond to the numbers in parentheses in the key near the map.

Bulleted lists provide information on which monsters appear generally throughout the section.

Unique areas, such as geographic (or architectural) landmarks, teleporters or other useful locations are called out on a location-by-location basis.

Treasure sites (where the good stuff tends to be found) are randomly generated throughout dungeons. Some of these are crates, some are wooden chests and some are metal chests. The treasure in these chests does recycle itself, but not so often as to make it feasible for you to hang around, opening the chest all day. Also, the goodies inside are chosen on a somewhat random basis. Just because a chest gives you the sword of a lifetime doesn't mean you can go into business as an arms dealer. Other times you might find gold, or other valuable items.

Once again, please note that these dungeons are correct at the time of printing, but that changes may occur as time passes. We recommend you make notes on the maps as you explore the dungeons.

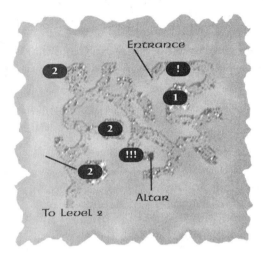

Level 1

♀ All monsters may be found on this level

(1) Lizard Men Lair

(2) Zombie Lair

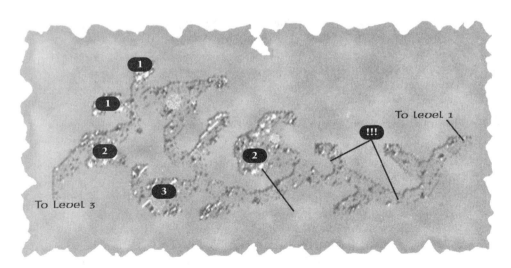

Level 2

♀ All monsters may be found on this level

(1) Lizard Men Lair

(2) Rat Men Lair

(3) Spider Lair

Level 3

☥ Daemons

☥ Ghouls

☥ Liches

☥ The painting is useful if you double-left-click on it.

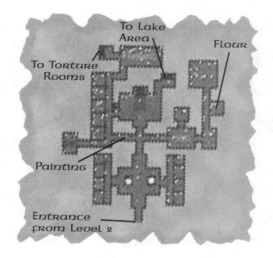

Lake Area

☥ Dragons

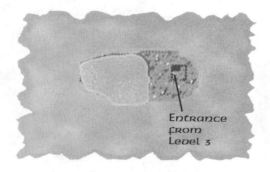

Torture Rooms

☥ Ghouls

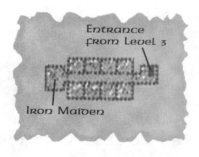

Deceit

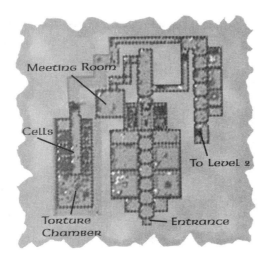

Level 1

☥ Giant Rats

☥ Sewer Rats

☥ Slimes

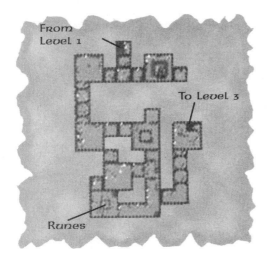

Level 2

☥ Air Elemental

☥ Earth Elemental

☥ Fire Elemental

☥ Giant Rats

☥ Headless

☥ Lizard Men

☥ Mongbats

☥ Scorpions

☥ Sewer Rats

☥ Skeletons

☥ Slimes

☥ Zombies

Level 3

- ♀ Gazers
- ♀ Giant Scorpions
- ♀ Giant Spiders
- ♀ Rat Men
- ♀ Snakes
- ♀ Zombies

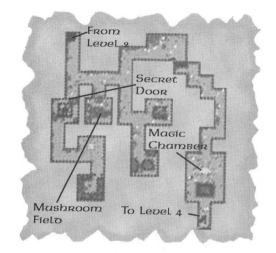

Level 4

- ♀ Daemons
- ♀ Dragons
- ♀ Drakes
- ♀ Elementals
- ♀ Ghouls
- ♀ Liches

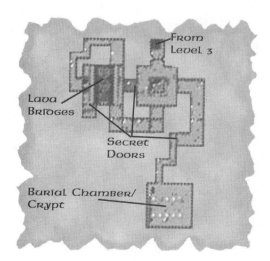

Despise

Entryway

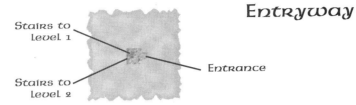

Stairs to Level 1

Entrance

Stairs to Level 2

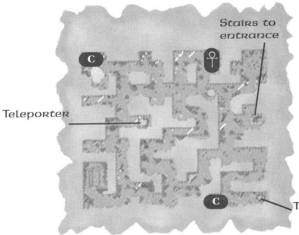

Stairs to entrance

Teleporter

Teleporter

Level 1

♀ Lizard Men

♀ Rat Men

♀ Scorpions

♀ Slimes

♀ Teleporters convey you back and forth between each other. They are two way.

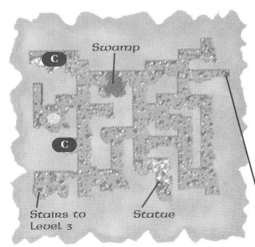

Swamp

Stairs to Level 3

Statue

Stairs to Entrance

Level 2

♀ Gazers

♀ Ghouls

♀ Lizard Men

♀ Rat Men

♀ Zombies

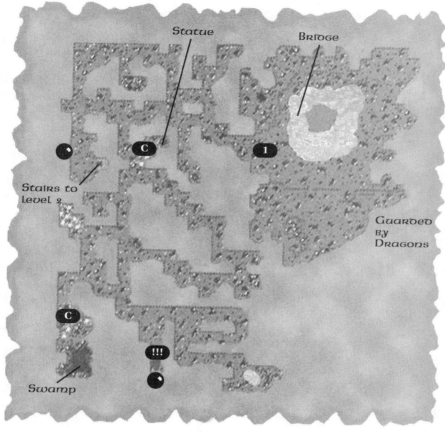

Statue

Bridge

C

1

Stairs to
Level 2

Guarded
By
Dragons

C

!!!

Swamp

Level 3

A few of the creatures from the upper levels of this dungeon can be found on this level, along with:

☥ Daemons

☥ Drakes

☥ Elementals

☥ Liches

(1) This large area surrounding the lake is the home of Dragons and Drakes.

⬤ Crystal Balls may reveal what has been recently said in the vicinity … if you're lucky.

Destard

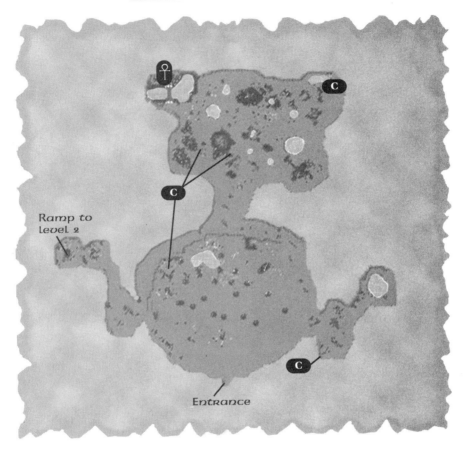

Ramp to
Level 2

Entrance

Level 1

☥ All monsters may be found on this level

☥ This is a favorite lair of dragons, so more dragons will show up here than would appear in a normal dungeon.

Level 2

♀ All monsters may be found on this level

♀ Higher frequency of dragons

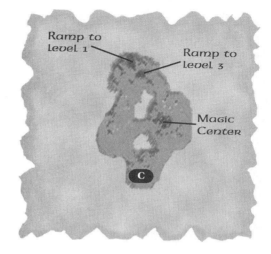

Level 3

♀ All monsters may be found on this level

♀ Higher frequency of dragons

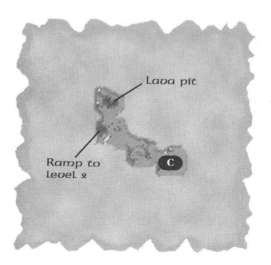

Hythloth

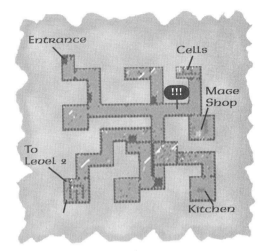

Level 1

♀ Lizard Men

♀ Giant Rats

♀ Rat Men

♀ Scorpions

♀ Spiders

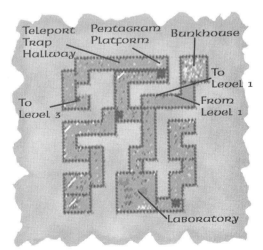

Level 2

♀ Lizard Men

♀ Giant Rats

♀ Rat Men

♀ Scorpions

♀ Spiders

Level 3

- ♀ Fire Elemental
- ♀ Lizard Men
- ♀ Giant Rats
- ♀ Rat Men
- ♀ Scorpions
- ♀ Spiders
- **(1)** Daemon Lair
- **(2)** Gazer Lair
- **(3)** Liche Lair

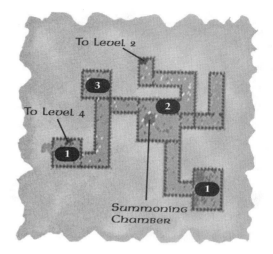

Level 4

- ♀ Fire Elemental
- ♀ Lizard Men
- ♀ Rats
- ♀ Rat Men
- ♀ Scorpions
- ♀ Spiders
- **(1)** Daemon Lair
- **(2)** Liche Lair

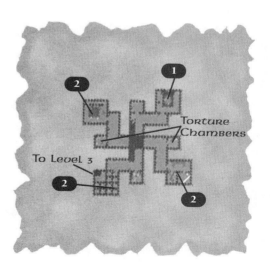

Shame

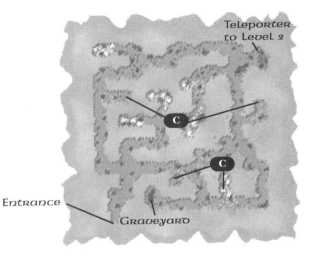

Teleporter to Level 2

C

C

Entrance

Graveyard

Level 1

☥ Lizard Men

☥ Orcs

☥ Rat Men

☥ Slimes

☥ Skeletons

☥ Zombies (a few)

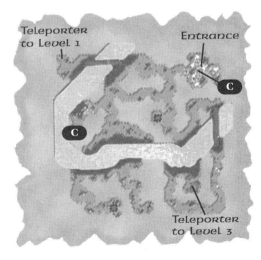

Teleporter to Level 1

Entrance

C

C

Teleporter to Level 3

Level 2

☥ Giant Scorpions

☥ Giant Spiders

☥ Lizard Men

☥ Mongbats

☥ Rat Men

☥ Slimes

☥ Skeletons

☥ Zombies

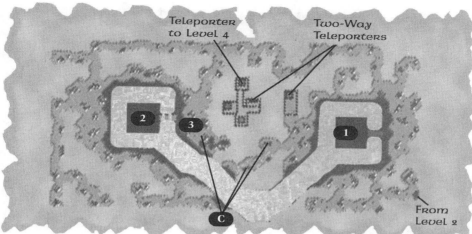

Level 3

All creatures on upper levels, plus:

(1) Lair of a single Gazer

(2) Lair of a single Fire Elemental

(3) Lair of a single Liche

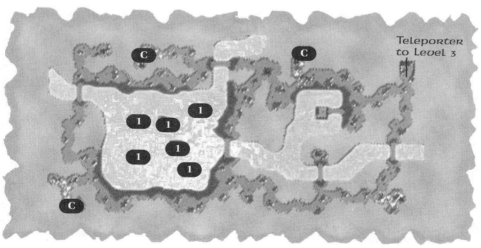

Level 4

All creatures on Levels 1 and 2 plus:

☥   Liches

☥   Earth Elementals

☥   Headless

(1) Lair of a single Gazer, on little islands in the middle of the lake

WRONG

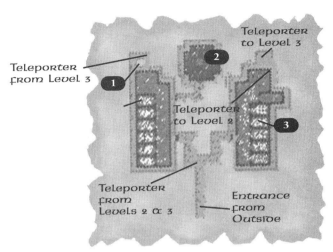

Teleporter to Level 3

Teleporter from Level 3

Teleporter to Level 2

Teleporter from Levels 2 & 3

Entrance from Outside

Level 1

♀ Lizard Men

♀ Rat Men

♀ Slimes

♀ Skeletons

(1) Liche Lair

(2) Lizard Men Lair

(3) Zombie Lair

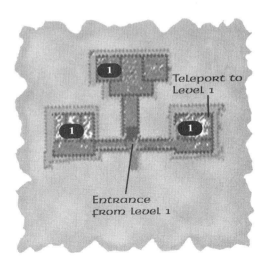

Teleport to Level 1

Entrance from Level 1

Level 2

♀ Lizard Men

♀ Rat Men

♀ Slimes

♀ Skeletons

(1) Zombie Lair

Level 3

No Creatures

Teleporters are all one-way.

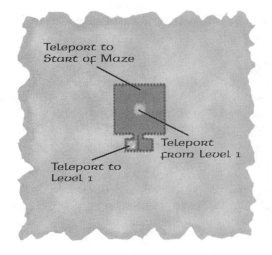

Details of Level 3 Maze

Walls will only appear as you walk next to them.

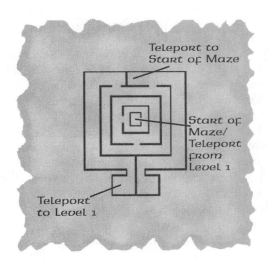

COMPUTER GAME BOOKS

The 11th Hour: The Official Strategy Guide	$19.95
9: The Official Strategy Guide	$19.99
The 7th Guest: The Official Strategy Guide	$19.95
Amok: The Official Strategy Guide	$14.99
Blood & Magic: The Official Strategy Guide	$19.99
Clandestiny: The Official Strategy Guide	$19.99
Close Combat: The Official Strategy Guide	$19.99
Command & Conquer: Red Alert Secrets & Solutions—The Unauthorized Edition	$19.99
Command & Conquer: Red Alert—Unauthorized Advanced Strategies	$19.99
Crusader: No Regret: ORIGIN'S Official Guide	$19.99
Cyberia 2: The Official Strategy Guide	$19.99
Daggerfall: The Unauthorized Strategy Guide	$17.99
Descent II: The Official Strategy Guide	$19.99
Diablo: The Official Strategy Guide	$19.99
DOOM II: The Official Strategy Guide	$19.95
Duke Nukem 3D: Unauthorized Secrets & Solutions	$14.99
Final Doom: Unauthorized Game Secrets	$19.99
Fury 3: The Official Strategy Guide	$19.95
Heroes of Might & Magic: The Official Strategy Guide	$19.99
Heroes of Might & Magic II: The Official Strategy Guide	$19.99
Hexen: The Official Strategy Guide	$19.95
Jetfighter III: The Official Strategy Guide	$19.99
Leisure Suit Larry: Love for Sail! The Official Strategy Guide	$19.99
Lighthouse: The Official Strategy Guide	$19.99
Lords of the Realm II: The Official Strategy Guide	$16.99
Master of Orion II: Battle at Antares—The Official Strategy Guide	$19.99
MechWarrior 2 Expansion Pack Secrets & Solutions	$12.95
MechWarrior 2: The Official Strategy Guide	$19.95
MechWarrior 2: Mercenaries—The Official Strategy Guide	$19.99
Microsoft Flight Simulator for Win95: The Official Strategy Guide	$19.99
Myst: The Official Strategy Guide	$19.95
NASCAR Racing 2: The Official Strategy Guide	$19.99
Pandora Directive: The Official Strategy Guide	$19.99
Phantasmagoria: Puzzle of Flesh—The Official Strategy Guide	$19.99
Privateer II: The Darkening ORIGIN'S Official Guide	$19.99
Quake Unauthorized Map Guide	$14.99
Quake Strategy Guide: Unauthorized	$19.99
Rama: The Official Strategy Guide	$19.99
The Residents: Bad Day on the Midway—The Official Strategy Guide	$19.95
Ripper: The Official Strategy Guide	$19.99
Sid Meier's Civilization, or Rome on 640K a Day	$19.99
Sid Meier's Civilization II: The Official Strategy Guide	$19.99
S.P.Q.R.: The Official Strategy Guide	$19.99

To Order Call 1-800-531-2343

Star Control 3: The Official Strategy Guide	$19.99
Star General: The Official Strategy Guide	$16.99
Steel Panthers II: The Official Strategy Guide	$16.99
Syndicate Wars: The Official Strategy Guide	$19.99
Timelapse: The Official Strategy Guide	$19.99
Wages of War: The Official Strategy Guide	$19.99
WarCraft II: Beyond the Dark Portal Official Secrets & Solutions	$14.99
WarCraft II: Tides of Darkness—The Official Strategy Guide	$19.99
War Wind: The Official Strategy Guide	$16.99
Wing Commander IV: The Unauthorized Strategy Guide	$14.99

VIDEO GAME BOOKS

Beyond the Beyond: Unauthorized Game Secrets	$14.99
Blood Omen: Legacy of Kain–Official Game Secrets	$14.99
Breath of Fire II Authorized Game Secrets	$14.95
Deception Unauthorized Game Secrets	$14.99
Donkey Kong Country 2 - Diddy's Kong Quest—Unauthorized Game Secrets	$12.99
Killer Instinct Gold: The Unauthorized Guide	$12.99
King's Field Unauthorized Game Secrets	$14.99
King's Field II Game Secrets: Unauthorized	$14.99
Mortal Kombat 3 Official Power Play Guide	$9.95
Mortal Kombat 3: Official Arcade Secrets	$9.95
Mortal Kombat Trilogy Official Game Secrets	$9.99
NiGHTS: The Official Strategy Guide	$14.99
Nintendo 64 Unauthorized Game Secrets	$12.99
PlayStation Game Secrets: Unauthorized, Volume 2	$12.99
PlayStation Game Secrets: Unauthorized, Volume 3	$12.99
Secret of Evermore Authorized Power Play Guide	$12.95
Secret of Mana Official Game Secrets	$14.95
Sega Saturn Unauthorized Game Secrets, Volume 1	$14.99
Shadows of the Empire Game Secrets	$12.99
Street Fighter Alpha Warriors' Dreams Unauthorized Game Secrets	$12.99
Super Mario RPG Game Secrets: Unauthorized	$12.99
Super Mario 64 Game Secrets: Unauthorized	$12.99
Tekken 2: Unauthorized Games Secrets	$12.99
Tobal No. 1: Official Game Secrets	$12.99
Tomb Raider Game Secrets	$14.99
Twisted Metal 2 Unauthorized Game Secrets	$12.99
Ultimate Mortal Kombat 3 Official Arcade Secrets	$9.99
Ultimate Mortal Kombat 3 Official Game Secrets	$9.99
Virtua Fighter 3 Unauthorized Arcade Secrets	$12.99
War Gods Official Arcade Game Secrets	$9.99

To Order Call 1-800-531-2343

To Order Books

Please send me the following items:

Quantity	Title	Unit Price	Total
_____	_____	$ _____	$ _____
_____	_____	$ _____	$ _____
_____	_____	$ _____	$ _____
_____	_____	$ _____	$ _____
_____	_____	$ _____	$ _____

Subtotal $ _____

Deduct 10% when ordering 3-5 books $ _____

7.25% Sales Tax (CA only) $ _____

8.25% Sales Tax (TN only) $ _____

5.0% Sales Tax (MD and IN only) $ _____

7.0% G.S.T. Tax (Canada only) $ _____

Shipping and Handling* $ _____

Total Order $ _____

---

*Shipping and Handling depend on Subtotal.

Subtotal	Shipping/Handling
$0.00–$14.99	$3.00
$15.00–$29.99	$4.00
$30.00–$49.99	$6.00
$50.00–$99.99	$10.00
$100.00–$199.99	$13.50
$200.00+	Call for Quote

Foreign and all Priority Request orders:
Call Order Entry department
for price quote at 916-632-4400

This chart represents the total retail price of books only
(before applicable discounts are taken).

By Telephone: With MC or Visa, call 800-632-8676 or 916-632-4400. Mon–Fri, 8:30-4:30.
WWW: http://www.primapublishing.com

By Internet E-mail: sales@primapub.com

By Mail: Just fill out the information below and send with your remittance to:

**Prima Publishing
P.O. Box 1260BK
Rocklin, CA 95677**

My name is _____

I live at _____

City_____ State_____ ZIP _____

MC/Visa#_____ Exp._____

Check/money order enclosed for $ _____ Payable to Prima Publishing

Daytime telephone _____

Signature _____

GREAT HINT BOOKS FOR ELECTRONIC ARTS™ GAMES!

Get the full inside scoop! Every book includes maps, hints, stats, strategy tips and a complete walkthrough of one of your favorite Electronic Arts games! Only official Electronic Arts books can tell you everything about our games — accept no imitations!

The Official Guide to Jane's Fighter Anthology...$24.99
(436 pages) (7868)

The Official Guide to Jane's 688(I) Hunter/Killer...$19.99
(192 pages) (10145)

The Official Guide to Jane's AH-64D Longbow $19.95
(224 pages) (10115)

Bullfrog's Official Guide to Dungeon Keeper...$19.99
(272 pages) (7853)

Bullfrog's Official Guide to Magic Carpet $19.95
(320 pages) (10119)

Bullfrog's Official Guide to Syndicate Wars $19.99
(240 pages) (10130)

ORIGIN's Official Guide to Privateer 2: The Darkening $19.99
(288 pages, plus full-color ship poster and map) (10117)

ORIGIN's Official Guide to Wing Commander IV...$19.95
(224 pages, 48 in full color) (10118)

ORIGIN's Official Guide to CyberMage..$14.95
(128 full-color pages) (10100)

ORIGIN's Official Guide to Crusader: No Regret $16.99
(192 pages) (10137)

ORIGIN's Official Guide to Crusader: No Remorse $19.95
(192 pages, 96 in full color) (10101)

ORIGIN's Official Guide to BioForge $19.95
(224 pages, 32 in full color) (10076)

ORIGIN's Official Guide to Wing Commander III $24.95
(Includes *Behind the Screens CD*) (10094)

ORIGIN's Official Guide to Wings of Glory $19.95
(Includes *Flight Recorder* disk) (10039)

Available at your favorite software or book retailer, or call 1-800-245-4525
anytime for MC/VISA/DISCOVER. (Prices subject to change.)

For details about every book, plus exclusive screenshots and previews
of all games, surf the ORIGIN Home Page:

http://www.ea.com/origin.html

An Electronic Arts™ Company
5918 W. Courtyard Drive • Austin TX 78730